Vencedor

Sloop *Vencedor* leading sloop *Canada* with *Pathfinder* looking on. An oil painting by Patrick O'Brien. By permission of the author.

VENCEDOR

The Story of a Great Yacht and an Unsung Herreshoff
Hero in the Golden Age of Yachting

CHARLES AXEL POEKEL JR.

SHERIDAN HOUSE

Essex, Connecticut

An imprint of Globe Pequot, the trade division of
The Rowman & Littlefield Publishing Group, Inc.
4501 Forbes Blvd., Ste. 200
Lanham, MD 20706
www.rowman.com

Distributed by NATIONAL BOOK NETWORK

British Library Cataloguing in Publication Information available

Library of Congres Cataloging-in-Publication Data
Names: Poekel, Charles A. JR, author.
Title: Vencedor: the story of a great yacht and an unsung Herreshoff hero in the golden age of
    yachting / Charles Axel Poekel Jr.
Description: Guilford, Connecticut: Sheridan House, [2021] | Includes bibliographical references
    and index. | Summary: "A history of a racing sailboat storied for its exploits and victories, and of
    the man who built it—a young Danish-American naval engineer, Thorvald S. Poekel"—Provided
    by publisher.
Identifiers: LCCN 2020048986 (print) | LCCN 2020048987 (ebook) | ISBN 9781493052929
    (hardback) | ISBN 9781493075379 (paperback) | ISBN 9781493075386 (epub)
Subjects: LCSH: Vencedor (Yacht)—History. | Yacht racing—United States—History. | Poekel,
    Thorvald S.
Classification: LCC GV822.V35 P64 2021 (print) | LCC GV822.V35 (ebook) |
DDC 797.1/4—dc23
LC record available at https://lccn.loc.gov/2020048986
LC ebook record available at https://lccn.loc.gov/2020048987

∞™ The paper used in this publication meets the minimum requirements of American National
Standard for Information Sciences – Permanence of Paper for Printed Library Materials, ANSI/
NISO Z39.48-1992.

To the Memory of
Thorvald Julius Schougaard Poekel

Contents

Contents

ACKNOWLEDGMENTS

TEN YEARS AGO, MY WIFE LYNN AND I MADE A PILGRIMAGE TO THE NEW England town of Bristol, Rhode Island. During our visit, I noticed the sign for the Herreshoff Marine Museum. I told my wife that I knew that my great-grandfather had worked for the Herreshoffs for a long period of time. I was curious to see what records the museum had. When we inquired about a "Poekel" working there, the museum representative said, "Poekel who?" and soon returned telling us, "We have no record of anyone by that time ever working here." At that point I started my quest to find out who Thorvald Julius Schougaard Poekel was and what he later accomplished.

Although my father was raised by him, there was very little information in the family. Apparently, T. Sch. Poekel, as he wanted to be known, was more interested in raising his grandsons that burnishing his reputation.

The one person who really helped to open my eyes was Kurt Hasselbalch, the former curator of the Hart Nautical Collections at the Massachusetts Institute of Technology (MIT) Museum. Kurt said there were thousands of boat design records in the Herreshoff collection but nothing of personnel records. He did find that on the construction print of *Defender* and three other prints of world-renowned yachts the name of T. Sch. Poekel had been inscribed therein. Kurt told me that this was quite rare since Nathanael Greene Herreshoff signed almost all the prints alone. Kurt also said that perhaps a handwriting analyist could one day examine the plans as to what role my great-grandfather might have played in the actual design process besides being a draftsman.

Kurt arranged to have my great-grandfather's toolbox included in an exhibition at the MIT Museum entitled: "Herreshoff—Lighter, Heavier and Faster." Here's what the description reads:

> T.S. Poekel was one of many highly skilled draftspeople and engineers at HMCO. Although workers' names rarely appeared

on early plans, Mr. Poekel's is visible on the lower right of *Defender's* construction drawing, His handwriting can also be found on the Newport 30 plan. Poekel later became a successful yacht designer in his own right.

Kurt's discovery inspired me also to research the life and works of T. Sch. Poekel. I was amazed to find that he had designed and built one of the most famous racing sloops in the history of the country, *Vencedor*, that brought world-class yacht racing to the Great Lakes. He also designed and built a 145-foot steamer that was one of the largest and most luxurious yachts to ever sail the lakes. He also perfected the Herreshoff boilers and designed other marine machinery. His accomplishments form the basis of this book.

Besides T. Sch. Poekel, there were other unsung heroes who worked at the Herreshoff Manufacturing Company (HMCO), who never got the credit they deserved: individuals like Darwin Almy who started his own boiler company after he patented a boiler; John F. Duthie who became a major boatbuilder in Seattle; and A. A. Packard who after helping to design the *Columbia*, joined forces with Starling Burgess.

My research was a fascinating journey, and along the way there were many people who helped make it so rewarding whom I want to thank:

Past Commodore Leif Sigmond of the Chicago Yacht Club whose gift of the annals of the Chicago Yacht Club gave me additional inspiration for this book;

Heather Marker, librarian at the Seattle Public Library for collating material on John F. Duthie;

Maribeth Bielinski, collections access manager at the Mystic Seaport Museum;

Rachael Robinson of the Hart Nautical Museum at the MIT Museum;

Mary Kay Nelson, archivist of the Racine Heritage Museum;

Sheilagh Doerfler, senior researcher at the American Ancestors & New England Historic Genealogical Society, who researched the geneaological records of T. Sch. Poekel in the United States and reviewed his Danish records;

Niels Moller Jensen of *My Danish Roots* who traced the lineage of T. Sch. Poekel in Denmark;

Joseph P. O'Flynn for use of his Nautical Dictionary published by Harbor House Publishers, Inc. which greatly contributed to the Nautical Glossary;

Professor Susan McMullen, research services librarian at Roger Williams University;

Karen Bouchard of the John D. Rockefeller Jr. Library at Brown University;

Leslie Martin, reference librarian, Chicago History Museum;

Katie Levi of the Chicago History Museum;

Beverly Darville of the Royal Canadian Yacht Club;

Vanessa M. Cameron, librarian and archivist of the New York Yacht Club;

Maureen Taylor, the great photo genealogist;

Patrick Gavin-Byrnes, professional sailor and rigger, who was able to identify most of the sails of *Vencedor*;

The members of the Trophy Committee at the Chicago Yacht Club;

Jesus Santos for photographing the Mackinac Cup and Trophy;

Commodore Lou Sandoval and General Manager Dwight Jenson and staff at the Chicago Yacht Club;

Ruth and John Verperian from the Oakville Historical Society;

Ken Bekin of Cowes on the Isle of Wight whose ancestors captured on film some of the most magnificent yachts the world has even seen;

The Board of Governors of the Larchmont Yacht Club;

The many dedicated employees of the New York Public Library;

My sister Anne Poekel McCauley, my cousins Peter Pockel, Jennifer Lockwood, Sally Harper, Thorvald Poekel, and Peter's daughter Elizabeth Pöckel who all shared stories and anecdotes about their extraordinary ancestor who came from Denmark at 25 years of age and lived to experience the American dream; and

Last but not least, my beloved and talented wife Lynn who wore out too many red pencils editing the manuscript during our quarantine for COVID-19.

Hammetts Cove
Marion, Massachusetts, September 1, 2020

Prologue

One of the great, triumphant achievements of man is the sailboat, a solid mass which can be directed through a volatile element without machinery to power it. Yet the achievement was incomplete: "the perfect hull and rig" were still to be attained. (even in our own days competent authorities have wondered whether the combination can ever be found!) The search was to produce geniuses among designers.

—Jerome E. Brooks

In the winter of 1895–1896, the Lincoln Park Yacht Club of Chicago challenged the Royal Canadian Yacht Club of Toronto to a series of races between a yacht belonging to the fleet of the R.C.Y.C. and *Vencedor*—a sloop currently being built at the Racine Boat Manufacturing Company (RBMCO).

The challenge came from a thirty-one-year-old cigar manufacturer from Chicago, Illinois. Edward C. Berriman, who besides running one of the biggest cigar-manufacturing businesses in the country with his brother Matthew, was also an avid yachtsman and the Commodore of the Lincoln Park Yacht Club. Berriman had confidence in the ability of the RBMCO. The company had built for him the forty-two-foot center board cutter named *Valiant*, which had won several regattas. Prior to that, the company had built a twenty-five-foot Sandbagger named *American Girl* for him. And unbeknownst to the Canadians, the Racine Company had informed Berriman that they were bringing in a young Danish American naval engineer by the name of T. Sch. Poekel to be its chief engineer and superintendent. Poekel had been a key draftsman with Nathanael Greene Herreshoff at the world-famous Herreshoff Manufacturing Company (HMCO) in Bristol, Rhode Island. The eager and aggressive owners of the Racine Company had decided to go on the world nautical stage. The challenge was to determine international yachting supremacy on that "great unsalted sea"—the Great Lakes.

After the challenge was received, there was some preliminary correspondence and then the R.C.Y.C. formally invited the Lincoln Park Yacht Club to send a committee to Toronto to work out the details. Thus, a proposal was set in motion to bring international racing to the Great Lakes. Before this, international yacht racing had been confined to the American northeast after the sloop *America* won what would become known as the America's Cup in 1851, and brought the British American competition to American shores.

This was game on. It was the first major international battle on the Great Lakes since 1812, when Commodore Oliver Hazard Perry triumphed over the British navy declaring, "I have met the enemy and they are ours." This friendlier contest would pit the talents of Will Fife Jr., scion of the famous Scottish family with over 150 years of designing the world's fastest yachts against those of an unknown thirty-three-year-old Danish-born engineer who had honed his skills, working hard in hand with Nathanael Greene Herreshoff, perhaps the greatest yacht designer the world has ever seen. This would be Poekel's first attempt at designing a yacht in had own name. Perhaps the race was not actually between the United States and Canada, but between Denmark and Scotland. In any event, the race would be a test to determine whether Canada or the United States had supremacy on the waters of the Great Lakes. The yachting world in 1896 was waiting to see if *Vencedor*, Spanish for conqueror, would live up to its name.

Part One

CHAPTER 1

I hereby challenge any representative yacht of your club to sail a
series of three races for a suitable prize or trophy with the sloop
Vencedor.

—C. O. Andrews
Secretary
Lincoln Park Yacht Club

ON MAY 24, 1895, INSIDE JUDGE HOGLUND'S CRIMINAL COURTROOM
in Chicago sat Edward C. "Ted" Berriman, who was also known as
Commodore Berriman, having been elected that title by the Lincoln
Park Yacht Club a month before. He was there as a witness to testify
against a former employee of his company who had embezzled $400.
That company was Berriman Bros., a cigar-manufacturing company.
But as the defendant's attorney stated that "the real thieves are the
owners of the company," Berriman couldn't control himself after his
integrity had been impugned by the wily defense attorney, and he suddenly leapt across counsel table and punched the defense attorney in
the face. After order was restored, Berriman was held in contempt of
court and fined $5.

Edward C. Berriman was born on March 29, 1864, in Oswego, New
York. Starting in 1881, he was actively engaged in the cigar-making
business in Chicago, Illinois. Together with his brother Matthew, he
built the business into one of the largest cigar companies in the United
States. Berriman Bros. manufactured such well-known brands as Don
Cosme, Jose Vila, La Sinceridad, La Evidencia, Marc Anthony, and
Light It.

A cigar ring from a popular brand of the Berriman Brothers

Berriman, like many other male Chicagoans of the day, was a Freemason. In fact, in 1896, the tallest building in Chicago was the Freemason's Building. Berriman was a member of Covenant Lodge No. 526 in Chicago. Berriman was elected to his Lodge on April 16, 1886, became an Entered Apprentice on October 15, 1886, a Fellowcraft on October 22, 1886, and raised to Master Mason on November 12, 1886.

Like many successful Chicago businessmen and manufacturers, Ted and his brother Matthew became avid sailors and yachtsmen on the waters of Lake Michigan.

Ted had a lot of great ideas for fostering sailing on the Great Lakes. During the 1893 Columbian World Exposition in Chicago, he advocated a "free for all Regatta."

During the 1895 racing season on the Great Lakes, *The Chicago Chronicle* became a strong advocate of international yacht racing between Canada and the United States. Many of its readers responded in the affirmative and wrote letters supporting the idea.

Commodore Edward T. Bolcom of the Milwaukee Yacht Club said this: "I am very glad to see *The Chronicle* boom the project for an international yacht race on the great lakes. In my estimation, nothing would give a greater stimulus to yachting and that is what every true yachtsman wants to see."[1] Also speaking up in support of the idea was the well-known yachtsman and former secretary of the interlake association

Earnest W. Radder who said, "I m [*sic*] heartily in favor of an international regatta."

One person decided to make it happen. He was E. C. "Ted" Berriman.

Ted Berriman had raced very successfully with a yacht named *Valiant*. It was built by the RBMCO of Racine, Wisconsin. Berriman returned to that company in late 1895, to build him a bigger and faster yacht.

Harper's Weekly in Volume 40 pointed out that "a Chicago syndicate placed an order with the Racine Com-

Commodore Edward C. Berriman

pany for a boat from the designs of Poekel." The *Weekly* added that "although Poekel was upwards of nine years associated with the Herreshoffs, and has had therefore unsurpassed opportunity for acquiring intimacy with the lines that have defeated all comers, still this *Vencedor* (Spanish for conqueror), as the defender is called, is his first boat. If he succeeds against a designer of such ability and so long experienced as Fife, he will have good occasion to be proud of his work." The article added that Poekel used the lines of *Defender* for the basis of his design.

As a sailor on the Great Lakes, Berriman had witnessed a growing animosity between American and Canadian sailors. This resulted from a highly disputed race in the early 1890s. At the time of his challenge, Berriman said that "there did not exist a very good feeling between yachtsmen of Canada and the United States," and his earnest desire of his challenge was "that it might establish better relations with our fellow yachtsmen across the border."[2]

On January 26, 1896, the *Chicago Daily Tribune* reported that Secretary C. O. Andrews of the Lincoln Park Yacht Club issued a formal challenge to S. Bruce Harman, secretary of the Royal Canadian Yacht

Club for a series of international freshwater races. The challenge read as follows:

Winter Quarters Lincoln Park Yacht Club
Chicago, January 23, 1896

S. Bruce Harman, Secretary
Royal Canadian Yacht Club
Toronto, Canada

Dear Sir:

On behalf of the Lincoln Park Yacht club of Chicago, and in the name of Messrs. Berriman Bros., members of said club, I hereby challenge any representative yacht of your club to sail a series of three races for a suitable prize or trophy with the sloop *Vencedor,* load water line not to exceed 45 feet to be sailed on waters to be hereafter agreed upon, during the season of 1896, and under the rules of the New York Yacht club, so far as the same apply to freshwater.

Should this challenge be accepted it is suggested that a committee of two be appointed by the Royal Canadian Yacht club, the four so selected to choose a fifth member. This committee to decide upon the time and place of holding the races, the selection of prize, the conditions governing the future challenges, and the exact rules under which the matches are to be sailed.

In furtherance of the foregoing the Lincoln Park Yacht club, at a meeting called for the purpose have appointed Messrs. E.P. Warner and W.A. Paulsen to confer with the two your club may name to conclude arrangements in the event of your acceptance.

Sincerely your obedient servant,
C. O. Andrews, Secy L.P.Y.C.

The *Toronto Evening Star* reported on January 28, 1896, that the Royal Canadian Yacht Club would have to turn down the challenge since Canada had no yacht the size of *Vencedor.* The only two available racing yachts were *Zelma* and the cutter *Aggie,* and both would come in about eight feet shorter than *Vencedor.* It questioned why the Canadian club couldn't build a boat of an equivalent size. The article praised the concept of an international race and what it would do to yachting, and with just a little bit of parochial bravado it added, "Canadians are well up in yachting and have more than held their own on every occasion. If enough energy were put into the present project, our American friends would soon be shown that although they may be able to outclass everything off Sandy Hook, still the men from the north can sail rings around them on the Great Lakes."[3]

The *Tribune* praised the challenge stating that "this is a step in the right direction, as everything pertaining to international yachting affairs has been carried on in the East and with the West left out in the cold as it were." The paper went on to predict that *Vencedor* would probably beat anything the Canadians could challenge since its designer "Mr. Poerkle [*sic*] is a graduate of Hereshoff's [*sic*] yard it is proof positive that the Berriman boat will be the best in this part of the country."[4]

After the challenge was made, hundreds of letters were sent to the Lincoln Park Yacht Club in its praise. Among the letters sent to Commodore Berriman was one from Commodore Lucas of the Royal Hamilton Yacht Club. Lucas congratulated Berriman, stating that he was sure the challenge would be accepted and that the event would transform yacht racing on the Great Lakes.

The Lincoln Park Yacht Club had been founded eight years before when D. D. Dutton and C. O. Andrews took their tiny sloop *Alice* up to Lincoln Park and moored it there. From this humble beginning, the yacht club took shape, and although in 1896, it had less than 100 members, it was known to be the most entertaining yacht club on Lake Michigan.

The Royal Canadian Yacht Club received the challenge and on February 1, 1896, unanimously chose to accept it although its acceptance never reached the Lincoln Park Yacht Club; so the Canadians sent it again in a new letter. It read as follows:

Toronto, February 6, 1896

C.O. Andrews, Esq.
Secretary
Lincoln Park Yacht Club
Chicago, United States

Dear Sir:

I am favored with yours of the 5th instant, and in reply have to say that I wrote you on the 3d instant, and am much surprised to learn that same has not reached you. I inclose copy herewith.

Inclosure

S. Bruce Harman
Honorary Secretary

Toronto
February 3, 1896

C. O. Andrews, Secretary
L.P.Y.C., Chicago

Dear Sir:

Your communication of January 23 proposing a series of races between the yacht Vencedor and a yacht of our club, was laid before the general committee on Monday, 27th ultimo, and by them referred to the sailing committee of our club, but unfortunately owing to the absence of some of the members they were unable top to meet until Saturday, February 1. I have now, however, great pleasure in stating that the committees are unanimous in their desire to bring about the proposed matches. They feel that before finally accepting and naming a yacht to meet *Vencedor* it will be necessary for us to have a more definite knowledge of her size, so that, in the event of our not having a similar sized craft, we may immediately take steps with a view toward building one.

I might say that at present we have no racing yacht between 36.5 and 46 feet L.W.L. or 40 by 38.5 corrected or sailing length respectively— measured under New York Yacht Club rules.

Will you, therefore, please inform me at the earliest possible moment as to the following points: The L.W.L. and corrected or sailing length measured under New York Yacht Club rules, with regard to the details. My committee feels there will be no difficulty in arranging then once they know that they have either a suitable sized craft already in our fleet, or that we can make satisfactory contract to have one built.

I remain yours truly,
S. BRUCE HARMAN
Honorary Secretary R.C.Y.C.

The Canadians had accepted but wanted *Vencedor*'s sail area and water length to be decreased, since their existing fleet had only forty-two-foot sloops. The following wire was sent:

If you will reduce your sail plan and perhaps a little on the water line until corrected lengh [*sic*] by actual area rule is forty-five feet and agree to allow double time allowance for all over forty-five feet, may be able to arrange race with a forty-two footer. Answer me in care of Commodore Lucas, Hamilton, Ont.

To this Commodore Berriman replied:

Vencedor can be made to sail a forty-six feet, corrected lengths, New York measurement. Mr. Poekel will be here today and will give you further information.

In order to resolve the demands of the Canadians, the Lincoln Park Yacht Club sent Mr. E. P. Warner to Toronto and summoned designer Poekel to Chicago. Warner wired the L.P.Y.C. the following: "If you will reduce your sail plan and perhaps a little on the water line until corrected length by actual area rule is forty-five feet and agree to allow double allowance for all over forty-five, may be able to arrange race with a forty-two footer."

After consulting with designer Poekel, Berriman wired the R.C.Y.C. that the sail area of *Vencedor* could be reduced.

According to Commodore Berriman, he received a wire from Warner on February 25, 1896, at 5:30 pm, that said, "Can't do better than already stated except not to exceed one-half foot."

To this Berriman wired back stating that "we could make corrected length by actual sail area rule and give forty-six feet seven inches double time allowance for over forty-five feet."

Concerning the size reduction Warner later said:

> They have practically abandoned their "first-class" rating on Lake Ontario, which comprised all boats over forty-six feet and for that reason it would have been impossible to get a race out of them if we hadn't materially reduced the *Vencedor's* sail area and brought her down to their "forty-six footer" class. While we were ready to do anything that was fair, this was an embarrassing position to place us in, for Mr. Poekel, the designer of the *Vencedor*, had all arrangements ready to go ahead as the plans stood. It was inevitable, however, and we had to make the best of it.[5]

On February 27, 1896, E. P. Warner of the Lincoln Park Yacht Club wired Berriman the following: "From this it can be seen by cutting down the sail area and makng [*sic*] other changes we have been able to reduce *Vencedor's* sailing length to within one inch of that required by the Canadian yacht club, and from the last message we take it there is every prospect of closing the race. We have made reductions of sail area of *Vencedor* in order to meet their demands whch may prove somewhat of a disadvantage."[6] The R.C.Y.C. had to have the full vote of its racing committee, but Mr. Warner felt that the committee would accept the compromise.

In spite of the agreement reached, most observers felt it wasn't fair to *Vencedor*. It forced the Berriman brothers to accept unfair conditions. Commenting on this the editors of *Forest and Steam* said this: "It is in every way unfortunate that the matter was not started in a different way, by a mutual agreement with the Royal Canadian Yacht Club as to the best size of yacht before the design was completed and the work of construction began. Now it is too late to alter the size of the new yacht."[7]

The Canadian papers, of course, thought otherwise.

The *Toronto Evening Star* reported, on February 25, 1896, the following:

"The members of the Lincoln Park Yacht Club have decided to alter their yacht *Vencedor*, so that a Canadian boat may be had which will correspond in dimensions. It is kind of the Chicago Club to consent to this, but then, it is only right that the craft in course of construction should be altered, and not the boat already built."

This analysis, of course, didn't figure on the Canadians building a new boat to compete.

Commodore Berriman, however, was happy that his dream for an international race would come into fruition and said this: "I am thoroughly satisfied with the arrangement for the race as they now stand. We would never have come to an understanding through correspondence in time to get the race off this year. It was the most sensible move that could have been made to send Mr. Warner down there. Everything was easily arranged when the exact situation was understood by all parties."[8]

What was being planned between the Royal Canadian and the Lincoln Park Yacht Clubs would be the first international yachting race on the Great Lakes, but it was not the first time Canada had entered the international racing scene.

From the inception of *America* winning the Cup in 1851, for a period of over twenty years, it was thought that any challenge for America's Cup would be from England. But in the spring of 1876, Major Charles Gifford, vice commodore of the Royal Canadian Yacht Club, acting on behalf of his club issued a challenge. The New York Yacht Club, which was experiencing tough times and was also fearful that an English challenge may not come during America's centennial accepted the challenge. The Canadian challenger would be *Countess of Dufferin*, designed and built by Captain Alexander Cuthbert of Cobourg, Ontario. Cuthbert had the reputation of being a fine yachtsman, if not a talented designer, and his boats had a good record of wins in the Great Lakes. The New York Yacht Club's entry was the sloop *Madeleine*. The skipper of *Countess of Dufferin* was totally unfamiliar with the local waters and finished the race ten minutes behind the *Madeleine*. The next day saw a new local pilot on *Countess* but it again lost—this time by over twenty-six minutes. To add insult to injury the Cup's first winner *America* joined the race just for fun and it too beat the *Countess* by twenty minutes.

After the disastrous races, there was a dispute between Cuthbert, Gifford, and several creditors who had backed the yacht. The yacht was seized by the New York City sheriff and chained to the docks at Stanton Street in the City. Cuthbert was able to unleash the yacht and sail it up the East River and it journeyed back to Canada before the sheriff could seize it again. It was soon sold and had a successful yachting career as part of the fleet of the Chicago Yacht Club.

Five years later in 1881, Captain Cuthbert again believed he had designed a winner of America's Cup. His wooden model resulted in the yacht *Atalanta*—named for the swiftest of mythical Greek maidens. This second Canadian challenge was issued through the Bay of Quinte Yacht Club in Belleville, Ontario. The New York Yacht Club readily accepted—waiving the six-month advance notice requirement.

In what would result in a lot of ridicule of the Canadians, *Atalanta* had to be disassembled and towed by mules to go through the Erie Canal on its trip to New York City.

The New York Yacht Club had only a small number of sloops that could compete. The fastest sloop available was *Arrow*, but since her owner wasn't a member of the New York Yacht Club, it wasn't eligible. The Club commissioned the builder of *Arrow* to create a new sloop commencing a soon-followed tradition of designing a yacht solely for purposes of being a Cup defender. The creation of David Kirby was *Pocahontas*. She, however, was a disaster and soon took on the moniker of "Pokey." After several trials between boats, the American entry was *Mischief*, a sloop designed by Archibald Cary Smith and built of iron and commonly known as the "iron pot."

In spite of its mythical Greek name, *Atalanta* performed miserably—finishing the first race thirty-one minutes behind *Mischief* and forty-two minutes behind it in the second race. The races also saw an uninvited guest—*Gracie*—challenge both yachts. The *Spirit of the Times* characterized the races as "a stupid comedy" and stated that the Canadian entry "bungled around the course by an alleged crew, who would have been overmatched in trying to handle a canal-boat anchored in a fog."

When Cuthbert intimated that he wanted another challenge in 1882, the New York Yacht Club quickly amended its rules to disallow another Canadian challenge that year.

Although *Atalanta* performed poorly, it holds one record that remains to this day—the only America's Cup contender to be designed, built, and skippered by the same man—Captain Alexander Cuthbert, representing the Bay of Quinte Yacht Club.

Fifteen years would elapse before the Canadians ventured again onto the world of international yachting—this time it would not be in the waters of the Atlantic but closer to home on the Great Lakes. And international racing on the Lakes was long overdue. By the late 1800s, there were more than 1,000 boats sailing the lakes all flying the burgees of some thirty to forty yacht clubs.

Upon accepting the challenge of the Lincoln Park Yacht Club, some members of the Royal Canadian Yacht Club formed a syndicate to mount their challenge. The syndicate consisted of the top echelon of Canadian businessmen. They were George Gooderham Sr., president of the Bank of Toronto; James Ross of Montreal, a street railway magnate, and although a Canadian, he was a member of the New York Yacht Club and owner of the schooner *Alcea*; S. F. Mckinnon, wholesale merchant and ex-president of Toronto Board of Trade; F. J. Phillips, Canadian Manufacturing Company and Consolidated Plate Glass Co.; George H. Gooderham, son of George Sr. and a leading member of the Royal Canadian Yacht Club; and Edward Æmilius Jarvis, stockbroker and banker, who was the elected Rear Commodore of the R.C.Y.C. Thirty-six-year-old Jarvis, manager of the Bank of Hamilton, being a take-charge man would serve as managing member of the syndicate. He would rule the syndicate and the yacht. He also had the reputation of being the best amateur sailor in Canada.

Together these leading Canadian businessmen would raise $6,000 and spend their summer in preparation for the first international yacht race on the Great Lakes. This amount would not be a problem for the six businessmen in the syndicate since their collective worth was estimated to be over $10 million.

The syndicate's Yacht Club had an inauspicious beginning. It started out in 1852, with a group of eight men sitting in a storeroom in the new city of Toronto forming a boat club and then a year later it became the Toronto Yacht Club. It was founded as a recreational yachting club and in the British tradition as unofficial auxiliary of the British Royal Navy in defense of Lake Ontario. When it applied for a royal warrant to be called the Royal Toronto Yacht Club, it was completely surprised when it was granted the title the Royal Canadian Yacht Club.

In the beginning, there was talk of Skipper Jarvis designing the new yacht, but since he had never undertaken the design for one as large and not willing to take any chances in the international competition, the group placed an order on or about March 16, 1896, with Will Fife Jr. in Scotland to design and build the yacht. Fife, coming from three generations of yacht designers and builders, had a world-class reputation of being one of the best in the business. The frames would be constructed in Scotland and then shipped to Canada for assemblage by James Andrew in Oakville, Canada.

CHAPTER 2

Poekel, the designer, just from the Herreshoff yard, had every reason to create a yacht of the first class. He had some reputation as
chief draughtsman for the Herreshoffs and designer of the fast
yachts they had turned out. But this reputation was shared with
his employers.[1]

—*Racine Daily Times*

IN NOVEMBER OF 1895, THE RACINE BOAT MANUFACTURING COMPANY
(RBMCO), Wisconsin, announced that Thorvald Sch. Poekel would be
its new superintendent and chief engineer. The company had origins that
went back over twenty years.

In 1870, a small company was started in Kenosha, Wisconsin, named
the Kenosha Hardware Company. It manufactured metal equipment for
florists and light brass and iron casting for seats. In 1874, some investors
infused it with cash and moved it to Racine where it became the Racine
Hardware Manufacturing Company. Racine is located ten miles north of
Kenosha and just about sixty miles north of Chicago on Lake Michigan's
western shore. The company expanded its manufacturing to hardwood and
veneer seats and also into parquet flooring which was called wooden carpet.
A salesman named Samuel Curtis Johnson who was in the flooring division would later buy the division, and in 1886, separate it forming his own
company, which eventually became Johnson's Wax, a Fortune 500 company.

From its manufacturing of wooden veneers, the company started to
manufacture wooden hulls for small boats. Boatbuilding became a large
segment of the company and continued to expand.

In 1891, the company hired Fred W. Martin as its chief designer and
superintendent.

15

The company achieved fame when it manufactured twenty-five electric motorboats for the 1893 Columbian World Exposition in Chicago. The electric boats were extremely popular at the Exposition with over 800,000 people using them to travel in the lagoons and canals. The company also manufactured the turnstiles used at the entrances.

In December of 1892, Fred W. Martin formed a new company called the Racine Boat Manufacturing Company(RBMCO) merging the old boat division from the previous company. The company specialized in canoes, rowboats, and other small boats.

Unable to meet its payroll, the Racine Hardware Manufacturing Company closed for business on June 17, 1893.

Fred Martin, in 1894, designed a forty-two-foot center board cutter named *Valiant* for the Berriman Brothers of Chicago. *Valiant* had 1,600 square feet of sail. That design brought a lot of publicity to the RBMCO. It went on to win several regattas for the Berrimans. Later in 1894, Fred W. Martin in a dispute with his partners left the company and went on to form another boatyard.

In 1895, the owners of the company were A. C. Frank and W. J. Reynolds who wanted to expand the company's manufacturing to larger boats. They hired Thorvald S. Poekel to replace Martin as chief designer and superintendent. According to Fred Gunther, Poekel "was an expert designer and brought with him all the latest technology of steam engines, boilers and large power and sail yachts, both steel and wood."[2]

During Poekel's tenure at the Racine boatyard, he added fin-keel racing sloops and steamer yachts to the yard's offerings, including the largest steel steamer to be built on the Great Lakes west of Cleveland.

Here's what the *Chicago Daily Tribune* said about the new boatyard in Racine:

> The new shipyard at Racine with its complete plant for construction of modern racing yachts, its force of skilled workmen and the crack designer, Theodore Peokel [*sic*] has opened the eyes of lake yachtsmen to the fact that they can have built and designed right at home fin-de-siecle racing machines.[3]

Poekel's position at Racine was that of a superintendent and chief engineer. In that position, he would design sailing yachts and steamers and supervise the construction of many vessels. In 1894, a writer for the *New York Times* wrote about yacht designers and summarized what it took to be one:

> Yacht designing is by no means easy work. To draw plans of a vessel that is to withstand the buffeting of the waves is to carry spars and sails that will be strong enough to meet the big winds and at the same time be large enough for days when the wind is light, to have good accomodation below, and to be a handsome craft and a fast sailor requires knowledge that can only be obtained by hard work, study and experience.[4]

On a personal note, T. Sch. Poekel, as a Danish American, was very much at home in Racine for it had, except for Greenland, the highest concentration of Danes outside of Denmark. In the late 1800s, 10 percent of all Danes in America lived in Racine. There was the Society of Dania; Dania Hall built in 1876, where receptions, dances, and dinners took place; and the Bethania Lutheran Church, which in 1897 started a tradition of Danish Christmas eve services. Up until the 1940s, the services at Bethania were all in Danish. There was even a Danish Old Peoples Home in Racine. Poekel after hours, provided lively entertainment at social functions by playing his violin.

RBMCO was extremely proud of having T. Sch. Poekel as the superintendent and chief engineer. Poekel would transform the factories into large yacht construction areas, and he would create ramps and other innovations for bringing the new creations into the adjacent Root River. Poekel would bring the company national awareness as well as international fame by designing the American entry for the first major international yacht race on the Great Lakes.

When word spread throughout the yachting world that T. Sch. Poekel was designing the American entry in the first international race on the Great Lakes, the yachting world wanted to know who Poekel was and what experience did he have. *The Boston Globe* reported that he was "a graduate of the Herreshoff works." Other papers said he had been the chief draftsman for the HMCO.

Here's what the *New York World* wrote about Designer Poekel:

Not only the Canadian but the yachting world in general will gain new ideas regarding Chicago's venture when they learn that the real power in the background is a man who has been Herreshoff's chief designer and superintendent for the past nine years. The most famous racers that ever floated have been turned out from the hands of this same man. *Defender* and *Vigilant* were superintended by him during the whole of their construction. So too were the *Dakota* and *Niagara*, which have had pretty much their own way in England *Navahoe*, *Ballymena*, *Vamoose*, *Gloriana*, *Colonia*, and many other well-known and speedy crafts.

The *Chicago Tribune* reported that Commodore Berriman had "placed his order with the Racine Boat Manufacturing Company for the best racing yacht that money can build. The company has secured the services of T.S. Poekel, who has had for some years the reputation of being one of the best yacht designers in the East."[5]

Racine Boat Manufacturing Co., in 1896, showing steamer *Pathfinder* with sloop *Vanenna* in front—Permission of Racine Heritage Museum

Another newspaper had this to say:

Mr. Poekel is now the chief designer of the Racine Boat Manufacturing Company of Racine, Wis. Prior to his nine years of service with the Herreshoffs he graduated at the Royal Danish Naval Academy of Copenhagen and his skill as a naval architect and mechanical engineer is sufficiently attested by the excellence of vessels which have passed through his hands, and for which he was at least partly responsible. How far he is to be credited as to personal assistance in the designing of the above mentioned world beaters is not generally known, but there can be no question about his carrying to the Chicago people a large part of Herreshoff's best knowledge, so far as construction is concerned.[6]

On December 3, 1895, the *Chicago Chronicle* wrote a story about a new steel steamer to be designed for F. W. Morgan and built for $75,000 by the RBMCO. The article said the following about its designer:

"Theodore [*sic*] Poekel, the designer, is a man of broad experience and a thorough yachtsman. He is a graduate of the Royal Danish Naval academy of Copenhagen, and comes direct to the west from Herreshoff, with whom he has served as chief designer and superintendent for nine years. Such work as the *Defender, Vigilant, Navaho [sic], Dakota, Niagara, Ballymena, Vamoosa [sic], Truant* and the torpedo boat *Cushing* have been turned out during his term there, and the success of these vessels is evidence of his skill and ability as a naval architect and mechanical engineer.[7]

When a Racine newspaper added this:

"Poekel was for nine years past had been the naval architect and general superintendent of the famous Herreshoff Manufacturing Company at Bristol, R.I. and as such had personally designed the great *Defender* and the *Vigilant*, the *Dakota*, the *Niagara*, and all of the famous fast sailing pleasure craft, for which the United States and the Herreshoffs have become world famous," a sportswriter for the *Milwaukee Sentinel* wanted the Herreshoffs to verify what was said.

An assistant editor of the *Sentinel* wrote a letter to Mr. N. G. Herreshoff. The announcement apparently drove Captain Nat into a rage. He alone was a naval genius. He alone designed every sail-steamer yacht that the yard built. He was the Wizard and there were no assistant wizards.

How to handle the glorification of a former employee who had the audacity to leave the company and to achieve greatness himself? First, don't dignify the response by penning your own letter. Have the secretary of the company sign the letter. Second, deny, deny, deny. Poekel was a nobody, not a naval architect, not an engineer, just one of many draftsmen who simply copied the Wizard's plans. He had simply been a gofer for the Wizard. And add that he recently asked for some help on designing some machinery.

No one perhaps will ever know the exact involvement Poekel had with the yachts designed and built at the Herreshoff yard during the golden age of yachting. What is known is that he worked there for nine years, and he had extensive training as an engineer in the Danish navy. He gave private lessons to John F. Duthie who became one of the greatest yacht designers and builders in the Northwest. He was extremely skilled and knowledgeable on yacht design, construction, boiler makers, and machinery, and he supervised the construction of *Defender* during N. G. Herreshoff's bout with pneumonia and typhoid fever.

So what role did the employees play to the success of N. G. Herreshoff? His son Francis would write in his father's biography: "I must say that the high standard of the employees at the Herreshoff Manufacturing Company contributed much to his success."[8]

The *Milwaukee Sentinel* wrote a letter to the HMCO to help verify what was being said of Poekel. On December 1, 1895, the *Sentinel* published a letter it had received from the HMCO. The letter was from C. W. Young, secretary—the same C. W. Young who had witnessed the patent application with T. Sch. Poekel in April of 1895. The letter read as follows:

November 25, 1895

Sporting Editor
The *Sentinel*

Dear Sir:

Referring to yours of November 22, the announcements lately made by the [RBMCO] of Racine, Wis., that they have engaged Mr. T. Sch. Poekel, "who for nine years had been general superintendent of the Herreshoffs, and as such had personally designed the *Defender*, *Vigilant*, *Dakota*, *Niagara* etc.," also that the torpedo boats we are now building were designed "exclusively" by him, is absolutely false in every particular. Mr. Poekel was never general superintendent of this company, and we have but one designer, Mr. Nathaniel G. Herreshoff, who designed the *Defender*, *Vigilant*, the torpedo boats and all other craft built by this company, and he is the only person having the right to make claim as such. The so-called "gifted naval architect (?) and designer (?) was in the employ of this company for several years in the simple capacity of one draughtsman among others, all of whom take their instructions from and make copies in development of preliminary drawings made by Mr. Herreshoff. He alone having to do with the modeling, designing, and calculations entering into the designs.

"The gifted naval architect" has not the ability to design such vessels as is claimed for him. Furthermore, we have knowledge of his having already telegraphed to a certain Eastern designer as to proper proportions for a steam yacht of a certain length.

We have no animus against Mr. Poekel, and these statements will not hurt us, for, as you well know, all persons making such, eventually reach their own level, but we hope you may be able, through the columns of your valuable paper, to prevent yachtsmen in the West from being gulled by such palpable lies.

The Herreshoff Manufacturing Company
C. W. YOUNG, Secretary
Bristol, Rhode Island

A *Sentinel* editor responded:

Please accept many thanks for information given in favor of Nov. 25 relative to Mr. [Thorvald Schougaard] Poekel [former draftsman at HMCO]. I send you under separate cover copy of paper containing the announcement which we trust will be satisfactory. If there is anything further about this matter kindly advise me. [request for article by NGH about half-raters . . .]

Poekel came to Milwaukee to give the Sentinel his statement, which is included in today's article. He was apprehensive that something derogatory to him was to be published. Am inclined to believe that the company that employed him may be more to blame for the 'bombastic' statement. The company is the 'Racine Boat Mfg. Co. of Racine', and should not be confounded with the Racine Yacht & Boat Works, of which Fred W. Martin is sup[erintendent] & naval architect, which is at Racine Junction.

Yours very truly,

A. W. Fiese, Assistant Editor
Milwaukee Sentinel

Mr. Poekel was made aware generally of the contents of the letter and gave the following statement to the *Sentinel* editors:

I never made any statements such as were reported at Racine and Chicago. It is not my intention to take any credit from the Herreshoffs. I had charge of the draughting department of the Herreshoff company for eight years. I have made plans and looked after the construction of sail and steam yachts, engines and boilers during that time, and I also took charge of the *Defender's* construction during Mr. Herreshoff's illness.

The following statement was given by the RBMCo:

Mr. Poekel, the chief designer of the company, is an entertaining gentleman of broad experience and a thorough yachtsman. He is a graduate of the Royal Danish Naval Academy of Copenhagen and comes direct to the West from Herreshoffs with whom he has served as chief designer and superintendent for nine years. Such work as the *Defender, Vigilant, Navahoe, Dakota, Niagara, Ballymena, Vamoose, Truant* and torpedo boat *Cushing* etc., have been turned out during his time there and the success of these vessels is evidence of his skill and ability as a naval architect and mechanical engineer.

After receiving these statements, the *Sentinel* wanted to end the controversy by concluding:

Mr. Poekel's connection with the Herreshoff's for long a time, no matter in what capacity, was sufficient to give him a standing in the West, without the announcements made by the Racine paper and *The Chicago Tribune.*

The design plans of all of the Herreshoff boats are maintained at the Hart Nautical Collection at MIT. A review of the plans shows that the name of T. Sch. Poekel appears on the plans of *Defender, Navahoe, Vigilant,* and *Vamoose* and his involvement in the *Newport* 30's is clearly seen.

Even after the attempt by the Herreshoffs to downplay the role that T. Sch. Poekel had at the company for nine years, newspapers across the country continued to extol Poekel's background. On January 27, 1896, the *Journal Times* of Racine wrote that "Poekel was Nat Herreshoff's assistant for years and formerly chief designer in the Danish Navy," and that the *Vencedor* was designed "to resemble *Defender* and to have the beauty and speed of Howard Gould's *Niagara.*"

It should be noted that it appears that Poekel had no direct involvement in any of the press reports since in not one is his first name correct.

In an article about *Vencedor* published by the *Buffalo Courier* on February 12, 1896, it was said that "she is from a Poekel design, and will be built at Racine, Wisconsin. Resigned Poekel and every workman employed on her construction are from the Herreshoff shops at Bristol, R.I. and worked on the *Vigilant, Defender, Niagara* and others." It was true that Poekel had brought with him several Herreshoff workers and that a group of expert steamfitters came across from Bristol.

The *Buffalo Morning Express* of February 28, 1896, wrote that Poekel "was the chief designer and superintendent for the past nine years," and that "he superintended the *Defender*, *Vigilant*, *Dakota*, *Ballynmore*, *Vamoose*, *Gloriana*, *Wasp*, *Colonia*, and many others. The article added that Poekel "graduated from the Danish Naval Academy." The article then tried to put its information in perspective by writing: "How far (Poekel) he is to be credited as to personal assistance in the designing of the above-mentioned world-beaters is not generally known, but there can be no question about his carrying to the Chicago people a large part of Herreshoff's best knowledge, so far as construction is concerned."[9]

Many newspapers simply mentioned Poekel's prior employment with the Herreshoffs without embellishment. In writing a story of *Pathfinder* both the *Saint Paul Daily Globe* on November 11, 1895, and the *Chicago Tribune* on November 9, 1895, simply wrote that "Theodore Poekel, manager of the company, is a graduate of the Herreshoff works at Bristol, R.I."

As of mid-February 1896, it wasn't a sure thing that *Vencedor* would be the entry for the United States in the international competition. The *Detroit Free Press* reported that a syndicate composed of Robert Hayes, Frank V. Newell, Lido Ramsdell, Judge Loren Collins, and Mr. Dyrenforth had placed an order for a steel-framed racing yacht to be named *Siren* at the Racine boatyard with the intention of bringing it into the international competition either in the future or in 1896.[10] The yacht was to represent the Lake Michigan Yachting Association and to sail under the auspices of the Columbia Yacht Club and fly its blood red burgee. The syndicate argued that a challenge race with *Vencedor* along the lines of the America's Cup qualifying customs should be adopted in the competition with *Canada*.

Some commentators felt that the challenge to Canada should come from the Lake Michigan Yachting Association of which the Lincoln Park Yacht Club was a component. They pointed out that *Siren* was sailing out of the Columbia Yacht Club, which in 1896 had the largest fleet of any yacht club on Lake Michigan.

It was the original intention that *Siren, Vanenna,* and *Vencedor,* all would engage in qualifying trials to see which sloop would race against the Canadian entry in the international races. However, before such trials could take place, the Lincoln Park Yacht Club sealed its deal with the Royal Canadian Yacht Club stating that its sole entry would be *Vencedor.*

Designer Poekel insisted that every wooden and metal part of *Vencedor* be of the highest quality. In order to find the ideal piece of wood for the ton-and-one-half keel, he sent an agent of the company on a nationwide hunt for the perfect timber. The agent often rode on horseback traveling the country in a journey that ended up totaling over 2,000 miles. The search ended in a remote area of the bluegrass country of Kentucky when the agent spotted a tall white oak standing alone in a clearing. At first the landowner was reluctant to have the oak cut down, but as the monetary offer increased so did his willingness to have it cut and sold. After much haggling, the Kentucky farmer finally parted with his prized oak tree. It was cut down and placed on two railway flat cars and on March 10, 1896, the sixty-five-foot-long oak log arrived in Racine.

Excitement was building for the race and it was reported that "letters come every day to Chicago yachtsmen congratulating the Lincoln Park Yacht Club in having inaugurated this interlake international contest and prophetizing that it will serve to build up yachting on the lakes to a place of equal importance with that it now holds on salt water."[11]

In February of 1896, the *Chicago Tribune* described in some detail, but not enough to give valuable information to the Canadians, the building of

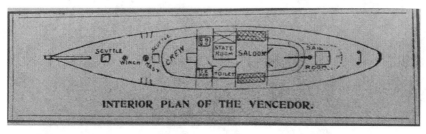

Interior drawing of *Vencedor* by T. Sch. Poekel

Vencedor in Racine. Poekel, taking a page out of N. G. Herreshoff's book, insisted that there be absolute secrecy during the construction phase. The Americans were out for a win and further evidence was a report that Commodore Berriman was negotiating with Charlie Barr, one of the best yachtsmen in the United States, to be the skipper of *Vencedor*. Barr was one of N. G. Herreshoff's favorite captains. Sir Thomas Lipton, who three times saw his America's Cup hopes end at the hands of Barr had this to say about the wiry Scottish skipper: "I can say without hesitation that Barr is the greatest helmsman to-day in racing a boat."

As word spread the Canadians were building a new yacht and were probably not going to use one of their existing yachts, it was thought that the rules of the race affecting measurement should be renegotiated. The *Chicago Daily Tribune* of March 22, 1896, had the headline: "Grave Question of Measurement—Building of a New Boat by Canadians Not Fair to Vencedor."[12] The article argued that *Vencedor* was designed to sail advantageously not less than forty-seven feet and since the initial agreement was based on the assumption that the Canadian boat would not be longer than forty-one feet. The rules allowed for a double time allowance if *Vencedor* measured longer than forty-five feet. The article made the point that if the new yacht of the Canadians were built to be forty-six feet, *Vencedor* would only give a small time allowance for the extra foot and would stand a better chance at winning.

In early March of 1896, after knowing that there would be an international race between the United States and Canada, there was much speculation as what yacht would be the Canadian entry. It was felt that if a new yacht wasn't going to be entered then the only other choice was the cutter *Zelma*. *Zelma*, also a Fife-designed yacht, was owned and sailed by Commodore R. A. Lucas of the Royal Hamilton Yacht Club. It had been launched in 1892, and was one of the best yachts deigned by Fife sailing on the Great Lakes. It had a stellar-racing record the year before, finishing first eleven times with one second. The *Calgary Herald* was of the opinion that although a race between *Zelma* at 39:36 feet and *Vencedor* at over forty-five feet was feasible but improbable, and adding that "the Lincoln Park boat will be a Poekel design, which is tantamount to a Herreshoff boat."[13]

The big question raised by the Canadian newspapers was: What would be a better race, *Vencedor* against a new boat or *Vencedor* against *Zelma*?

In the early part of 1896, the representatives of both clubs met to determine length at the Argonaut Rowing Club in Toronto. The meeting took place there due to a fire at the R.C.Y.C.

Back in Bristol on March 22, 1896, it was reported that Poekel's protégé, John F. Duthie, had engaged in his spare time in designing and building a boat of his own. It was a miniature version of *Vigilant* made with three-sixteenth inch galvanized iron sheeting and Duthie named it the *"Young Vigilant."* It was about eighteen feet in length with a mainsail and jib and was thought to be the smallest steel sailing boat afloat.[14]

By April 1896, *Vencedor's* construction was proceeding at a swift rate. Next to it in the construction shed of the RBMCO were two other yachts under construction—*Siren* and another yacht being constructed for William R. Crawford of Chicago. It was reported that as good as Poekel was he couldn't handle another design besides *Vencedor* and *Pathfinder*. The design of the new yacht would be given to Joseph I. Meyers of Chicago. It would later be named *Vanenna* and although not a pure fin keeler she would have her ballast outside of the keel.

Crawford, *Vanenna's* owner, was an avid sportsman and prominent Chicago resident. He was the general counsel of the Chicago Southwestern Railway, and a member of the Calumet, Chicago's most exclusive club. At Yale he had been a substitute quarterback of the football team. Currently, he was the captain of the football team of the Chicago Athletic Association and on the lakes he had crewed on the forty-five-foot sloop *Rambler*, which had a remarkable win record.

Both *Vencedor* and *Siren* were to have fin keels. The pace for construction quickened as it was hoped that all three large yachts would sail against each other prior to the international race against the Canadians scheduled in August. The goal was to have all three yachts ready for the Columbia Yacht Club's opening race to Michigan City and, if not, certainly for the July 4th race of the Lake Michigan Yachting Association in Milwaukee.

There was some debate among yachtsmen on the Great Lakes as to whether fin keel sloops could be adapted for the lakes. They could not go into shallow ports and many dry-dock facilities couldn't handle them.

Also, that month revealed that Commodore Berriman had not been able to obtain Charlie Barr as skipper but retained the services of Irving G. Barbour to be *Vencedor*'s helmsman. Barbour had been the quartermaster on the successful America's Cup victory of *Defender* in 1895. He was from the group of sailors from Deer Isle, Maine. All twenty-nine crew members of *Defender* were from Deer Isle and were known as the "Deer Isle Boys." According to Tom Duyn, who taught at the Deer Isle Stonington High School, the "boys" were all fierce competitors and strong-minded.[15] Irving and his brother Bentley were both crew on *Defender*. They were descended from Solomon Barbour who had arrived on Desert Isle in 1793. Poekel no doubt knew Irving Barbour from his Herreshoff days when the Deer Isle crew came to Bristol to assist with the construction of *Defender*. Based on his reputation with *Defender*, he was considered to be a ringer as skipper of *Vencedor*.

But Henry C. Haff, the former skipper of *Defender* who had led it to victory in America's Cup and was in the best position to judge Barbour, seemed to have some reservations of Barbour's abilities when questioned saying this: "He is certainly a reliable quartermaster, though I never heard of him being in command of a racing yacht. Yet he may have sailed small craft down East. He teaches school in winter, and I think he has been a deep sea sailor in large ships."[16]

Back in Chicago, Commodore Berriman was trying to figure out where and how he would moor his prized yacht once it arrived in the Windy City. He had experienced what Chicago's industrial soot and smog had done to the sails on his yacht *Valiant*, and he didn't want the white sails and the almond-colored decks of *Vencedor* to turn gray from the soot coming from the smokestacks of Chicago. The solution would be to moor it out in Lake Michigan but how to insure its safety. The answer, according to an article in the *Chicago Times-Herald* was to have a large wooden buoy with a steel shaft inside anchored by ten tons of rock or casting. Two sets of swivels and chains would tie the yacht down and prevent any damage.[17]

The annual meeting of the Lincoln Park Yacht Club, which took place on April 14, 1896, saw E. C. Berriman reelected as Commodore. But the biggest news, besides an update on the upcoming international races from the meeting, was the club's amendment of its constitution, which permitted women to be full members of the club. The revision stated that any woman who owned a yacht or was part owner of a yacht would become a "nag member." Initiation fees were waived for nag members but dues would be in place, which at the meeting were raised from $5 to $10 per year. This was an era that saw women gain some, if not all, rights to the heretofore male yachting enclaves. Two years before the New York Yacht Club admitted Lucy Carnegie, the widowed sister-in-law of Andrew Carnegie, when she applied as the owner of the 135-foot steam yacht *Dungeness*. Although admitted as a full member, she had no voting rights. Carnegie's admission came shortly after the highly revered Yacht Racing Association of Great Britain admitted women.

Kaiser Wilhelm II

Members present were excited to hear the news of the upcoming international races with *Vencedor*. Also present at the meeting was Commodore Paulsen of the Chicago Yacht Club who denied rumors that his club was attempting to absorb both the Lincoln Park and the Columbia Yacht Clubs. Twenty-four years later the Lincoln Park Yacht Club was absorbed into the Chicago Yacht Club but its burgee lived on as the burgee of the Chicago club. The Columbia Yacht Club, founded in 1892, survives to this day.

As for yacht designers and builders in England, besides Fife of Fairlie, there was Watson of Glasgow. While Fife was working on the Canadian entry, Watson had designed a cutter that was being built by D & W Henderson & Co. Its name was *Meteor* and was launched on the Clyde on May 13, 1896. Its owner was Kaiser Wilhelm II, Emperor of Germany. It was extremely fast. Its boom and bowsprit were longer than those on Lord Dunraven's *Valkyrie*. On June 8, 1896, in the Royal Cinqueport Regatta in the English Channel, *Meteor* beat the *Britannia, Ailsa,* and *Satanita.* It was thought that it could beat *Niagara.*

In describing the building of *Vencedor,* the *Daily Ocean News,* on August 22, 1896, wrote the following:

> The construction of the boat was proceeded under the directions of the designer with the greatest care. Every piece of wood put in her passed first under his scrutiny, and many of the more important pieces were selected after a great expenditure of time by the designer himself. The work on the boat progressed slowly, simply because of the great pains taken in getting out her parts and putting them together. When the *Vencedor* was launched and given a trial, the creator was satisfied he had turned out the best boat of her class afloat. (p. 4)

Vencedor was described as a canoe with a flat floor with an enormous keel, which at its bottom had a bulb containing the ballast. It was said that it was patterned after *Niagara,* a Herreshoff-designed yacht owned by Howard Gould. That yacht had tremendous success in regattas off the coast of the United Kingdom, as well as *Defender,* which Poekel was heavily involved with the design and the construction. It was said that Poekel combined the best qualities of *Defender* and *Niagara* with his own novel designs to come up with the design for *Vencedor.* According to a news report, "Poekel, the designer, just from the Herreshoff yard, had every reason to create a yacht of the first class. He had some reputation as chief draughtsman for the Herreshoffs and designer of the fast yachts they had turned out. But this reputation was shared with his employers."[18]

It was designed so that the captain and crew could live aboard— quarters were for nine crew members complete with a galley that had a cooking range and an ice box.

It would be steered by a tiller instead of a wheel. A small winch would operate the main sheet and halyards.

Poekel introduced a new form of yacht-building that he brought from the Herreshoff yard—the frames upside down with the keel in the air.

By May 20, 1896, the cabins were on *Vencedor* and the fin was made.

Vencedor under construction at RBMCO

Kaiser Wilhelm II, the grandson of Queen Victoria, was an avid yachtsman and enjoyed racing in European regattas. He was extremely proud of his presence on the world stage of yachting and would never be intimidated by his English relatives and their yachting activities. It was said he had a hate–love relationship with England. This was exemplified on one occasion when he heard King Edward VII was onboard *Shamrock* with Sir Thomas Lipton. He asked someone, "Why is my uncle sailing with his grocer?"

In June 1896, there were stories around the world that Kaiser Wilhelm II was considering mounting a challenge for the America's Cup with his yacht *Meteor*. A group of Chicago yachtsmen had a meeting with Superintendent Poekel at the RBMCO and discussed the Kaiser's

Toolbox of T. Sch. Poekel

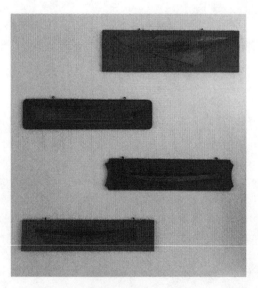

Half hull models from yachts designed by T.Sch. Poekel learned
to design boats from N.G. Herreshoff, who carved half hulls, took
measurements, and then created drawings.

plan to challenge for Ye Olde Mug. Poekel told the yachtsmen that "I can build a yacht that will beat *Defender*." *The Saint Paul Globe* explained the rationale behind the bravado statement in its Sunday, June 21, 1896, edition:

> Designer Poekel is confident he can design a boat of the *Defender's* dimensions which will prove much faster than the Herreshoff sloop that sent the last of the Valkyries home vanquished. He had virtual supervision of the construction of the *Defender* and made all the working plans from which she was built.[19]

One of the men who heard this replied, "If you can do that, I will furnish the money to build it," upon which another yachtsman said, "You will not furnish it all for I want to do part of that myself."

The Chicago men then discussed how to bring it about, including having membership in the New York Yacht Club, which they said some of their friends had, as well as the giving of a nine-month notice of their challenge. The Chicago yachtsmen, however, wanted to remain anonymous for the time being.

When asked about the possibility, Commodore Berriman commented, "There is no reason why a cup defender should not be built on Lake Michigan."[20]

Another product of Poekel's nautical design genius was the Poekel Steam Yacht Engine. Although similar to the Herreshoff's engine, it was far superior. In its 1902 catalog, the RBMCO had this to say about its marine engines:

> We manufacture single, compound and quadruple expansion engines from one to 2,000 horse-power, designed to meet any requirement and adapted to high duty. The material used in the construction of our engines is the best obtainable, and in keeping with modern practice, and as our designer has had many years' experience on torpedo boats and steam yacht machinery, we feel justified in saying that we produce the best marine engine on the market. Let us demonstrate this to you,[21]

A Poekel-designed triple-expansion engine.

A reporter for the *Racine Daily Journal* wrote this about a 100 horse-power model in operation:

> Although it was going at the rate of 600 revolutions per minute, it worked like a sewing machine. The reversing of the engine is one of the strongest points, and marvelous. The reverse is executed instantly and there is hardly a perceptible jar. In fact, it is impossible to detect that the machine has been reversed unless a person is looking directly at it.[22]

Poekel-designed triple-expansion steam engines were installed in most of the large Lake Geneva steamers constructed by RBMCO.[23] These would include such famous steamers as *Loreto* in 1896, for J. M. Smyth, furniture baron of Chicago, and *Kaiulani* in 1900 for Tracey Drake, owner of Chicago's famous Drake Hotel.

CHAPTER 3

Everyone's life is a fairy tale, written by God's fingers.
—*Hans Christian Andersen*

THE TOWN OF NAESTVED, DENMARK, IS LOCATED ON THE ISLAND OF Zealand about forty-four miles southwest of Copenhagen. Although not directly on the coast, water surrounds it and goes through it. The River Susa, the longest river in Zealand, passes through it on its way to Lake Tystrup. It was here that, on December 12, 1862, Thorvald Julius Schougaard Pöckel was born. He was the son of Axel Broder Poekel, trumpeter in the second regiment of dragoons in Naestved and Anna Conradine Elisabeth Hansen. His namesake Thorvald Julius Schougaard Pockel was the musical director of the famed Tivoli Gardens and composer of music including two marches that are still played today—Signal Galop and Under I Kongens Hare Galop. Two members of the Poekel family, Carl Friedrich August Poekel and Carl Frederik Theodor Poekel, were both awarded the Silver Cross of the Order of Dannebrog for meritorious service.

Fourteen-month-old Thorvald Pöckel was baptized on February 20, 1863, in St. Martins Church (Danish: Sankt Mortens Kirke) in the Parish of Praesto in Naestved, Denmark. The medieval church traces its roots to 1200 and is dedicated to St. Martin of Tours. The baptism took place in the newly added porch which was built in the 1850s. By being baptized in St. Martins, Poekel became a member of the Church of Denmark—or as it is officially known the Evangelical Lutheran Church. Today, approximately 75 percent of all Danes are members.

Following a family tradition, young Thorvald was taught to play an instrument. He mastered the violin and the music he could make with it. But music was not to be his obsession—water and the crafts on it were. His first experiences were being in a canoe on the Susa River. He was mesmerized with how a man-made piece of wood could conquer the water and slide effortlessly across it. He was also fascinated with boats that lined the harbor in the center of Naestved.

Poekel embarked on a career in marine engineering. He was an apprentice in 1879, at the age of seventeen. He became a full engineer in 1880 and an engineer in the Danish navy in 1883. Engineering taught Thorvald to be extremely detailed and precise. He realized at an early age that penmanship and writing legibility were crucial for an engineer. He would learn, perfect, and maintain this trait for his entire life. He was known for his analytical thinking and cleverness. And from his days at sea, he grew more attached to the water and to the craft that had to traverse it. As for the ocean, he would always say that it was never the same—it changed second by second.

As Denmark faced an economic downturn in the 1880s, Poekel became interested in seeking new opportunities in America.

Scandinavian immigration to America had started with Leif Ericson, a Norseman from Iceland, who is widely credited with being the first

At twenty-one years of age T. Sch. Poekel was an engineer in the Royal Danish Navy—Author's collection

European to discover the North American continent, preceding Columbus by some 500 years. Emigration from Denmark to America started slowly. Between 1820 and 1850, the average number of Danish immigrants averaged just sixty per year. And in 1864, the tiny country of Denmark became even tinier losing 25 percent of its area with the German annexation of Slesvig-Holsten.

It was not until after the Civil War that Danish immigration to America occurred on a larger scale. Danes would easily blend into the American melting pot—they were white, Protestant, and had a unique capacity for learning English. They also weren't clanish.

In 1887, Thorvald Julius Schougaard Poekel fit into the typical demographic mold for emigrants from Denmark—he was twenty-five years of age and a single man. He, like so many other European immigrants seeking a new life, would pack all his worldly possessions into a large wooden steamer trunk and set sail for America. Included in the wooden trunk would be his prized violin.

He had already promised his parents, Anna and Axel, that once he was established in America they could join him. They understood that life in America held out great promise—more than life in Denmark.

In October of 1887, Thorvald took his steamer trunk and journeyed to Liverpool, England, where he purchased a one-way ticket to Boston on the Cunard Line *Scythia*. The ship had been aptly named being for the ancient Nomads who occupied Persia and now thousands of European nomads would cross the Atlantic on a journey from the "old country" to "the new." According to the *New York Times*, the fares on the

In immigrating to America, T. Sch. Poekel used this wooden trunk to bring his possessions from the old world to the new.

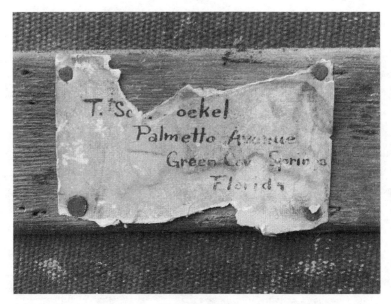

As a draftsman and a designer, Poekel had excellent penmanship his entire life.

Scythia ranged from $60 to $100 for cabin class, $35 for intermediate, and "very low rates" for steerage—probably around $20. Seemingly cheap today, the cost of a transatlantic steamship ticket would cost a Danish farmhand in the 1880s almost a year's wages. The trip would take nine days with an intermediary stop in Queenstown, Ireland.

Pöckel, who changed his Danish-spelled surname to Poekel, arrived in the Port of Boston on October 27, 1887. Going through immigration to America thoughts went through his head similar to Oscar Wilde's experience when he stated to officials that he "had nothing to declare but his genius."

CHAPTER 4

The Herreshoff operation also included brothers James (the boy Wonder) and John (the Blind Genius). Altogether the family was nicknamed the Great Ones by locals, who gave them credit for the jobs, money and acclaim they brought to Bristol, but who were also struck by Nat's cold eccentricity.

—*Author Michael D'Antonio*

LATE IN 1887, FRESH OFF THE BOAT FROM DENMARK, POEKEL WAS TOLD that there were opportunities for employment as a naval engineer at the Herreshoff shipyard in Bristol, Rhode Island. It was said that the company paid some of the highest wages in Rhode Island and even supplied housing for many of its workers.

The Herreshoff family had immigrated to America almost 100 years before Poekel arrived. Charles Frederich Herreshoff came to America in 1790 from Germany. The Herreshoff family initially settled on farmland in Point Pleasant, Rhode Island, before relocating to the town of Bristol.

But the history of the area goes back much farther than the Herreshoff's arrival. Prior to the arrival of the *Mayflower*, it was the center for the Wampanoag Indians. Their early leader Metacom, who was referred to by the colonists as King Philip, ruled from the land of Mt. Hope and it was around the lands surrounding Bristol that colonists and Native American Indians engaged in a bloody battle known as King Philip's War (1675–1678). In the war the colonists lost over 1,000 lives and the Native American Indians over 3,000. The colonists were able to prevail and killed King Philip in Misery Swamp. They felt he was unworthy of burial and had him beheaded and quartered, placing his head on a pole, which was conspicuously displayed in Plymouth for over a generation.

It wasn't long before the twenty-five-year-old Danish immigrant arrived in the town of Bristol, Rhode Island. He immediately liked the quaint coastal town that strongly reminded him of Naestved. It also wasn't directly on the coast but had a water access and a nice port. Just as Naestved had a direct train to Copenhagen, Bristol had train service to Providence via the Providence, Warren, and Bristol line. It was also a complete town with seven churches, and both an Odd Fellows' Hall and a Masonic Hall. As a reminder of its colonial history, one of the main arteries in town was named Metacom Avenue.

Soon Poekel reached the main office of the HMCO on Burnside Street. He announced that he was there to apply for a job. He was soon ushered into the office to meet with the president of the company, John Brown Herreshoff. It was inwardly located through two outer offices. To his utter amazement, he immediately realized that Mr. Herreshoff was blind. Tragically John B., as he was commonly referred to, had lost the sight of one eye at seven years of age and then he lost sight in the other one while horseplaying with his brother Charles at the age of fifteen. Blindness had hit the Herreshoff family hard—of the seven Herreshoff brothers J. B. and three others were blind. John B. was heavily built with gray hair and a gray beard. His voice was gruff with a quick temper but "he had the impressive face of the blind."[1]

However, he also realized that John B. was extremely bright and sharp in his questioning of Poekel's naval engineering skills from Denmark. Poekel related that he had studied as an apprentice and an engineer and as such he had served in the Royal Danish Navy. He told Herreshoff he had experience with nautical machinery and the drafting of plans. He also said that he had a keen interest in ballast—the heavy weight that adds stability to a boat. Poekel then met the "blind boatbuilder's" brother—Nathaniel Greene Herreshoff. He had been named, actually misnamed, after a descendant of the famous American Revolutionary War hero Nathanael Greene of Rhode Island. For some reason his Christian name was spelled Nathaniel. In the early 1900s, after visiting the grave of Nathanael Greene in Savannah, Georgia, Herreshoff changed the spelling of his to Nathanael.

Nathanael was a tall, handsome man with sensitive features and a large golden beard. He was always stooped and extremely taciturn.

One author would write that "the family was nicknamed the Great Ones by locals, who gave them credit for the jobs, money and acclaim they brought to Bristol, but who were also struck by Nat's cold eccentricity."[2] Suggestions for design by clients to Nat were immediately rejected on the first asking, ask again and you were shown the door.

The Herreshoff brothers decided to hire the young Danish immigrant and assign him to the drafting room located directly above the main office. Little did the trio know that they all would be working together during the greatest years in the history of the HMCO during the golden years of yachting.

Nathanael had studied for three years at MIT. One of his professors was William B. Rodgers, the founder and President of MIT. He then worked from 1869 to 1879, at the Corliss Steam Engine Company in Providence, Rhode Island. The company gained international fame with designing and building the largest steam engine in the world for the country's Centennial Exposition in Philadelphia in 1876. On the Opening Day, President Ulysses S. Grant and Emperor Dom Pedro of Brazil pushed the button to start the behemoth engine that through tunnels and shafts powered over 800 machines located throughout the Exposition. It generated 2,500 horsepower and drove 8,000 parts simultaneously. Responding to the button being pushed and working below the platform was Nathanael Greene Herreshoff who always remembered Mr. Corliss presenting the president and the emperor with the gold-plated cranks which they had used to start the engine.

With an innate quest for innovation, in 1875, with an idea that he had sailing on the French Riviera some years before, N. G. Herreshoff designed a unique boat—a special catamaran. It was patterned after the proas of the Pacific region and N. G. Herreshoff had his brother John B. build it in Bristol. In 1876, the International Centennial Committee sponsored regattas in Philadelphia and in New York, which were the largest of their kind in the history of the country. N. G. Herreshoff entered his catamaran called the *Amarylis* in a race for any yacht fifteen tons or less scheduled for Friday, June 23, 1876. Even in those early days of American yacht racing, there was an attempt to classify boats.

In June of 1876, N. G. Herreshoff, after getting the Providence Yacht Club to sponsor the boat, sailed *Amarylis* from Bristol to New York—making the 200-mile trip in the remarkable time of fourteen hours. It was said that *Amarylis* even beat steamers in Long Island Sound on its way to New York.

Its entry into the race was met with derision by the crew of the monohulled sandbaggers. Some said it was "neither a yacht nor a boat." Even after ridiculing its appearance, none of the yachtsmen filed a formal challenge with the race committee believing that the strange-looking boat would never win. The race went off and with a shortage of wind *Amarylis* crept along, but after the wind picked up so did the Herreshoff's catamaran and it went like a rocket skimming over the water. It ended up finishing first beating the favored *Pluck and Luck* by twenty minutes and the second place yacht *Sophie S.* by seven minutes. After the race, challenges were filed and on the grounds that *Amarylis* had no cabin facilities (N. G. Herreshoff would argue that a tent could be erected onboard) the yacht was disqualified and the win given to *Pluck and Luck*. Although *Amarylis* didn't receive a winner's diploma, it did receive a certificate stating that it had attained the highest speed ever made by a vessel of its length.

Francis Herreshoff in his father's biography, being a loyal hagiographer, simply states that *Amarylis* won.

The *New York Times* reporter praised the speed of *Amarylis* and added that a catamaran had two other great attributes "to sail a vessel like the *Amarylis* requires about as much seamanship as is needed to handle a wheel barrow" and "the fiercest squall cannot capsize a flying-proa, even if she is handled by a Presbyterian minister from an inland town, and infested with a dozen frightened women who stand up and scream in the presence of apparent danger, according to the pleasing practice of the sex."[3]

About 125 years later America's Cup would see the return to the type of yacht that N. G. Herreshoff designed and raced in 1876—just a bit ahead of his time.

In 1879, N. G. Herreshoff would leave Corliss and join with his brother John and form the HMCO. The company started out exclusively designing and building steam yachts.

T. Sch. Poekel was hired by the Herreshoffs to work in their drafting department. Upon leaving the offices, he was told that work started at the sound of the shop bell in the cupola and stopped at the sound of the bell. The ringing of that bell on his first day at work signaled to Poekel that his great American dream was about to begin.

When T. Sch. Poekel started work at the Herreshoff yard in Bristol, he was told of the fixed rule that governed the boatyard—no yacht from an outside design would be built there and that no design would be furnished to be built outside. He also learned an unwritten rule: any employee would remain anonymous for anything he did there.

Poekel also quickly found out that only the folks in Bristol knew how to properly pronounce the Herreshoff name—it was not—Hershoff but Herris-shoff. Concerning the pronunciation of his own surname, Poekel told those who asked that it's the same as to "Poke-Hell" out of someone.

When the young Dane started at the Herreshoffs, the yard was totally focused on the design and construction of high-speed steamers. The Herreshoffs had basically stopped designing and building sailboats.

In 1887, the HMCO was awarded a contract from the U.S. Navy to build a steel torpedo boat. It was Seagoing Torpedo Boat No. 1, which was christened *Cushing* by J. B. Herreshoff's daughter Katherine on January 23, 1890. It would see action in the Spanish-American War. This was the first torpedo boat that T. Sch. Poekel would be involved in but not the last.

Next being built came the steamers *Now Then*, *Say When*, and *Ballymena*.

While T. Sch. Poekel was learning the intricacies of steam boilers, tragedy struck.

On December 8, 1888, there was a trial run for the Herreshoff-built *Say When*. The boat had been built for Norman L. Munro, a wealthy New York publisher. Munro had a collection of Herreshoff boats, including the fast *Now Then*. He wanted a faster one. Nathanael was determined to goose up the engine. Early that morning employee Albert S. Almy complained to James Herreshoff: "Your brother is monkeying with the boiler." "Let him," replied James, "he has to learn."[4]

After Nathanael tampered with the valves to increase the speed and just off Bristol Ferry there was an explosion on *Say When* at about 10 o'clock in the morning. Charles Newman and Charles Horton working in the engine room were badly scalded and Newman was taken to the Rhode Island Hospital in Providence. Newman suffered immensely in the hospital where his skin had to be ripped from his bones. He died an agonizing death on January 6, 1889. He was survived by a wife and a young child. Herreshoff quickly made a payment of $2,500 to the family, which was almost immediately reported in the *Bristol Phoenix*. The amount in 2020s money would be approximately $69,000. On that day, Herreshoff noted in his diary that "Charles Numan [*sic*] died this morning from injury on *Say When*."[5]

A few months after the accident, a formal inquiry took place as well as a suit for damages from the Administrator of the Estate of Charles Newman. As a result of the lawsuit, on March 4, 1890, the HMCO was ordered to pay $4,000 in restitution. The result of the inquiry board was that Nathanael Greene Herreshoff's boiler's operating license was taken away forever.

Another high-speed steamer built in 1889 that T. Sch. Poekel worked on was the 148-foot *Ballymena*. It was built for Alexander Brown of the Brown Brothers financial firm. Ballymena was the family's ancestral home

Nathanael Greene Herreshoff-a man of many ideas—but few words—Permission of Mariner's Museum and Park

in Ireland from where Alexander's great-grandfather had emigrated from. The Brown family initially imported Irish linen. The business would go into banking and would one day become Brown Brothers Harriman, one of the most prestigious financial companies in the world.

When T. Sch. Poekel commenced working at the HMCO, the boatyard was the sole center of activity for the town of Bristol. The rest of the waterfront had seen better days in the early part of the nineteenth century when it was a fairly thriving port. Now it was full of decaying docks with a mostly unused waterfront. The exception was the Herreshoff yard that stood out against the dilapidated waterfront. The Herreshoff yard consisted of a boatbuilding compound with various small buildings. There were two buildings—north and south along Hope Street fronting on the water. Going up Burnside Street was a building that housed the main administrative offices and designing rooms. This building had formerly been a rifle manufacturing factory owned by General Burnside of Civil War fame. There were other buildings for lumber storage, a rigging and sail loft, a foundry, forge, boiler, cabinet, pattern, joiner, and paint shops. It was a boatyard compound with John B.'s house up the hill toward town, and Nathanael's on a rocky peninsula jutting out into Bristol Harbor. It was named Love Rocks, which was what the townsfolk called the peninsula. The Herreshoff yard provided everything needed to construct steam and sail boats, and with an extremely talented workforce of hundreds of employees, it had the capability of designing and building the finest yachts in America. And it would make the quaint town of Bristol, Rhode Island, famous throughout the world.

During the beginning of Poekel's tenure, when the yard focused on steamers, he met, Darwin Almy, who was the foreman of the boiler department and would become another unsung Herreshoff hero. Darwin's brother Albert S. Almy worked in the carpentry shop. As a carpenter, Albert Almy would play a major role in the construction of the Cup defenders *Vigilant*, *Defender*, *Columbia*, and *Constitution*.

Darwin Almy, Albert's brother, had a varied background. He began working for the Herreshoffs in 1879. He was self-taught after quitting school at age sixteen. After dropping out of school, he worked on his father's farm, served as a sailing master on a fishing steamer engaging in the menhaden oil business, and partnered in a jewelry manufacturing business in Providence. As an unsung Herreshoff hero, he worked at the Herreshoff yard for eleven years, becoming the foreman of the boiler and engineering departments. Darwin Almy and T. Sch. Poekel had some common bonds—they both were clever engineers, who enhanced their reputations with their employer's reputation, and both belonged to fraternal organizations that promoted honesty and integrity. Poekel was a member of the International Order of Odd Fellows, and Darwin Almy was a Freemason belonging to the St. Albans Lodge No. 6 in Bristol. Poekel and Darwin Almy learned the intricacies of steam boilers for yachts at the Herreshoff yard. Almy left the Herreshoffs in late 1889, and formed his own company in the fall of 1889, shortly before he was granted a patent on a new type of boiler that he had invented. His company began to manufacture water tube boilers and he received a patent on the very successful Almy water tube boiler. He became the president and treasurer of the Almy Water Tube Boiler Company located in Providence, Rhode Island.

In July of 1890, there was excitement in the Herreshoff yard upon the arrival of a young millionaire newspaper publisher named William Randolph Hearst. He had come for a steam yacht and not just any yacht, but the fastest yacht in the world. Hearst decided upon a ninety-four-foot steamer named *Javelin*. After construction had begun, Hearst changed his mind and said he wanted a larger steamer, so it was agreed he would buy the 112-foot *Vamoose*.

Hearst had another request. He and the Herreshoffs stipulated that if the yacht couldn't do twenty-six knots, he could refuse delivery. The yacht was steam only and didn't even have a fixed mast. *Vamoose* was named after the then in-vogue expression of "vamos" in Spanish or "let's go" in English. In order to insure that it did go the steamer had an 875-horsepower quadruple expansion steam engine. The steamer was capable of reaching speeds of 23.5 knots. Poekel, who was proud of his involvement with Hearst's yacht, affixed his name to the construction plans that became a practice he would follow during his tenure working for Nathanael Greene Herreshoff.

T. Sch. Poekel saw firsthand with Hearst that wealthy Americans wanted to own yachts and they wanted them to be fast.

Vamoose, built for publisher William Randolph Hearst—Library of Congress

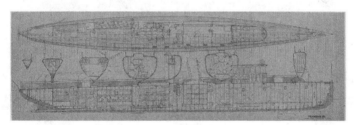

Construction Plan of Vamoose showing the name T. Sch. Poekel— Permission of MIT Museum

Three weeks after taking over the yacht, Hearst had *Vamoose* race a steamer named *Mary Powell* on the Hudson River. After soundly beating *Mary Powell*, Hearst told his engineer to keep up with a passenger train of the New York Central that was seen traveling north near Yonkers. *Vamoose* kept up with the train until it reached the station in Hastings. At that point Hearst's engineer Heilborn stated: "I will wager my life that this is the fastest steam craft in the world."[6]

Hearst attempted to bring the *Vamoose* to San Francisco. It was sailed down to the Isthmus of Panama where it was to be loaded onto a specially built crib consisting of three railroad cars. Even a bridge along the railroad right-of-way was taken down for the trip. But suddenly Colonel Rives, president of the Panama Railway Company, intervened and stopped the Isthmian trip. The reason was because the Hearst-owned *San Francisco Examiner* had published a bad review of Colonel Rives's daughter Amelie's new novel, *The Quick or the Dead*. The *Vamoose* had to backtrack and return to Eastern waters where it finished its career racing in interclub regattas. In one race sponsored by the American Yacht Club in September of 1891, with the winner receiving a $500 prize, every other challenger stood down after the *Vamoose* arrived at the starting line.

Kenneth Wyte, a biographer of Hearst, felt that *Vamoose* might have been the fleetest thing on water, but its builders had sacrificed everything in the way of comfort and stability to velocity, and Hearst put it up for sale almost the moment it set its speed records.[7]

Vamoose came back into play in November 1896, when Hearst needed to get dispatches from the civil unrest in Cuba. He announced that he had "the fastest craft that ever left a trail of foam up on the waters of New York." Hearst had leased *Vamoose* back from its new owner. He headed it to Key West and crowds cheered it on its way. *Vamoose* was to transport the famous writer Richard Harding Davis as war correspondent in Cuba accompanied by Frederic Remington who in his own words said, "I was expected to illuminate the genius of Mr. Richard Harding Davis." Hearst, who was in stiff competition with Pulitzer, had paid them both $3,000.00 apiece to go to Cuba and cover the war for his *New York Journal*.

Vamoose as a dispatch ship never succeeded, as after a two rough attempts the second crew turned the boat around and brought it back to Key West.

So instead of arriving in Cuba on *Vamoose*, Remington summed it up this way: "Mr. Davis proposed that, since we could not get in the old-cellar window, we had best go around and knock at the front door. I should never have dreamed of such a thing, but Davis has the true newspaper imprudence, so we arranged passage on the regular line steamer *Olivette* for Havana."[8]

Javelin, having been partially completed for Hearst, was sold by Herreshoff to Edwin Dennison Morgan III, who assumed the contract. E. D. Morgan was often confused with John Pierpont Morgan, although

Beacon Rock, known as "The Acropolis of Newport"

distantly related. He was the grandson of the Civil War general, New York governor and senator of the same name, a financier, and a true yachtsman. In the beginning of the twentieth century he was called "America's Greatest Yachtsman." He had joined the Seawanhaka Corinthian Yacht Club in 1879, and would have a presence in the nautical world for over fifty-five years. From 1893 to 1894, he was commodore of the New York Yacht Club. He collected yachts like some people collect stamps. From his beautiful villa named Beacon Rock designed by Stanford White and perched above the cliffs overlooking the entrance to Narragansett Bay, and Newport, Rhode Island, his yachts were moored below—most of them designed and built by the Herreshoff yard.

With good employment at the Herreshoff yard, T. Sch. Poekel was in a position to get married and on Christmas Eve, 1890, he married a fellow Scandinavian—blond haired, blue eyed nineteen-year-old Anna B. Nilsson of Malmo, Sweden.

Poekel actually had been engaged to marry Anna's cousin the previous year. However, at a huge engagement party in Bristol the year before he met his fiancee's cousin Anna and it was love at first sight, which resulted in a trade between the cousins.

Anna had been working in Boston as a domestic. Although they were from neighboring Scandinavian countries, they spoke one common language in America—English. They were beginning a marital journey that would last for over fifty years.

Like Poekel and Almy, many of the craftsmen and workers at the HMCO were members of fraternal organizations. Francis Herreshoff, N. G. Herreshoff's son, in describing the workmen at the HMCO stated that "many of them belonged to the Odd Fellows or the Masons, or both, and this seemed to create a brotherly feeling among them. In fact, it was more like a big fraternity than a workshop, where each member tries to help the other and always called one another by his first name."[9]

T. Sch. Poekel, like many other Herreshoff workers, was a member of the Independent Order of Odd Fellows. The creed of the Odd Fellows stated the following:

I am an Odd Fellow
   I believe in the Fatherhood of God, and the Brotherhood of man.
   I believe in Friendship, Love and Truth as basic guides to the ultimate destiny of all mankind.
   I believe my home, my church or temple, my lodge, and my community deserve my best work, my modest pride, my earnest faith, and my duty "to visit the sick, relieve the distressed, bury the dead and educate the orphan" and as I work with others to build a better world because in spirit and in truth, I am, and must always be, grateful to my Creator, faithful to my Country and Fraternal to my fellow man.
   I AM AN ODD FELLOW

Besides fostering a love of God and their fellow man, the Odd Fellows and the Freemasons also provided social interaction. Poekel would use many of those occasions as well as church socials to play his violin. He was extremely versatile performing solos and joining with others to play dance music. His jovial manner coupled with old European manners made him extremely popular at the social events he attended.

Membership in the Odd Fellows in New England was high at the *fin-de-siecle*. In 1898, over 16,000 loyal members marched in a parade through the streets of Boston. Colloquially known as the "poor-man's Masonry," the Odd Fellows had more members than the Freemasons in the mid-1890s.

Although not a Freemason himself, T. Sch. Poekel had a great deal of respect for the Freemasons. He would often comment that all the ones he ever met in business were honorable men of integrity. "Their word was their bond," he said.

Author John Dickie writes, "In the United States, after the Civil War of the 1860's, there began a golden age of fraternalism that would last until the end of the nineteenth century."[10] This age would parallel the golden age of yachting.

However, N. G. Herreshoff wanted no part in sharing fraternal feelings or recognition of achievement. All 300 of his employees were there to burnish his genius, and they weren't his equals or his brothers. The employees never accepted Nat or John B. as part of their club even though they knew who their bosses were. Herreshoff himself said very little to his employees. Most of his interaction was with the superintendents. For the most part, he never learned the real names of most of his employees, and he adopted the workmen's tradition of calling them by the work they performed or by their appearance.

One day when a salesman had lunch with N. G. Herreshoff and started a conversation, N. G. abruptly cut him off saying, "Young man, when we sit down to the table we sit down to eat, not chatter."[11] Even N. G.'s son would write that his father was too busy working to be human. It was said that N. G. kept his long beard, so he wouldn't have to waste time shaving every day.

Making his daily rounds at the HMCO Nathanael G. Herreshoff would be very quiet and barely engaged with anyone. He was inordinately fearful of spies and interlopers coming on to his property. When Cup contenders were being built, he would often hire armed guards to surround the workshops.

Although many of his employees as Masons and/or Odd Fellows believed in God, it appears that N. G. Herreshoff was not religious—at least he didn't believe in an afterlife. Late in his life, when asked by

Starling Burgess about an afterlife, he told him that in his opinion "when a man died he went out like a candle."[12] While membership in fraternal organizations helped to unite the Herreshoff workforce, there is no evidence that any of the Herreshoffs themselves belonged to either the Masons or the Odd Fellows.

During the beginning of Poekel's employment, the Herreshoff yard was focusing on steamers, but two events brought about a huge change. One was the death of Edward Burgess in 1891, and the other was the design and building of the yacht *Gloriana*.

Both Edward Burgess and Nathanael Greene Herreshoff were born in 1848. Herreshoff studied at MIT and Burgess graduated with honors from Harvard in 1871. Burgess was a Boston Brahmin in the truest sense. One of his classmates at Harvard was another Brahmin Henry Cabot Lodge. Edward was the son of a prosperous West Indies trader from Boston. He enjoyed yachting as a sport but was learned in mathematics.

As a professor of entomology at Harvard, Edward or Ned as he became to be called met Professor Alpheus Spring Packard of Brown University who also specialized in entomology. Professor Packard was the author of the seminal work *A Study of Insects*. The two insect professors had sons who would one day become partners in yacht designing.

Soon after his father suffered some severe financial losses, Burgess decided to make a career as a yacht designer. Burgess had no formal training but was a self-taught amateur in boat designing.

He established a small office in Boston with his brother. Business was very slow at first and the Burgess brothers only designed a few small boats. However, due to the social connections that Edward had, that was about to change.

After the Royal Yacht Squadron challenged for America's Cup with Sir Richard Sutton's *Genesta*, a syndicate of Burgess's aristocratic friends led by F. Malcolm Forbes decided to commission Burgess to design the American contender. The result was a cutter based on a revolutionary design. It was named *Puritan*. It was the first attempt at designing a racing yacht for Burgess, and it showed the world that he was a genius at design. Burgess turned to a young George F. Lawley of Boston who built it. Together Burgess and Lawley made nautical history and *Puritan* kept the cup in American hands. It was followed by *Mayflower*, captained by Hank Haff, which also won America's Cup beating *Galatea*. The third winner for Burgess was *Volunteer*, which won racing against *Thistle* that had been designed by the Scottish designer George Lennox Watson. *Volunteer* won handily despite the fact *Thistle* was skippered by veteran John Barr with his brother Charlie Barr as a member of the crew.

Cut from a different mold from Herreshoff, Burgess was kind, genial, and generous. He married a beautiful Virginia belle named Cardine Louisa Sullivant, known as "Kitty." Her beauty was recognized by Giuseppe Fagnani who used her as a model for his painting "Erato." Burgess had two sons with Kitty: William Starling and Charles Paine.

The yachting world was shocked when Burgess died on July 12, 1891, from typhoid fever at the young age of forty-three. Remarkably, during his brief seven-year period as a yacht designer with no formal training, he had designed over 137 vessels. His beloved wife Kitty died a few weeks later on September 16, 1891, from pneumonia leaving their two sons orphans to be raised by relatives.

When son Starling was a young man of eighteen years of age at Milton Academy, N. G. Herreshoff, his "Uncle Nat," designed and had built a seventeen-foot jib and mainsail sloop for him named *Sally II*. Uncle Nat gave a discount on the price, charging Starling or rather his trustee $700 for the boat. During the construction Starling would stay with N. G.'s family at Love Rocks. However, when Starling told "Uncle Nat" that he wanted to be a yacht designer when he grew up, Herreshoff barred him from ever entering the model room at Love Rocks where he kept all of his models.[13]

Before 1890, the Herreshoff brothers had built only eight sailboats—four of which were for themselves. The arrival of a clever marine engineer who was an expert in ballast was exactly what the Herreshoffs needed and T. Sch. Poekel's tenure at the HMCO would not be a coincidence in the transformation of the small Bristol boatyard into one of the leading designers and builders of racing sailboats in the world.

In 1891, N. G. Herreshoff was commissioned by Royal Phelps Carroll to build a large racing yacht. After construction had begun, Carroll who was engaged to marry and busy with other activities informed the Herreshoffs that he wanted out. Serendipitously, another Herreshoff client Edwin D. Morgan saw it being built and decided to purchase it. The forty-six-foot yacht was named *Gloriana* and had a unique design. Morgan had chosen the name from the heroine of Spenser's "The Faerie Queene." Its revolutionary design, coupled with the death of Burgess, brought the Herreshoffs to the forefront of racing yacht designers. Soon N. G. would be known as the "Sorcerer of Bristol." And during this time he also had the assistance of T. Sch. Poekel who would be recognized as a clever designer himself. Exactly what input Poekel might have had with *Gloriana* and other yachts may never be known, but it is inconceivable that his involvement would not have helped to create the speedy and unique Herreshoff racing yachts. As a known expert on outside ballast, it is quite possible that Poekel invented the heavy keel.

Gloriana had a unique spoon-bow ("*Gloriana* bow") and a fin keel. According to yacht expert William P. Stephens, "From keel to truck *Gloriana* was a masterpiece of original thought, careful selection of elements and attention to minute detail."[14] Its overall length was a third larger than its length at waterline and it was light with the ballast being 60 percent of its displacement. The yacht had a deepened, rounder, and fuller waterline that enabled it to carry huge sails.

Another innovation on *Gloriana* was the use of machinery. Its hollow bronze centerboard could be raised and lowered by powerful differential lifts.

According to author Jerome E. Brooks, the *Gloriana* designers were able to evade the current rules for load-waterline measurement and *Gloriana*, *Wasp*, and others were known as "the rating cheaters."[15]

Nathanael Herreshoff would claim to have invented the fin keel but he was challenged by General I. Garrard of Frontenac, Michigan, who claimed that he had invented it and used a similar device in 1881. The spoon bow was all N. G. Herreshoff's invention and was soon copied by yacht designers the world over.

During the 1891 season nine 46- footers were built with *Gloriana* being the best. Its racing record for its first season was incredible—eight first place finishes and no losses.

The revolutionary design of *Gloriana* brought worldwide fame to the
Herreshoff yard in Bristol—Permission of MIT Museum

On June 9, 1891, less than three years after arriving in America, T.
Sch. Poekel went to the Court of Common Pleas in Bristol and petitioned for naturalized citizenship. One of his witnesses was Christian
Hermann, machine shop foreman at the HMCO, who started work at
the yard in 1878, and would stay on for forty years until 1918.

From 1892 to 1893, more large racing sailboats were built than at
any other time in yachting history and T. Sch. Poekel was at the center
of that building. During that period, besides *Vigilant*, Poekel was actively
involved in the 138-foot steamer *Truant* that was launched in 1892 and
the *Dakota* (1893).

The steel-hulled *Truant* was launched on August 23, 1892, and christened by its owner Helen Handy Newberry of Detroit, Michigan. She
was the wealthy widow of John Stoughton Newberry who had made millions in building railroad cars and who started the Detroit, Mackinac,
and Marquette Railroad. The steamer cost $60,000 and featured a triple-
expansion steam boiler. T. Sch. Poekel would learn to be an expert in

Triple-expansion steam engine from *Truant*—Permission of The Henry Ford

designing, building, and perfecting this type of engine. When the yacht was finished in September, it was sailed to Detroit via the Gulf of Canso and the Northumberland Strait. In 1936, it was purchased by Henry Ford who completely refitted it. But he took the original triple-expansion engine and put it in his museum in Dearborn where it is today.

Gloriana and its successor, *Wasp*, would be two of the most highly successful racing yachts built by the Herreshoff yard.

Wasp, built for Archibald Rogers of Hyde Park, New York, and designed to defeat *Gloriana*, was launched on February 29, 1892. Over 100 people attended the launch superintended by Captain Nat and his brother John B. Also in attendance was Mr. Hyslop, the official measurer of the New York Yacht Club. Although *Wasp* was similar to *Gloriana*, it had noticeable differences including its length, forward lines, and mast, which at twelve feet was nearly three feet higher than that of *Gloriana*. The yacht had twelve tons of lead in its keel.

On May 2, 1892, *Wasp* sailed out of Bristol Harbor headed for Roger's home in Hyde Park. At the helm was Charlie Barr. This was the first Herreshoff yacht to be captained by Charlie Barr. Thereafter, Barr would sail almost exclusively on Herreshoff-designed yachts and would achieve worldwide fame for them and for himself. N. G. Herreshoff considered the diminutive Barr (friends called him "Wee Charlie") to be a genius on the water. Soon the Scottish-born Barr would do as Poekel did and petition to become a U.S. citizen, which ingratiated himself to American yachtsmen.

For the yachting season of 1892, *Wasp* was headed for regattas at the Larchmont, Seawanhaka, New York, and Atlantic yacht clubs. The public would follow the nip and tuck battles between *Wasp* and *Gloriana*. The amount of publicity that these yachts received brought a lot of orders to the HMCO for racing sailboats. Before *Gloriana*, the Herreshoff yard had only built ten sailboats—and all under thirty feet in length. As *Wasp* left for New York, it was observed that the Herreshoff yard had ten new boats under construction.

One fascinating story about the head draftsman for Herreshoff who quite possibly was Poekel is related by Burnett in her book *Let the Best Boat Win*. It tells the story of draftsman working on the design of a steam engine and asking N. G. Herreshoff, "How about the size and taper of the connecting rods we are to draw up full size?" Herreshoff, she relates, stumbled in his pocket, produced the stubby pencil that he always carried and drew a profile on a piece of paper of the required part stating, "There, that ought to do." The draftsman's jaw dropped but said he said nothing. The part in question had a complicated function so the draftsman, having been trained as an engineer, embarked on making mathematical calculations and the result was that Nat's sketch was the exact size and shape according to his mathematical calculations. Based on this story, Burnett posits that this is but another example of how Herreshoff got to be known as the "Wizard of Bristol"—a term she says Herreshoff disliked as it indicated unworkmanlike skills.[16] However, it also illustrates that in all probability the draftsmen were the ones who through methodical mathematical calculations helped make the designs of N. G. Herreshoff work.

N. G. Herreshoff designed all his boats by first making wooden models or half hulls. From these models, he would trace them and make notes by pencil in small books. Herreshoff would make twice daily rounds to his draftsmen, usually employing from three to four. The draftsmen would take the rudimentary pencil drawings and notations then turn them into inked construction plans. The draftsmen would put N. G. Herreshoff's name was on all the plans. Some, however, had the name of T. Sch. Poekel who would rise up to be N. G. Herreshoff's chief draftsman.

In the fall of 1892, the HMCO received an order from Royal Phelps Carroll for a forty-five-foot sloop to sail in European regattas. *Navahoe* was launched in January 1893. The construction plans of *Navahoe* bore the name of T. Sch. Poekel, as did *Vamoose, Vigilant, Defender,* and the *Newport 30's*. During 1893, the yachts *Colonia* and *Vigilant* were also under construction. Both yachts would be contenders for the America's Cup challenge by the *Valkyrie II*. In the words of Nathanael Herreshoff, "This was a busy winter for me, [and] as well for the working men. I had not time, with my force in the drafting room, to work out complete detail drawings for each yacht, so both the defender's rigs were alike, and many of the details were the same as worked out for *Navahoe*."[17] *Navahoe* was launched in May of 1893. With N. G. Herreshoff too busy to attend to every detail, T. Sch. Poekel as his chief draftsman would have been allowed a greater than usual role in the planning and designing of the large racing yachts.

Navahoe was built for Carroll at a cost of $42,500. It was named in honor of the Navajo Indians but because of maritime tradition the name was changed to the English version so that it had the lucky seven letters.

When N. G. Herreshoff was ready to launch a boat, nothing would stop him—even a missing owner. On the morning of a snowy February 18, 1893, the eighty-four-foot yacht slid down the south slip of the Herreshoff yard. Not able to make the launch as the snow delayed their train ride from Providence was the owner Royal Phelps Carroll and his family. Most disappointed in the group was his sister Helen Carroll who had journeyed from Washington, D.C., to christen the yacht. Also missing the launch was Royal's father Robert Kee Carroll, the former governor of Maryland.

Navahoe—another Herreshoff racing sloop that had the name of T. Sch. Poekel on its construction plans—Permission of Beken of Cowes

So the launch took place without the owner and his guests and under tight security. Herreshoff wouldn't even release its dimensions. Reporters and photographers had to resort to piling in rowboats to cover the launch.

Carroll wanted to sail *Navahoe* over to England to enter regattas there. With his wife onboard and Charlie Barr at the helm, he set out in the spring of 1893. Barr, not quite the captain he would eventually become, encountered a heavy fog bank after leaving Newport and sailed the giant sloop directly into the Nantucket Lightship. After making an unscheduled stop in Boston for repairs, Carroll, his wife, and Barr sailed the sloop over to England with the hopes of winning the Cape May, Brenton's Reef, and Royal Victoria Cups. It had mixed results but managed to win the Brenton's Reef Cup beating the top English yacht *Britannia* in a race across the English Channel and back—winning by only a few seconds.

In a 120-mile race across the English Channel and back for the Brenton's Reef
Cup on September 12, 1893, in what was described as one of the best and
closest yacht races ever seen in European waters, victory was awarded to
Navahoe after a protest by its owner Royal Phelps Carroll. Initially, the Prince of
Wales's *Britannia* was given the corrected win by two seconds—Courtesy of Paul
Aronson, photo by Carrie Bradburn

Edward, the Prince of Wales, eldest son of Queen Victoria was
the owner of *Britannia,* which was launched on April 20, 1893,
one week ahead of *Valkyrie II.* Both *Britannia* and *Valkyrie II* were
designed by the Scottish designer George Lennox Watson. The
Prince would help promote yacht racing on the world stage, and he
was also a Freemason who would serve as Grand Master of Masons
in England.

Carroll, in an interview with the *New York Times* on September 16,
1893, was highly critical of the construction of *Navahoe.* "Evidently there
was some mistake in her design," he stated adding, "She does not carry as
much sail as she was designed to carry. She has not sufficient stability in
my opinion—her weight and ballast are not properly adjusted."[18] *Navahoe*
returned to the States in October of 1893.

A formal challenge for America's Cup came from Sir Wyndham Thomas Wyndham-Quin, fourth Earl of Dunraven and Mount-Earl, of Dunraven Castle, Brigend, Glamorgan, Wales, and of Adare Manor, Sadare County, Limerick, Ireland. The Earl, whose seat was the magnificent Adare Manor in Limerick, challenged for America's Cup with his yacht *Valkyrie II* for a race in 1893. The challenge was accepted. This was the second attempt by the earl with a yacht named after a warder of Odien from Norse mythology.

A syndicate formed by Archibald Rogers, William K. Vanderbilt, and J. P. Morgan contracted on December 13, 1892, with the Herreshoff yard to build a possible cup defender named *Colonia*, which was to replicate Rogers's *Wasp*. The cost was $45,000. Also, in the Herreshoff yard was *Navahoe*.

As yacht racing grew in the United States, yachtsmen realized there had to be a solution for disparate boats racing against each other to insure fairness. England had used a classification system based on tonnages. On the East Coast, the Seawanhaka Rule was adopted. Beginning in 1893, and extending through to 1903, the Seawanhaka Rule applied to all races for the America's Cup.

The Seawanhaka Rule was: Rating = (Water Length + Square Root of Sail Area/2).

In 1903, N. G. Herreshoff would come up with the Universal Rule that replaced the Seawanhaka Rule.

But according to William P. Stephens, "The yachts designed under the Seawanhaka Rule between 1883 and 1900 represent the high point of designing in America."[19]

Nathanael Greene Herreshoff knew what the rule covered and what it didn't cover, so for the next several years actively exploited it. He designed narrow boats with long overhangs and huge sail areas.

The *Puritan*'s sail area was considered enormous at 7,982 square feet. Herreshoff's first Cup winner *Vigilant* had a sail area of 11,272 square feet and the *Defender* in 1895, 12,602.30 square feet. Finally, Herreshoff's last Cup winner *Reliance* had a sail area of 16,169.03 square feet. It was pointed out in the *New York Times* that *Reliance*'s sail area was equivalent to a square 127.16 feet on each side that would blanket anyone's view of New York City's General Post Office as seen from Lower Broadway.[20]

In early 1893, a syndicate consisting of Charles Oliver Iselin, August Belmont Jr., Cornelius Vanderbilt, Charles R. Flint, Chester W. Chapin, George R. Clark, Henry Astor Carey, Dr. Barton Hopkins, E. M. Fulton Jr., and Adrian G. Iselin commissioned the Herreshoffs for a Cup defender.

As work commenced, John B. Herreshoff on March 15, 1893, announced that the new yacht would be plated with Tobin bronze below the waterline and steel above. This was not a surprise, however, since large amounts of the bright metal had been delivered weeks before to the yard. Tobin bronze is brass containing tin and is resistant to seawater.

N. G. Herreshoff would write in his personal recollections that "after studying the original design with no lead outside, it was decided to increase the draft, and place part of the lead ballast outside."[21] This was a most significant change from his original design, and it is most interesting that N. G. doesn't take personal credit for the change which he does in other matters. It is quite possible that the idea came from T. Sch. Poekel who had a reputation of being a ballast expert.

On June 14, 1893, at 7:55 pm the new yacht was launched from the north shop of the HMCO. Only C. Oliver "Ollie" Iselin was present to witness the launching. As Florence DeWolfe, N. G. Herreshoff's sister, took a bottle of champagne and christened the yacht its name for the first time was announced—*Vigilant*. The public was allowed into the yard but not into the shops. As the Tobin bronze-coated centerboarder slid into the water, T. Sch. Poekel stood by with prideful eyes.

In those days there were no rules limiting crew size. *Vigilant* with its wide deck often had a crew of seventy to provide more stability, while yachts of similar length usually had a crew of forty. It was estimated that the crew of seventy amounted to "live ballast," weighing almost six tons and gave the yacht an advantage of about one foot of unmeasured waterline. Having no room to house the crew, an old schooner named *Hattie Palmer* was chartered to serve as chaperone for the season for housing and towing purposes. *Vigilant*'s exploitation of the defect in the rules was not unnoticed. *Forest and Stream* magazine of November 2, 1893, wrote, "Assuming the right of *Vigilant*, in default of any express prohibition, to avail herself of this kind and amount of ballast, there is still the nice question of ethics—whether such a course is to be considered fair and sportsmanlike." The seventy member crew

Vigilant, the Herreshoffs' first America's Cup winner in 1893—Library of Congress

were mostly Scandinavians. Because of their enormous power and strength, they were known collectively as "Norwegian steam."

Later on in the summer, *Vigilant* beat *Colonia*, *Jubilee*, and *Pilgrim*, and on September 11, it was announced that the centerboarder would be America's entry to compete against Lord Dunraven's *Valkyrie II* in defense of America's Cup. *Jubilee* and *Pilgrim* were sponsored by Boston syndicates and *Vigilant* and *Colonia* by New York syndicates. Both of the New York contenders were designed and built by the Herreshoff yard. *Vigilant* would be the first Herreshoff-designed boat to race for yachting's most prestigious contest—America's Cup.

The fact that the Americans had a choice among the four possible contenders to defend the Cup highlighted another inequity in the rules facing the British. They could select only one challenger.

The evolution of American yacht design started in the eighteenth century. One of the first yachts was the pink or pinkie, which was a boat designed for cod fishermen in New England. Soon thereafter Captain

Andrew Robinson in 1713 perfected the schooner which was a double-masted yacht with sails fore and aft.

The advent of yacht racing in England and America brought on the establishment of yacht clubs. On June 1, 1815, in the Thatched House Tavern in St. James, London, the Royal Yacht Squadron was founded. It was the first and would become the most prestigious yacht club in the world. The exclusive club in Cowes on the Isle of Wight required its members to be gentlemen who owned yachts not under ten tons. In America on July 30, 1844, John Cox Stevens of Hoboken, New Jersey, and eight other yacht owners met aboard Steven's yacht *Gimcrack* in New York Harbor and formed the New York Yacht Club.

The history of America's Cup goes back to when *America* won the first cup race against Great Britain in Cowes, England, in 1851. It had been built for John Cox Stevens. It beat over sixty-five English yachts in the presence of Queen Victoria. According to myth, it had won by such a large margin that when the Queen was told the American boat had won and she asked who was second, the reply was "Madam, there is no second." Whether true or not, this story gave great encouragement to yacht racing in the United States.

The win by *America* gave it possession of what was originally commonly referred to as the "Queen's Cup," the "Royal Cup," and even "Ye Olde Mug." But by 1874, thanks to a poem by Hamilton Morton, a former secretary of the New York Yacht Club, it became known as "America's Cup."

Winning the Cup by the United States was so momentous that when Daniel Webster was giving a speech in the Statehouse in Boston, and he received word of *America*'s win, he announced, "Like Jupiter among the gods, America is first and there is no second."[22] The win was not just a race between two yachts but signified that the torch of world power had passed to America.

Giving T. Sch. Poekel encouragement while working at the Herreshoff yard was the knowledge that the only foreign yacht to ever beat *America* was the Swedish-designed *Sverige*.

Poekel, as a well-respected draftsman at the HMCO, was indeed living the American dream and he proudly became a naturalized U.S. citizen on September 13, 1893. As an American, Poekel could root not just for a yacht that had his name on its construction plans but also for his country's effort to retain the America's Cup. The citizenship ceremony took place in the Court of Common Pleas in Bristol. And what better town in America to gain it. Bristol was known for having the oldest Fourth of July parade in America. It was established in 1785, by Reverend Henry Wight of the First Congregational Church—himself a veteran of the Revolutionary War.

Both John B. and N. G. Herreshoff realized at an early point in Poekel's employment that he was a clever engineer and as such would supply them with revolutionary ideas for their yachts. They would make him their chief draftsman.

Having been accepted as the challenger for the 1893 America's Cup, Lord Dunraven brought the *Valkyrie II* across the Atlantic in a twenty-nine-day journey, which had the yacht facing severe headwinds and for days was incommunicado. *Valkyrie II* was designed by Scotsman George Lennox Watson of Glasgow. It would face *Vigilant*, which was the first Cup contender to have a bronze bottom. C. Oliver Iselin, was the managing partner of the syndicate as owner and the skipper of *Vigilant*. Iselin, with an estate in New Rochelle, New York, was the scion of a wealthy Swiss family of importers and a life-long sailor. Starting with the *Vigilant*, he would rival E. D. Morgan as the leading yachtsman in America.

Soon after he arrived in New York City, Lord Dunraven went to the New York Yacht Club to discuss a delay of the races. Upon entering the hallowed club none of the members recognized the Irish Earl. A young man approached him and told him that he was in a private club and he had to be accompanied by a member. After straightening the young man out, the Earl was escorted to where the Cup committee was meeting. He met with them and asked for a postponement of the races due to the unexpected time-consuming trip across the Atlantic of the *Valkyrie II*. The committee granted his request.

Lord Dunraven had the highest respect for Nathanael G. Herreshoff, which was exhibited a few years later when asked if he thought *Valkyrie III* would beat *Defender* his response was, "I have a wholesome regard for the genius of Herreshoff."[23]

The America's Cup competition between *Vigilant* and *Valkyrie II* took place on October 5, 7, 9, and 13, 1893, off Sandy Hook, New Jersey, just south of New York City. Nathanael Greene Herreshoff was at the helm for the first two races and for much of the third. The first race was called off for lack of wind. *Vigilant* won on October 7 by five minute forty-eight seconds corrected time. The October 9 race was the toughest with *Valkyrie II* leading by over two minutes at the first mark. At that point, seasoned sailor C. Oliver Iselin took over and put every sail out—the spinnaker, the balloon jib, the club topsail in place of the working topsail, and then *Vigilant* breezed across the water to victory. After the second win, everyone was convinced that *Valkyrie II*—even its designer Watson—couldn't hold a match to *Vigilant*.

Vigilant won the third and deciding race on Friday the 13th of October, 1893, by forty seconds.

Even though *Valkyrie II* put up a strong battle, *Vigilant* had won three straight in the best of five contests. But what a remarkable feat for N. G. Herreshoff—he had designed, built, and sailed *Vigilant* to victory for the U.S. Eighth America's Cup win. Forever after, he would be known as "Captain Nat."

A writer for the *New York Times*, although prematurely, eloquently commented on the outcome: "It is all over—and the uncomely silver urn that was wrested years ago as a symbol of sovereignty from her who claims to rule the waves still remains on alien soil, as the Ark of Israel was ruthlessly stored in the Temple of Dagon. In other words, with a singular propriety, the America's Cup remains, as it will probably remain forever, among the trophies of American conquest."[24]

History was also made during the races as Lord Dunraven's daughter became the first female to sail in an international yacht race in the United States. Hope Goddard Iselin, second wife of C. Oliver Iselin, would have the distinction of being the first American female crew member in America's Cup competition on the *Columbia* in 1899.

After complaining of the presence of too many spectator boats near the course during the 1893 races, Dunraven went on to issue another challenge for 1895.

With *Vigilant*'s victory in America's Cup, the HMCO became famous throughout the world and put Bristol on the map.

A few weeks after the America's Cup races, an impeccably dressed young man of about thirty years of age appeared at the Herreshoff offices on Burnside Street in Bristol. His suit was custom-tailored and he wore a tall silk hat. The Herreshoffs were used to dealing with some of the wealthiest men in America—men like C. Oliver Islin, Edwin Dennison Morgan,

John Pierpont Morgan, and William Randolph Hearst. This gentleman appeared to be cut from the same cloth. He was ushered into the inner office of John B. and was joined by N. G. Herreshoff. He told them he wanted them to build a yacht for him, and not just any yacht but a twin-screwed steamer. It was to be one of the largest and most luxurious yachts in the world and at 185 feet in length, the largest ever built by the Herreshoffs. He told the brothers he was Howard Wade Ream of New York City.

Mr. Ream, who brought with him no letters of introduction or endorsements from Herreshoff customers, stated he was a New York City stockbroker currently living at the Waldorf Astoria Hotel and in the process of relocating his offices to 40 Wall Street. He wanted the Herreshoffs to design and build for him a luxury steamer incorporating some of the same details of *Vigilant*, including the Tobin bronze bottom. Money would be no object. The Herreshoffs quickly drew up a contract, gave Ream some manganese and aluminum samples that they said would be used in construction. Captain Nat made a preliminary sketch. The yacht would have a twenty-two-foot-six-inch beam and its interior would contain the finest furnishings that money could buy. The agreed upon price was $150,000, which was to be paid in installments. It would be the largest amount the company had ever charged. The equivalent in 2020, would be $4.2 million. The Herreshoff brothers immediately ordered materials to build the yacht and took on extra workmen at the yard. They said the yacht would be completed by June 1st of 1894, and proudly made an announcement in the press.

The Herreshoffs would never see Howard Wade Ream again.

In December of 1893, two men were arrested in Boston on charges of larceny of a gold watch. One of the men was Howard W. Ream. A search of Ream by the police found he had a sketch for a magnificent yacht, a contract with the HMCO, and some samples of aluminum and Tobin bronze. When the co-defendant copped a plea and was sent to jail, Ream was held but subsequently released by the judge on the condition that he take the next train out of Boston.

Ream, it turns out, was a confidence man from Chicago who had once served time in Chicago's Bidewell Prison for vagrancy—being a masher in front of a Chicago theater. He was known to mingle in Chicago society posing as the nephew or son of Norman B. Ream, one of the wealthiest men in the United States. Norman had a high position with Chicago's Board of Trade and was on the board of some twenty-two corporations in the country. When Howard had gone to New York City, he booked a room for two nights at the Waldorf Astoria, which gave him an address there. He left owing $7, which he never paid. Neither did he pay the Herreshoffs, only telling reporters that he purchased the yacht on behalf of some of his New York friends whose identity he wouldn't reveal.

Mr. Howard Wade Ream was never heard from again.

On April 19, 1894, *Vigilant* was sold by the syndicate to George Jay and Howard Gould, wealthy sons of Jay Gould. Jay Gould, the railway magnate, was one of the wealthiest Americans of the nineteenth century. He was most commonly referred to as a "robber baron" for his allegedly shady business practices. Such practices included receiving a $3 million bonus which was undisclosed to his shareholders when he merged his Kansas Pacific and Union Pacific railroads.

Jay Gould, typical of the very wealthy in the nineteenth century, was into yachting. In 1883, he spent $230,000 to have built his luxurious 230-foot yacht *Atalanta*. It had a crew of fifty-two and contained a dining room that could accommodate thirty-two guests. Despite Gould's money, he was rejected by both the New York Yacht Club and the Eastern Yacht Club. So he established his own club—the American Yacht Club in Bay Ridge, New York. The American Yacht Club, founded in 1883, was initially a club for owners of steam yachts and became known for its fabulous cuisine.

The article stated that the price being paid for *Vigilant* was $25,000, which was considered a bargain since the syndicate had paid the HMCO $60,000 for it. This was less than an unaccepted offer of $30,000 made by James Gordon Bennett Jr., publisher of the *New York Herald*, who also wanted to own it in order to challenge the Prince of Wales's *Britannia*.

It was arranged that *Vigilant* and *Valkyrie II* would race each other again in European waters. This never happened as *Valkyrie II* was broadsided by *Satanita* during a race and sank in the Clyde early in the 1894, season.

T. Sch. Poekel, like many others, felt that the United States always had an advantage in winning America's Cup since the rules of the New York Yacht Club required any challenger to arrive by water "on their own bottoms"—either by sailing or being towed. Thus, the English had to construct a heavy enough boat with suitable rigging to withstand the North Atlantic in order to compete in American waters. To try and disprove this theory, Gould had the *Vigilant* refitted and sailed to England in 1894. *Vigilant's* fourteen-day trip to Ireland and its return in 1895 in seventeen days under the command of Charlie Barr set the record of the fastest transatlantic roundtrip by a sailboat.

Besides having an interest in yachts, Howard Gould had an unfettered interest in stage actresses. Shortly before he purchased *Vigilant*, Howard got engaged to the twenty-five-year-old actress Odette Tyler, from Savannah, Georgia, who was the daughter of a civil war general. Her godfather was Robert E. Lee. Although he gave her a ring valued at $9,500 ($285,000 in current dollars), it was widely rumored that his elder brother George Jay Gould and other family members were against the engagement because Howard was twenty-three years old—two years younger than Odette. The engagement was called off before Howard left to be with *Vigilant* in England. It's not clear if he ever got the engagement ring back.

On July 28, 1894, crowds thronged the Mount Bay Regatta to watch a race between the *Vigilant* and the Prince of Wales's (later King Edward VII) yacht *Britannia*. Within its first year of racing, it won thirty-three times out of forty-three starts. Britishers came by train from all over to watch the race. *Britannia*, captained by Philip Nichols of Penzance, whose brother Benjamin skippered *Vigilant*, won by over seven minutes.

In sixteen races with *Britannia*, *Vigilant* lost twelve, including one skippered by Nathanael Herreshoff. Many observers speculated that *Vigilant* didn't do very well in European waters due to the fact that the races there covered much shorter courses than in America. Others felt that *Valkyrie II* was really a better boat (it was practically the same as *Britannia*) but lost to *Vigilant* due to its home court advantage sailing in American waters.

Also, heavily engaged in yachting at the time was the Prince's cousin Kaiser Wilhelm II, the Emperor of Germany, whose yacht racing would be followed throughout the world.

It was the golden age of yachting and royalty had a large role. Besides the English royalty and the Kaiser, there was also King Alphonso XIII of Spain who loved yacht racing.

Yachting in the 1890s was not without peril. Even the Kaiser's yacht
Meteor could go aground—Permission of Beken of Cowes

Also, in 1894, besides Mr. Ream, the Herreshoff yard was visited by
Augustus Stout Van Wickle and his ten-year-old daughter Marjorie. Van
Wickle was a Pennsylvania industrialist heavily involved in mining coal
and other ores. During his visit, John B. showed him a seventy-eight-and-
half-foot steamer that he had built for himself and named *Eugenia* after
his wife. Van Wickle out of impulse bought it at once. He would later
rename it *Marjorie* after his daughter. Also, during his trip to Bristol, he
was shown some land not far from the Herreshoff yard. He would soon
purchase it and build a country estate with magnificent gardens naming it
Blithewold. Marjorie would later inherit it and, after a lifetime of botanical
enhancements, she bequeathed it to the public upon her death in 1976.

In early 1895, the Herreshoff yard launched the *Niagara* (HMCo. #451)
—a sixty-five-foot fin-keel sloop built for Howard Gould. It was forty-five
feet long on the waterline, with twelve-feet beam, and ten-feet draught. It was
one of the largest fin-keelers that the Herreshoff yard ever built.

Gould took the *Niagara* over to the United Kingdom in the spring
of 1895, and entered it in almost every regatta. Its initial record was

Niagara—Permission of Beken of Cowes

stupendous—winning forty-one races out of fifty starts, coming second nine times and third once. Among the trophies which *Niagara* won that first season were the Lord Dunraven Castle Yacht Club Challenge Cup, silver punch bowls from the Clyde, Corinthian, and Royal Albert Yacht Clubs, silver loving cups from the Royal Western of England and the West of Scotland Yacht Clubs, the Maitland Kersey Cup presented by the Castle Yacht Club, and a silver set and tray from the Royal Western Yacht Club.

John Barr was the skipper of *Niagara*. He had been the captain of *Thistle*. At the end of the European yachting season, both Barr and Gould returned to America.

Niagara's second season, not quite as great as its first, saw the sloop win twenty out of forty races. No American yacht ever made such a record in English waters.

Howard Gould, as the owner of *Niagara*, was made a life member of the Royal Ulster Yacht Club of Belfast, an honorary member of the Royal Cork Yacht Club, the Start Bay Yacht Club of Dartmouth, and the Douglas Bay Yacht Club of the Isle of Man. He was also elected a member of

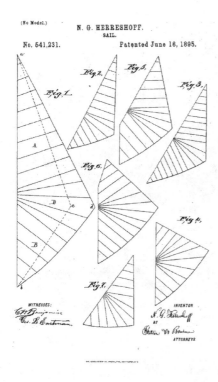

the Royal Largs Yacht Club, the Royal Alfred Yacht Club, and the Royal Temple Yacht Club.

On April 8, 1895, Nathanael Greene Herreshoff applied for a patent for an invention of new and improved triangular sails, including jibs, foresails, and staysails. Attesting as witnesses to Herreshoff's application were the longtime Office Manager C. W. Young and Chief Draftsman T. Sch. Poekel.

Letters of Patent (No. 541,231) were granted to Herreshoff on June 18, 1895.

With the invention of the crosscut sails, Herreshoff couldn't find a manufacturer to execute such a radical departure, so he set up a sail loft and manufactured them himself. According to Herreshoff's son, "It is my belief that the cross-sails gave Mr. Herreshoff a great advantage over other designers until other sailmakers cut their sails in the same way."[25] He added that it was "probable that the crosscut sail has been copied more than any of his inventions, and it is used today on almost every racing sailboat throughout the world."

In 1894, Lord Dunraven formalized his next challenge for America's Cup for 1895. After that challenge, a syndicate was formed with C. Oliver Iselin as managing partner to commission a yacht for the American defense of the Cup. Iselin and the HMCO agreed to a price of $75,000 for the design and construction of *Defender*. It would be paid in six installments of $12,500 each. It was the most money the company had ever received for the construction of a yacht. The contract, however, provided that in the event the yacht was not launched by June 15, HMCO would lose $1,000 down and $100 per day for every day beyond June 15.

UNITED STATES PATENT OFFICE.

NATHANIEL GREENE HERRESHOFF, OF BRISTOL, RHODE ISLAND, ASSIGNOR OF TWO-THIRDS TO THE HERRESHOFF MANUFACTURING COMPANY, OF SAME PLACE.

SAIL.

SPECIFICATION forming part of Letters Patent No. 541,231, dated June 18, 1895.

Application filed April 8, 1895. Serial No. 544,838. (No model.)

To all whom it may concern:

Be it known that I, NATHANIEL GREENE HERRESHOFF, a citizen of the United States, residing at Bristol, in the county of Bristol, in 5 the State of Rhode Island, have invented a certain new and useful Improvement in Sails, of which the following is a specification.

The invention applies to all approximately triangular sails, as jibs, foresails and staysails.
10 Sails are exposed to tensile strains in all directions, but the forces in different directions widely vary. The greatest strain in a sail of this form practically coincides with the directions in which it is most important to attain
15 permanence of dimensions. The parallel cloths in the upper and lower parts of my sail receive the greatest strains in directions substantially transverse to their lengths, and the arrangement also attains permanence of di-
20 mensions in the same directions. In the central area the tapering cloths each extend smoothly and continuously across the sail, and the upper and lower parts are properly joined by continuous tapering cloths which
25 extend quite across, and all oblique junctions with the weakness, elastic yielding and liability to shrinkage incident thereto, are avoided.

It is common to manufacture sails from
30 comparatively narrow strips of canvas, technically cloths, strongly and smoothly sewed together, and much attention has been given to the arrangement thereof. As sail canvas is usually manufactured it is stronger and
35 firmer and less subject to stretching and shrinking transversely than longitudinally of the cloth, and it is desirable to so arrange the strips in sails that the cloths shall be presented transversely to receive the heaviest
40 strains and to maintain the most permanent dimensions. Arrangements have been proposed and tried with more or less success to attain this end, but as heretofore carried out, such arrangements have, in triangular sails,
45 been believed to require a diagonal seam across the sail and oblique junctions of the ordinary seams therewith. There are objections to such, for the reason, among others, that there is an unavoidable want of uni-
50 formity in the elastic yielding, stretching and shrinking between such bias junctions and the other portions of the sail. I have discovered that it is practicable to avoid such angular junctions and attain the desired presenta-
55 tion of the cloths over a large portion of the sail area, and to present the cloths all in continuous lengths each extending quite across the sail.

In my improvement, instead of employing
60 the usual diagonal or mitered seam running across the sail from the clew to the luff and joining the upper and lower parts which have the cloths extending in different directions, I make the sail so that the upper and lower
65 parts are composed of ordinary parallel cloths, joining them by means of cloths cut tapering, the seams of which radiate from a point or from several points on or outside the luff of the sail and opposite the clew. From the
70 edges of these tapering cloths, parallel breadths are joined by sewing or in any other manner, until the whole sail is completed. These parallel cloths may be perpendicular to the leech in the upper part and perpendicular
75 to the foot in the lower part. I prefer arranging them perpendicularly to imaginary lines running to the head and tack from a point in the sail a little distance inside of the clew.

80 The invention keeps the weft of the fabric in the general direction of the greatest strain when the sail is in use, and at the same time avoids the use of oblique joints.

The accompanying drawings form a part of
85 this specification and represent what I consider the best means of carrying out the invention.

Figure 1 is a side view of a jib. The remaining figures are on a smaller scale. Fig.
90 2 shows a modification in which the seams in the fan-like portion radiate from more than one center. Fig. 3 shows the invention applied to a sail in which the length of the foot is greater relatively to the length of the leech.
95 Fig. 4 is a jib-headed top-sail. Fig. 5 is a yacht yard top-sail. Fig. 6 is a barge's topsail. Fig. 7. is a yacht's stay-foresail. All show the joints plainly marked by single lines. It will be understood that the joints
100 may be made with double seams, and with all the ordinary or suitable provisions for strength and smoothness.

Similar letters of reference indicate corresponding parts in all the figures where they appear.

Referring to Fig. 1, I will describe the entire sail area as divided into three parts, A indicating the upper portion, and B the lower portion. An imaginary center line c, extends from the head a to a point c near but considerably within the clew d. The cloths in the portion A are of full breadth and arranged at right angles to this line. The cloths in the portion B are similarly of full breadth and arranged parallel to each other and at right angles to an imaginary line c, b, which extends from the same point c to the tack.

D is the area of the sail between the parts A and B. For this the cloths are cut tapering and are inserted fan-wise, with their broader ends presented to the leech and foot respectively, and the narrower ends to the forward edge, the luff of the sail.

Modifications may be made without departing from the principle or sacrificing the advantages of the invention.

In Fig. 1 I have shown the taper as converging to a single point considerably forward of the luff. I prefer such in order to give an attractive appearance, but this may be varied. Thus the uppermost of the several tapered cloths in the part D may taper at such rate that if continued the boundaries would come to a point at a certain distance beyond the luff, and the adjacent tapering cloth may converge at a different rate so as to come together at a more distant point. Fig. 2 shows such an arrangement.

In Fig. 3 the tapering cloths all converge to a single point, as in Fig. 1, but the proportions of the sail are different.

In Fig. 4, a jib-headed topsail, the area D bears a larger proportion to the areas A, B, but the arrangement of the gores is the same.

Fig. 5 shows the application of my invention to a sail in which the form departs slightly from the triangular or jib form. In this the area of the part D is less than in the last.

In Fig. 6 the seams in the part D range toward a point which is only a little outside of the luff rope.

Economy may be attained with my tapering forms of the cloths in the mid portion by reversing the arrangements of the cloths, cutting sufficient lengths of ordinary fabric obliquely longitudinally, retaining one selvage on each portion and utilizing both the tapering pieces thus produced by turning one relatively to the other. This presents the yarns but slightly oblique and may serve for ordinary use but in preparing the sails for the best class of yachts, such economy may be overruled, and the required taper be given by cutting equally from each side of each of the tapering cloths. For small sails with sufficiently wide material it is possible to make the part D of a single cloth properly tapered.

I claim as my invention—

1. In the manufacture of jibs or other approximately triangular sails, the combination of a middle portion having tapering cloths arranged fan-wise and extending each continuously across the sail, with two other portions, one above, in which the seams are parallel, and run across the sail from the leech to the luff, and the other below in which the seams are parallel and run across the sail from the foot to the luff, as herein specified.

2. A triangular sail composed of cloths having the seams in the upper portion, extending perpendicularly to a line from the head to a point within the clew, and in the lower portion perpendicularly to a line extending from said point within the clew to the tack, the two portions connected by a portion in which one or more tapering cloths are used, arranged radially so as to fill up the space between the upper and lower portions, substantially as described.

In testimony that I claim the invention above set forth I affix my signature in presence of two witnesses.

NATHANIEL GREENE HERRESHOFF.

Witnesses:
TH. POÉKEL,
C. W. YOUNG.

Even though the Cup races were scheduled for September, Iselin's syndicate needed a June launch so that the yacht could have trial runs and the crew trained. And this time Iselin wanted an all-American crew. He would find such a crew among the sailors of Deer Isle, Maine. He traveled there and hired the group whose families had been sailing the Maine waters for decades. Many of the crew would arrive at the Herreshoff yard during the construction period and actually assist with the construction. The Herreshoffs subcontracted the rigging to Charles Billman of Boston and the Deer Isle boys worked with this group as well as with the regular Herreshoff yard workers. This was a great idea, since the crew could gain experience on the workings of the yacht that would enable them to make on the spot repairs while the yacht was racing.

Time was therefore of the essence and Poekel would play an important role.

C. Oliver "Ollie" Iselin, the managing partner of the syndicate that owned *Defender*, was one of the most recognized yachtsmen in the country in the late nineteenth century. Starting with *Defender* and through *Reliance*, he would be part owner and syndicate manager of four of America's Cup defenders. It was said that "Mr. Iselin was born to wealth, married heiresses, and is not harassed by the practical necessities that fall to the lot of most men. While other men are storing up useless millions he is giving his ceaseless energy to the sport of sports, and by his splendid nerve and skill is upholding America's ascendancy in the yachting world."[26]

Both *Valkyrie III* and *Defender* were built to be lightweight and fast-racing machines designed to race once. *Defender* itself was full of metal. It had magazine bronze on the bottom of the hull, frames of steel, bronze and steel fastenings, and aluminum for topsides. Besides being a weak metal, aluminum was subject to galvanic corrosion by salt water. According to noted author Jerome E. Brooks, "The action of sea water on different metals in close proximity is to induce electrolysis—a scientific fact of which Herreshoff was obviously unaware."[27] In fact, Herreshoff had touted his use of aluminum to Iselin and other members of his syndicate. A few months after the big race, corrosion set in and the beautiful *Defender* became a rust bucket moored at Iselin's

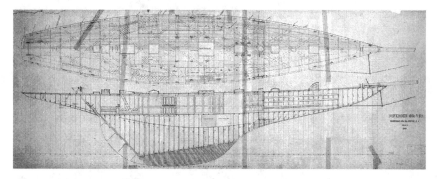

Defender's construction plan—Permission MIT Museum

75

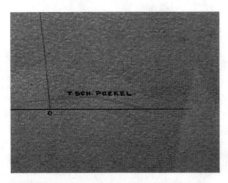

The name T. Sch. Poekel—on *Defender*'s construction plan

grand New Rochelle estate. When it had to be scrapped, Captain Nat became defensive and said that the yacht had served its purpose.

Poekel's name also appears on the final drafting plans of *Defender*. Of thousands of construction plans maintained by the HMCO, only a few more names other than N.G. Herreshoff's. So it is most unusual to have a draftsman's name appearing. Much more visual inspection of the plans and handwriting analysis are required to advance this sort of archival archaeology to determine the actual role of Poekel in the design. It does seem apparent, however, that Poekel thought his involvement in the design warranted his name to be on the plans.

In 1895, N. G. Herreshoff, during the construction of the *Defender*, took very ill. On March 6 Herreshoff's illness took an unfavorable turn and Dr. Miller was quickly called for. Miller's diagnosis was bronchial pneumonia in the right lung.

Herreshoff turned over the construction of *Defender* to Poekel. Herreshoff himself was confined to Love Rocks where inspite of his illness, he was reportedly ranting and raving and giving orders.

After his first diagnosis of pneumonia, there was a second of typhoid fever. What terrified the Herreshoff family was that this was the exact disease that had felled Edward Burgess at age forty-three. Herreshoff did manage to send missives to his workmen and his brother John.[28]

Taking time off from overseeing the construction of *Defender*, T. Sch. Poekel on May 14 performed a violin solo before a large gathering at the Burnside Lodge No. 34 of the Knights of Pythias in the Grand Army Hall in Bristol. After the formal program, he stayed and played for dancing.

The Knights of Pythias was another popular fraternal organization of the late nineteenth century. It was the first such organization to be granted a charter from the government—President Lincoln issued it one

During the illness of Nathanael Greene Herreshoff, T. Sch. Poekel took charge of *Defender's* construction—Library of Congress

in 1864. Founded by Justus H. Rathbone, who had been inspired by the Irish poet John Banim writing about the legend of Damon and Pythias. Its motto is "Friendship, Charity, Benevolence."

T. Sch. Poekel was not the only talented fiddler in maritime circles in 1895. Lord Dunraven himself was a talented violinist with a very special violin. Dunraven's violin was a Stradivarius made by Antonio Stradivardi in 1710, during his "golden period." Like many of the 700 "Strads" in existence, it is named after a famous owner—in this case it is the Lord Dunn-Raven Stradivarius. Lord Dunraven owned it from 1890 to 1923, and its current owner is the world-renowned German violinist Anne-Sophie Mutter.

On June 29, 1895, thousands filled the streets and others took boats out into Bristol harbor for the launching of *Defender*. T. Sch. Poekel, however, was close to the launch party and viewed with pride the launching, which saw Captain Nat's young daughter Catherine break the champagne bottle over *Defender's* bow.

The master and his disciple. N. G. Herreshoff and T. Sch.
Poekel—Permission of Mariners' Museum and Park

Hank Haff was the skipper for *Defender*, and the crew from Deer Island
included the Barbour brothers. Irving G. Barbour would be the quartermaster and take direct orders from Skipper Haff.

Henry "Hank" Haff was a very popular yachting skipper at the time.
He was known as a captain who could take a fast yacht and make it go even
faster. He was fifty-seven years old and had a most interesting background.
For the first twenty years of his life, he had been a farmer and had no nautical experience whatsoever.

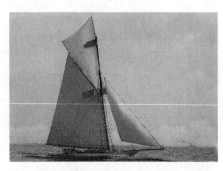

Defender—The 1895 America's Cup
Winner—Library of Congress

Dunraven, still upset over
the crowded spectator-filled
course conditions off New York
Harbor in 1893, petitioned the
New York Yacht Club to hold
the races off Marblehead, Massachusetts, but was turned down.

The races commenced off
New Jersey on September 7,
1895, with hundreds of yachts
and boats surrounding the course

with an estimated 60,000 spectators. Lord Dunraven protested the inability of the New York Yacht Club to keep the excursion boats away from the racing areas.

The 1895 America's Cup races have been aptly characterized as "a fluke, a foul and a fizzle."

Defender won the first race, which was marred by a steamship blocking the yachts on the course. Dunraven accused *Defender* of being higher in the water than its official measurement accusing the Americans of adding more ballast the night before the race.

September 10, 1895, saw the second race and Dunraven's challenger *Valkyrie III* crossed the finish line first, but only after dodging interference caused by the steamer *Yorktown*, a spectator boat, and sweeping across *Defender*'s deck ripping apart its starboard shrouds. C. Oliver Iselin, the manager of the syndicate that owned *Defender* issued a protest and the judge awarded the win to *Defender*. Iselin offered to resail the race but Lord Dunraven said such an offer should properly come from the racing committee, but the committee ruled it didn't have the authority to order a do-over and the win went to *Defender*. This incident received nationwide attention and in Chicago the *Tribune* posted a bulletin asking for public comments. Commodore Berriman of the Lincoln Park Yacht Club said this: "I believe the decision is perfectly just and proper. It is in strict accordance to the club rules and no fair sportsman could complain of it. However, I believe we can well afford to be generous and I would be glad to hear the *Defender* people had offered to declare the race off and sail it over again. This would be generous and would leave no room for complaint from the *Valkyrie* people."

That same day the *Times* of London ran a small article stating that J. L. Ashbury had died. What the brief obituary omitted was that James Lloyd Ashbury was the first Englishman to challenge for America's Cup in 1870, with *Cambria*, a schooner which he had sailed to the opening of the Suez Canal. It lost to *Magic* and then again he challenged with the *Livonia* which lost to the *Columbia* and *Sapho* in 1871. Ashbury who had inherited about $2,000 twenty-five years earlier had squandered most of it and in 1895 he was struggling financially. He died from an overdose of chlorodyne.

Lord Dunraven was extremely cognizant of the deleterious effect of spectator boat interference. He had been at the helm of *Valkyrie II* when in order to avoid a spectator boat, its racing opponent *Santanita* rammed it broadside causing it to sink into the Clyde.

On September 12, 1895, Lord Dunraven was still reeling from the interference of *Yorktown*, which caused the collision of the two racing yachts, and he wanted a representation that if there was spectator interference, the committee would have the race resailed or else he threatened to stand his yacht still and not race. The committee again would not offer a resail in the event of spectator interference, so the Earl made good on his threat and had *Valkyrie III* withdraw after the start. *Defender* finished the course alone and became the America's Cup winner.

Dunraven complained again about interference by the spectator boats. In fact, both Iselin and N. G. Herreshoff protested the interference by the spectator boats. Captain Nat who never said much after a race had this to say: "I am disgusted with the way *Defender* was treated. The steamers following crossed our bows, and took the wind out of our sails and we were badly backwashed. The patrol service was inadequate and no attention was paid to orders to keep away. I hope the next race will be a fairer test."[29]

After the three races, Lord Dunraven filed charges alleging tampering with its ballast. Hearings were held at the New York Yacht Club. The inquisition consisted of live testimony—N. G. Herreshoff testified as well as sworn affidavits. At the end of the proceedings, the allegations were dismissed. The New York Yacht Club had had enough of the objections of Dunraven and took action to expel him as a member. This was a bit unusual since the Earl was an honorary member. Dunraven would later claim that his resignation letter had preceded his expulsion.

Author Ed Holm in his book *Yachting's Golden Age: 1880–1905* stated that much of the success of Herreshoff had to do with his manipulation of the measurement rules in effect. Here is how he analyzed it:

All of Nathanael Greene Herreshoff America's Cup defenders between 1893 and 1903 were designed to take advantage of weaknesses in the racing measurement rule then in effect. Because the Seawanhaka Rule measured waterline length, Herreshoff took liberties with overall length; because sail area was taxed less than other factors, his yachts carried as much canvas as possible; and because displacement was not considered in the formula at all, he employed every possible stratagem to reduce weight where it did not contribute to speed.[30]

Another fraternal organization in addition to the Odd Fellows and the Freemasons was the Royal Arcanum. On February 7, 1895, Poekel played a duet with a pianist playing "The Merry Mountaineers" at social gathering of the Mount Hope Council of the Royal Arcanum. The motto of the group was "Mercy, Virtue and Charity."

Because of Poekel's genius in design, he was approached to mentor the scion of a great English ship-building family. He took under his wing a teenage boy who had emigrated with his parents from Liverpool, England. According to Clarence B. Bagley, the great chronicler of the history of Seattle, Washington, after attending high school in Baltimore for several months, the boy J. F. Duthie went to Bristol, Rhode Island, "where he received private instruction in shipbuilding under Mr. Poekel, chief engineer, with the Herreshoff ship building concern, builders of fast sailing yachts."[31]

Duthie was another unsung Herreshoff hero. After being trained by T. Sch. Poekel, he became the foreman of the plating and riveting department. He was a master craftsman, and the *Boston Herald* on June 30, 1895, in publishing a story on the Cup challenger *Defender*, wrote this about him: "The firm building a yacht generally gets all he credit, but in this case, so far as experts can judge, much of the credit for the clever job of plating should be given the foreman plater Mr. John Duthie. The work, on close inspection, shows the hand of a skilled, practical mechanic. The seams, while lapped are chipped off, so that no sharp edges appear. On workmanship, the *Defender* is good."[32]

One of the last projects T. Sch. Poekel was involved with at the Herreshoff yard during 1895 was the design and construction of the *Newport 30's*. From looking at the construction plans, one can clearly see T. Sch. Poekel's handwriting everywhere. Although Poekel did not stay to see them introduced in 1896, he was extremely involved in their design and production. The concept was for identical boats which could be raced against each other, and the winners were determined based not on their individual designs but on the skillfulness of their captains and crew. Their dimensions were forty-two feet O.A., twenty-nine feet six inches W.L., eight feet four inches beam, and seven feet one inch draft. There were ten built and the price tag put on them was $2,850. These fin-keelers were extremely popular with the Newport millionaires like Edwin D. Morgan, J. McDonough, and Cornelius Vanderbilt III. Most of the owners hired crews to race them for a season consisting of about forty or more races. Including the *Newport 30's*, the HMCO would make over 100 fin-keelers.

In the fall of 1895, after seeing the yacht that he actively was involved in and help to construct win the America's Cup, T. Sch. Poekel saw himself as an unsung hero. In November Poekel left the HMCO to go to be in charge of a boatyard in Racine, Wisconsin. One hundred and twenty-five years later the Herreshoff Marine Museum would acknowledge his departure cryptically commenting that "on November 5, 1895 a head draftsman in the HMCO offices heads out west to make his mark!"

Waking up in Love Rocks on November 24, 1895, N. G. Herreshoff would have read the following article in the *Boston Globe*:

Mr. Theowald Poeckel [*sic*], for many years head draughtsman at the Herreshoff work, has accepted a position with the Racine, Wis. Boat company as manager, and has begun his duties with the Wisconsin builders. Mr. Poeckel's large experience in draughting fast boats here will no doubt prove valuable to him in his new field of labor. He will have the personal supervision of the new steel steam yacht to be built by the Racine company for F.W. Morgan of Chicago. This yacht will have a ram-shaped bow, and will be 140 feet on the waterline and 130 feet on deck, and will resemble modern torpedo boats of the Ericsson type.[33]

T. Sch. Poekel would leave Bristol and Captain Nat. For almost nine years, he had worked alongside one of the greatest yacht designers the world had ever known. He had mastered molding half hulls, drawing up construction plans, designing and building boilers, and had become a ballast expert. He understood speed, what fin keels could do along with ballast. He had hands-on experience with steamers, racing yachts, torpedo ships and engines. During his tenure at the Herreshoff yard Poekel was involved in the design and building of the following famous yachts and America's Cup winners*: *Gloriana* (1981), Vamoose (1892), *Wasp* (1892), *Navahoe* (1892), *Niagara* (1895), *Colonia* (1892), *Vigilant** (1893), *Defender**(1895), as well as the *Newport30*'s and torpedo boats. For a period of time he had been in charge of the construction of *Defender* that won the America's Cup. He had heard the shop bell in the cupola ring for the last time. Now he was headed to the Midwest. With his engineering experience from the Royal Danish Navy and his firsthand experience at the Herreshoff yard, he was fully capable of designing, building, and superintending a boatyard and well equipped to be the superintendent and chief engineer of the RBMCO. He was thirty-three years of age.

CHAPTER 5

Keeping your courage comes from breeding. No teaching on earth ever gave anyone character, it's like red hair, you've either got it or you haven't got it.

—*Æmelius Jarvis*
Managing Owner and Skipper
Canada

DURING THE BIRTH OF ÆMILIUS JARVIS ON APRIL 25, 1860, IN THE family home named Bonshaw in northern Canada, a comet appeared in the northwest skies over the barn. The family's Scottish nurse said it "was a lucky sign. It meant that Æmilius would love animals, particularly horses."[1] Her interpretation should have also included love of boats. Both horses and boats would go as fast as a comet under the command of this extraordinary man.

When Æmilius was five, he had a miniature saddle. Æmilius was only ten years of age when he had his first glimpse of the sea. He moved with his widowed mother to Hamilton, Canada, where the family could be near his mother's brother, Æmilius Irving. He was almost immediately attracted to Burlington Bay. In 1871, at the age of eleven, he jumped off a pier and had his first sail on *Dart*. He quickly became a very proficient sailor and was soon asked to be part of the crew of *Wanderer*, sailed by some older boys in his neighborhood.

At twelve years of age, he and two of friends got together fifty cents and an old gun and purchased a dilapidated old dinghy to sail around Lake Ontario. Onboard the boys carried a pail of tar to constantly fix the leaky seams and appropriately named the boat *Tarpot*. The three boys had planned to sail around Lake Ontario, but when the time came, two of the boys backed out leaving Æmilius to sail alone. This he did on a two-week cruise, which took him to the Niagara River, Wilson, New York, Whitby, Rouge River, Scarborough Bluffs, Gibraltar Point on Toronto Island, and Port Credit. Although the seams had been heavily tarred, he still had to constantly bail the water out of the boat. He made this incredible trip covering several hundred miles, without provisions, without a compass or sextant, and sailed into ports he had never been before—quite a remarkable feat for a twelve-year-old boy.

After his solitary sojourn around Lake Ontario, he gained the reputation of being a fine young sailor. When a syndicate purchased *Saunterer*, Jarvis was asked to help skipper the yacht. *Saunterer* won a regatta giving Jarvis his first victory at thirteen-and-half years of age.

In 1874, Jarvis's friends from *Dart* and *Wanderer* moved up to the sixty-ton *Annie Cuthbert* whose designer and builder Alexander Cuthbert was the skipper. Captain Cuthbert was the same man who would go on to fame skippering Canada's contenders in the America's Cup in 1876 and 1881. Jarvis was asked to be a part of the crew and sail down to Put-In-Bay in the western part of Lake Erie. Jarvis would later say that in the crew "were number of professional chums—real sailors—and from them I learned a great deal of seamanship."[2] At Put-In-Bay, *Annie Cuthbert*, with Jarvis part of the crew, beat *Cora*, the American champion of Lake Erie for the Godwin Cup. Æmilius was fourteen-and-half years of age.

Æmilius was a tough boy with tremendous courage. He was raised knowing to be tough, meant that a boy had to withstand caning from his teachers and fist fights from other boys.

At age sixteen, Jarvis sailed on the schooner *Edward Blake* to England where he would serve as an apprentice seaman. *Edward Blake* was the same ship that some years later was used by the notorious W. J. McGarigle, the former warden of the Cook County Hospital convicted of bribery, for his escape from prison in Chicago. During its crossing to England, the schooner, which was carrying timber, was tied up in Montreal for six weeks. During that time, young Æmilius learned how to box firsthand in the bar room of the Hochelaga Hotel. He would later parlay his skills into winning the Canadian Amateur Boxing Championship.

After sailing on ships that brought him to Europe and South America, Jarvis returned to Hamilton, Ontario, where he became a banker.

He was no stranger to Lake Erie's waters, winning six races on *White Wings* there in 1882.

On October 14, 1886, Æmilius married Elizabeth Margaret Harriet Augusta Irving, his childhood sweetheart and his first cousin. Although newly married and working as the branch manager at the Bank of Hamilton, Æmilius still made considerable time for sailing. In 1887, he purchased *White Wings* for $1,400. The boat became one of the most suc-

Captain Æmilius Jarvis

cessful racing yachts on the lakes and with it Jarvis won twenty-four out of twenty-six races and came in second twice. The following year, Jarvis passed the examinations of the Canadian Board and became certified as a Master Mariner.

In 1888, Jarvis drew up membership applications for the Hamilton Yacht Club, which held its first annual meeting on April 2, 1888, and its first regatta on July 28, 1888. On May 30, 1891, the club received a royal charter from Queen Victoria and became the Royal Hamilton Yacht Club.

In 1896, he was a successful stockbroker and had the reputation of being one of the greatest sailors on the Great Lakes. He had also personally designed yachts such as *Samoa*, *Whistlewing*, and *Chaperone I and II*. Soon, he would supervise the construction, train the crew, and be the skipper of the Canadian entry in the most important yachting race of his life. He was thirty-six years of age.

CHAPTER 6

When the spirits are low, when the day appears dark, when work becomes monotonous, when hope hardly seems worth having, just mount a bicycle and go out for a spin down the road, without thought on anything but the ride you are taking.

—Sir Arthur Conan Doyle

AT THE *FIN DE SIÈCLE* OF THE NINETEENTH CENTURY, AMERICANS LOVED bicycles, and their love made Fred W. Morgan a wealthy man.

In 1896, Congressman Thomas Reed of Maine stated that the biggest problem confronting Americans was "how to dodge a bicycle."[1] There were close to 1 million bicycles in 1893, in America, and the number doubled to 2 million by 1896. There would never be this many bicycles in the country until 1936, when the total population was much larger.

The golden age of yachting would merge in the 1890s with the golden age of bicycling. Prior to automobiles, bicycles were the fastest passenger vehicles in the world. Bicycles were the transportation link between horses and automobiles.

Fred W. Morgan and Rufus Wright founded a company in 1891, for the manufacturing of bicycle tires. With the slogan "Morgan and Wright are Good Tires," the company sold bicycle tires from its Chicago plant. On October 9, 1894, Morgan received a patent for a quick-repair bicycle tire. The newly invented tire allowed for on-the-road repairs through the injection of cement into a flap covering the inner tube. A patent was granted on April 9, 1895. With its newly patented bicycle tire, Morgan and Wright soon became the largest manufacturer of bicycle tires in the world.

To promote its tires, Morgan and Wright sponsored races and racers throughout the country. One of the biggest events for which it supplied

Ad for the world's largest bicycle tire manufacturer in 1896

over one-third of the bicycle tires was the race between Washington, D.C., and Denver, Colorado, in 1894. Over 450 riders participated in the event, which saw the riders make the trip in six-and-one-half days. The race clearly demonstrated that besides the "spin down the road," bicycles could be used for long-distance transportation.

With the advent of the automobile era, Morgan & Wright began manufacturing automobile tires as well and their company eventually became the United States Rubber and Tire Company, which later became Uniroyal. But in 1896, Fred Morgan wanted a yacht and he wanted the fastest and most luxurious yacht that ever sailed on the Great Lakes.

On November 24, 1895, the *Boston Globe* reported that Poekel had accepted a position with the Racine Boat Company as manager and would have personal supervision of the designing and building of a steel steam yacht for F. W. Morgan of Chicago.[2]

T. Sch. Poekel had such a relationship with his coworkers at HMCO that around December of 1895 he persuaded a dozen steel workers from the HMCO to relocate to Racine to work on some new steel yachts, including *Pathfinder*.[3] It would be difficult for Captain Nat and John B. to explain why twelve talented Herreshoff employees chose to leave their employ and follow an untalented draftsman half way across the country. But they never tried.

Mr. Morgan requested that the famed naval architect George Warrington work with Poekel on his yacht—especially in regard to the machinery. Warrington started his career working at his family's iron works, the Vulcan Iron Works, and then in 1887, he established the Warrington Iron Works. For the next decade, he produced a number of fine steam and sail yachts—many of which were for wealthy Chicagoans who desired yachts at their summer homes in Lake Geneva.

Because of the upcoming construction of *Pathfinder* and the large racing yachts *Vencedor*, *Siren*, and *Vanenna*, a large workshop was constructed under Poekel's supervision. It was about 180 feet by 40 and on the roof was painted in large letters "Racine Boat Manufacturing Company." The huge workshop was just what was needed to allow work during the extremely cold Wisconsin winters.

One of the steel workers who didn't follow Poekel to Racine was John F. Duthie, his protégé and the foreman of the plating and riveting department at the HMCO. However, in January of 1896, Duthie came up with his own creation, a three-foot miniature steel model of the *Defender*. Duthie was already dreaming of greater things to come.

Since *Pathfinder* would be steel-plated, resemble a torpedo boat, and easily be converted, some thought that its construction might violate the Rush-Bagot Treaty.

On April 20, 1817, the Rush-Bagot Treaty was signed. This was a treaty between Canada and the United States to regulate naval armaments on the Great Lakes. It was negotiated between John Rush, the acting secretary of state in the new James Monroe administration, and Sir Charles Bagot, an English diplomat. Negotiations had taken place at the British Legation in Washington, D.C. The treaty restricted the number of naval war vessels permitted on the Great Lakes and Lake Champlain as well as establishing the 5,527 mile border between Canada and the United States—the largest north-south border in the world.

Pathfinder was 145 feet in length and said to be the only steel yacht built for the Great Lakes west of Cleveland. She had plenty of Herreshoff heritage as designer Poekel was an alumnus of the Bristol yard as were the steel workers who helped to construct it. The young Danish engineer did all the design work and personally supervised its construction.

The large building which RMBCO had constructed soon had three additional yachts alongside it—*Vencedor*, *Vanenna*, and *Siren*. *Pathfinder's* hull would be built there as well as most of her machinery and interior work. RMBCO had its own steel and brass foundaries and a well-equipped machine shop.

Pathfinder had a ram-shaped bow, a displacement of 150 tons, steam heat, and hot and cold running water. It had its own telephone system and electricity at a time when the majority of homes in the United States had neither. She had accommodations for ten passengers and a crew of nine. With its water tube boilers and four cylinder triple-expansion engines, it had the power to travel at eighteen miles an hour—making it the fastest yacht on the Great Lakes.

The steel steamer had four steel watertight bulkheads, making it unsinkable in the event of a collision.

By early February 1896, *Pathfinder's* four-ton iron keel, which had been cast in Milwaukee, arrived.

Mahogany filled its luxurious interiors and there was even a cabinet Baby Grand piano in its main saloon. She had the capacity for enough coal to carry her across the Atlantic. Its cost of $75,000 in 1896's U.S. dollars would be equivalent to $2,250,000 in 2020.

Morgan wanted his yacht to be the fastest on the Great Lakes, and there was speculation in yachting circles that he would get a chance to test it by racing it against the swift steamer *Virginia* of the Goodrich line and *Christopher Columbus*. *Christopher Columbus* had been built for the 1893 World's Columbian Exposition where it was used to ferry attendees to the White City. *Pathfinder's* initial trials had it going at seventeen knots per hour, but it was thought when her engines loosened up she could make twenty-two knots per hour. The burgee of the Lincoln Park Yacht Club flew on her forward mast.

Still another innovation on *Pathfinder* was its tender—it was made entirely of aluminum. It was thought to be the first all-aluminum boat on the Great Lakes and the Racine Company offered them for sale in its latest catalog.

A reporter from the *Chicago Tribune* posed an interesting question: It is often announced in the press someone has ordered a yacht to be built at a certain length and at a certain price but how does a yacht designer actually go about his job? The reporter was intrigued with the question and thought the general public would be too. And what better example to give but what was being designed as the finest yacht on the Great Lakes and to have the design all explained by T. Sch. Poekel. The article was published on October 25, 1896, and spared no details. It was titled "Evolution of a Yacht." The article underscored the talent and expertise that Poekel possessed in regard to designing and building steam yachts and their machinery. This time there were no letters from the Herreshoffs to the editor. The article in its entirety can be found in Appendix 2.

Although T. Sch. Poekel had left the HMCO in the fall of 1895, the *Bristol Phoenix* reported, on May 26, 1896, that "Mrs. Poekel left last week for Racine, Wisconsin, where her husband recently went to take charge of a boat building establishment in that place."[4] Anna Poekel had unselfishly given her husband six months to establish himself and the RMBCO. without any spousal distractions. After a short visit, Mrs. Poekel and her young daughter returned to Bristol.

On sunny July 7, 1896, five thousand people, about half the population of Racine, Wisconsin, turned out to witness the launching of the $75,000 *Pathfinder*—the largest boat ever built by the RBMCO. Nearby were docked the other RBMCO yachts *Vanenna* and *Vencedor*, which were both flying signal flags and American flags. Owner Morgan and his wife proudly stood on the docks admiring their magnificent yacht. As a cannon was fired from *Vanenna*, Helen, the young daughter of Walter Reynolds, the manager of the Racine boatyard, smashed a bottle of champagne on the bow and christened *Pathfinder*. Thousands roared as the huge steel-plated steamer slid stern first into the Root River. However, the river at that point was dangerously shallow and narrow and as *Pathfinder* slid down, it struck bottom, and one of her guide lines snapped causing her to heel to port. Suddenly during the launch dignitaries were thrown against the railing and thousands gasped for fear that the steamer would capsize. But, it was righted, and as it stabilized, there was a tremendous roar from the crowd. Thousands standing on shore waved flags and pennants.

Captain Denstaedt of Detroit brought the huge steel steamer to Chicago in four hours and forty-five minutes traveling at an average speed of eighteen miles per hour. Mr. Morgan and designer Poekel were both ecstatic with the way his new yacht performed, and Morgan said that he never saw a new boat prove as satisfactory on its first trip.

Pathfinder's arrival into Chicago was full of pomp and majestic ceremony. Horns were blown and bands played. Close to the Lake View Crib, the yacht *Sentinel* with L. C. Wachsmuth gave her a warm welcome. Just before the anchor was dropped, the launch *Beulah* came aside and a party from the Lincoln Park Yacht Club boarded. The group included Rear Commodore Dutton and Secretary Andrews. They presented Mr. Morgan with a club pennant, which was raised, and everyone saluted.

It was a grand celebration for a yacht, which was widely considered to be the finest that ever sailed on the Great Lakes.

After a few days in Chicago, Captain Morgan and his family boarded *Pathfinder* for a trip to Detroit. Accompanying them was designer Poekel who left the yacht in Detroit and took the train to Bristol, Rhode Island, to visit with his wife and daughter who were still living there. After Detroit, *Pathfinder* journeyed to Toledo to be present for the international yachting races between *Vencedor* and *Canada*. It would be from the deck

The launch of *Pathfinder* on July 7, 1896, with sloops *Vencedor*, *Vanenna*, and *Siren*, all fully dressed, behind it—Racine Heritage Museum Archival Collection

of *Pathfinder* that, T. Sch. Poekel would watch his sloop *Vencedor* in the race of a lifetime.

August 6 saw *Pathfinder* carry a group of members of the Holland Society of Chicago on an excursion to Holland City, Michigan. The Society had been founded a few months before on December 14, 1895, and its members simply had to prove U.S. citizenship and Dutch lineage but not lineage with colonial New Netherlanders as did members of the New York Society. Early leaders of the Chicago Society included retail store executive John Broekema and William Van Benthuysen, managing editor of the *Chicago Tribune*.

Together with *Sentinel*, the sparkling new steamer carried the distinguished group of members on an excursion that took them to Ottawa Beach with a dinner at the Ottawa Hotel in the evening. Mr. Morgan spoke briefly and said it was the first speech he had ever given. The next day there was a VIP tour of Holland City before returning to Chicago. T. Sch. Poekel was on board and heard many compliments of his work.

Pathfinder would remain in Chicago for another ten days before it left for Toledo to root on *Vencedor*.

CHAPTER 7

A yacht must be fast and bonnie.

—William J. Fife III

THE SCOTTISH COASTAL TOWN OF FAIRLIE, SCOTLAND, PRODUCED ONE of the finest yacht designers and builders in the world. Following his grandfather and father into the business was William Fife III, known in 1896, as Will Fife Jr. and in his family boatyard as "the Boss." It was now the task of Will Fife Jr. to design a yacht to represent the Dominion of Canada in the international Great Lakes Championship.

Will Fife Jr. was born in 1857, in Fairlie on the Firth of Clyde. He started his career in the family boatyard, then worked at the yard of J. Fullerton & Co. in Paisley and then moved on to be the manager of the Marquis of Ailsa's Culzean Yacht & Steam Launch Works in North Britain. There in 1884, he designed and built the twenty-ton *Clara*. *Clara* racing in the United Kingdom finished first seventeen times in twenty-one starts. Although its skipper, Captain John Barr, traveled by steamer to New York, a crew of professionals, including the skipper's brother, Charlie Barr, sailed it to America. In America, *Clara* also had an outstanding racing record and established Fife as one of the world's greatest yacht designers. By 1886, he was back in Fairlie at the family yard.

Like Nathanael G. Herreshoff, the Boss was extremely taciturn and a prolific yacht designer. Fife never married but devoted his free time to his mother and three sisters. He also served as a justice of the peace and was an elder in his church.

Fife would design and build *Canada* following his rule for any yacht he designed: "It had to be fast and bonnie." As an extra bonus for the Jarvis syndicate, Fife, who was given *carte blanche* in regard to the design, was only charging a modest fee since he felt worldwide publicity would generate more business for his boatyard. Fife was familiar to Canadian yachtsmen having designed and built *Cyprus*, *Zelma*, *Vox*, and *Vidette*. He was also familiar to American yachtsmen for having produced *Clara*, *Minerva*, *Uvira*, and *Barbera*.

The great yachting commentator A. J. Kenealy writing for *Outing Magazine* described the yacht designers of Scotland in this way: "There are two yachting factions on the Clyde. One worships at the shrine of George L. Watson, who designed the *Britannia* for the Prince of Wales, *Meteor* for the Kaiser and the three *Valkyries* for Lord Dunraven. The other bows down before the altar of William Fife Jr."[1]

On May 1, 1896, Will Fife gave an interview from Gourock, Scotland, stating how he got involved with the design of *Canada*: "I had designed two boats the *Yama* and *Zelma* for members of the Canadian club, which were successful and in consequence a syndicate of Canadian clubs commissioned me to design a boat to defend their interests this I have done."

An interesting contrast in designers was pointed out by the *Chicago Daily Tribune* on July 12, 1896 (p. 31). It pointed out that the *Vencedor* was designed by Poekel who also was "one of the best designers of Herreshoff's famous works" who had "chiefly designed the *Niagara*," which had been winning many races in England for its owner Howard Gould. What the *Tribune* pointed out as an irony was that recently *Niagara* had been losing races to the sloop *Saint* that was designed by Fife. The *Tribune* pointed out that "it is singular also that these boats, competing against each other in England, shall have companion boats designed by the same men contesting for the blue ribbon of the Great Lakes, thousands of miles away."[2]

In 1895, the fastest racing yacht in the world was *Britannia*, owned and sailed by the Prince of Wales who later became King Edward VII. *Ailsa*, which was named after a Scottish island, received international celebrity when it beat *Britannia* off the coast of Cannes, France, in early March of 1895. On March 14, *Ailsa* beat both *Britannia* and *Corsair* by twelve minutes with the Prince of Wales himself onboard *Britannia*. Onboard *Ailsa* were both its owner and its designer Will Fife.

The yachts racing in Europe not only sailed for trophies and mugs but also for cash prizes. For instance, the regatta on March 14, 1895,

The gaff-rigged cutter *Britannia* was built in 1893 for HRH The Prince of Wales, who was Commodore of the Royal Yacht Squadron. It was one of the most successful racing yachts of all time—Library of Congress

awarded 2,000 francs to the winner plus a gold medal, 500 francs to the second place finisher plus a silver medal, and 100 francs plus a bronze medal for the third place finisher. The United States and Canada were different. Yachtsmen from those countries felt that yacht racing was for the pure sport of it and the gentlemanly thing to do was to award a mug or trophy with no monetary incentive. That was soon going to change in the upcoming international competition in Toledo. This would be the first major yachting race in the United States for a moneyed prize.

Ailsa received its first defeat by losing to *Britannia* in the Prix Prince Albert I at the Monaco Regatta but by only several seconds. Also, playing a major role in international yacht racing was the Prince of Wales's cousin—Kaiser Wilhelm, the Emperor of Germany. The Kaiser's *Meteor* would soon beat *Ailsa*, but what was paramount now was a trial to determine if *Ailsa* or Lord Dunraven's Watson-designed *Valkyrie III* would challenge for America's Cup. A friendly match race took place on July 5 and Lord Dunraven's yacht beat the *Ailsa*. The following year would see the Kaiser's *Meteor* beat *Ailsa* for the Queen's Cup. *Valkyrie III* would be the one to race against *Defender* in 1895.

Some yachtsmen said that Fife copied *Ailsa* in designing *Canada*, while others said Poekel copied *Defender* or *Niagara* or *Wasp* in designing *Vencedor*.

The frames and woodwork for *Canada* were from the Henderson Brothers yard, the Anchor steamship people, also in Scotland.

Ailsa. Some observers said that Will Fife Jr. copied its design for *Canada.*

—Permission of Beken of Cowes

On April 20, 1896, Captain James Andrew of Oakville, Canada, received his commission to build *Canada*. He had the reputation of being a very capable and enthusiastic builder.

Captain Andrew also had a Scottish connection. He had been born in Dundonald, Scotland, and as a young man came to the lakes to work. Oakville was fast becoming a summer resort and a center for yachting. The Royal Canadian Yacht Club, which had been founded in 1854, ran a yachting race from Toronto to Oakville in September of 1857. Andrew established a shipyard on the west bank of the Sixteen Mile Creek adjacent to Doty's sawmill. In October of 1887, Andrew christened his first ship *Aggie*, which became a renowned racing winner on the lakes. He had also built *Winnetka*, which also had a successful record.

In preparation for the construction of the Canadian yacht, Andrew found out that at the bottom of nearby Sixteen Mile Creek there were white oak logs that had sank by their own weight to the bottom. Oakville had supplied white oak to the Royal British Navy since 1845. These logs were a rare find, and after being cured at the bottom of the Creek for fifty years would be fantastic for the decking of the new yacht. Andrew had them brought up and sent to Charles Doty's local sawmill where they were sawed into

Aggie. Built in 1887 by Capt, James Andrew.
—From the Archives of the Oakville Historical Society

Canada under construction—From the archives of the Oakville Historical Society

planks. However, the special oak was not to see its way into the new yacht, since residents of a local shantytown, known facetiously as "Tramp Castle," purloined the wood and used it for their evening camp fires.

Captain Jarvis put a lot of pressure on Captain Andrew for a quick assembly of the yacht. Since Andrew had received the plans for the yacht ahead of time, he was able to cast the lead keel in advance and was able to meet Jarvis' deadline.

More evidence of the Canadians' dogged determination to win the international race was the selection of the famous sailmaker Ratsey & Lapthorn Ltd. to make the *Canada*'s huge canvas sails. Ever since 1790, the company had been making sails in Cowes on the Isle of Wight. The company had a long and distinguished history and pedigree, having made some of the sails for the HMS *Victory*, which Lord Nelson sailed on in 1805 at the Battle of Trafalgar. It had made sails for both America's Cup challengers and defenders starting in 1887, with the challenge of George Watson's *Thistle*.

Ratsey & Lapthorn would make the large sails of *Canada* out of cotton and the light sails a mixture of cotton and silk. How much did they cost? The answer was a lot. As Ratsey pointed out, "The makin's was 'arf the price" meaning that the plans were half the price. It was rumored that Ratsey charged Lord Dunraven once $5,000.00 for his "advice and handling." There was no attempt by the Berrimans to secure Ratsey & Lapthorn sails, since it had been recently been publicized that the Iselin syndicate for *Defender* had wanted them but the company flatly refused out of patriotic pride.

Besides the planning and design, there would be the material and workmanship. On a sloop such as *Niagara*, *Canada*, and *Vencedor*, you would need material for the mainsail, the topsails, the jib, the balloon staysail, and the spinnaker. It was said that Howard Gould, after purchasing the *Niagara* for $100,000 would pay another $20,000 for sails in order to have its "white wings."

But what about the cost of maintaining a racing yacht? Winfield Scott Hoyt, grandson of the War of 1812 general, was a personal representative to William K. Vanderbilt and in charge of all of Vanderbilt's yachts. In 1896, he stated that "it takes $100,000.00 yearly to keep a first-rate yacht afloat." T. Sch. Poekel would often repeat the familiar adage that "if you have to ask how much it takes to maintain a yacht, you can't afford it."

Yacht racing in the later part of the nineteenth century was a sport for millionaires. It was said that to maintain a yacht you had to break the bank at Monte Carlo. If horse racing was the "sport of kings," yacht racing was the "sport of industrialists, robber barons, princes and kaisers."

On the East Coast, it would be the sport for the Vanderbilts, Morgans, Belmonts, and Goulds, and in the Midwest it would be the sport for the Berrimans, Morgans, Drakes, and Smyths. And in Canada, it would be the sport for wealthy bankers and businessmen.

Upon being named the skipper for the *Canada*, Jarvis and his young family moved to Oakville to supervise its construction. To get there he loaded his four children, his pregnant wife, a dog, and a cat on a barge and sailed up the lake to Oakville. When a violent storm arose, Jarvis himself took over the helm from the bargeman. With Jarvis at the helm the only item that was lost during the storm was a single pram.

Fife built the forty-five-foot yacht, which was set up in frame with the parts carefully numbered and taken down. The sails and ironwork spars were all prepared and packaged. May Fife McCallum, a descendant and author, would refer to it facetiously as a "kit boat" (p. lxv).

The Fife boat was shipped from Glasgow on April 20, 1896, on *Furnessia* and arrived in New York City on May 12, when it was shipped in fire big cases to Toronto where it arrived before May 15. From Toronto it went to Oakville to Captain James Andrew's shipyard. According to the *Toronto Evening Star*, the boat was wrapped so well and "boxed so tightly, so that the New York newspapers will not be able to learn anything, even if cathode rays are used."[3]

In Oakville, under intense pressure from Skipper Jarvis, Captain Andrew finished assembling the yacht in record time to be ready for launch in early June.

Author William Townsend described *Canada* this way: "Viewed end on, out of water, Canada's silhouette was that of a lily plant, springing

Preparing to launch *Canada*—From the archives of the Oakville Historical Society

from its bulb (the ballast) on a sweetly curved stalk (the deadwood) and swelling out into cup-shaped bloom (the hull)."

The yacht had an innovative design. It was the first Canadian yacht to have a spoon bow (for this Fife could credit the Herreshoff yard), and it had a cutaway forefoot together with a raking sternpost and long overhang for quick turning.

The finishing touches made *Canada* appear to be a yacht fit for royalty. The sloop was painted with black enamel above and white enamel below. At deck level, a gilt ribbon band circled the yacht. On the port bow, the arms of Canada's seven provinces were shown in full color surrounded by a wreath of maple leaves. Located on the starboard side was the blue-white burgee of the R.C.Y.C., which displayed a crown above, a beaver below, circled in naval oakleaves.

Yet it wasn't even known if *Canada* would be the yacht to challenge *Vencedor*.

Chapter 8

Captain Joe Nicholson whose memory antedates the flood, said that he remembered an international race in the 1870's that the Americans won.

—Detroit Free Press, May 10, 1896

A joint committee established with Ex-Commodores E. P. Warner and Dwight Lawrence of the L.P.Y.C. and C.A.B. Brown and Æmilius Jarvis of the R.C.Y.C. met in executive session at the Cadillac

Hotel Cadillac in Detroit, Michigan, where the final arrangements were made for the international yacht races. The organizers allowed for an unprecedented purse of $1,500, which was later modified with the two competing yachts dividing it up 60/40—Library of Congress

Hotel in Detroit on May 9, 1896, to select a time and place for the international races and to establish the rules.

Lobbyists for site selection came from Toledo, Cleveland, Toronto, Port Dover, and Put-in-Bay, each with grand proposals. Hard to believe but Detroit, the meeting site for the selection, failed to send promoters, though its representatives attended and supported other locations.

Toronto submitted a proposal by letter. Although the Joint Committee considered its proposal, it felt the location would not attract enough spectators from all over the lakes. A Canadian newspaper recently published an editorial extolling the worldwide benefits to Toronto in hosting the races. It said that it "would be an advantage to have Toronto mentioned several times during the course of several weeks in every one of thousands of newspapers that are published in the United Kingdom, in the United States, in Australia, in France and even in Germany."

Mayor Ansley presented a proposal from his city of Port Dover. The committee felt that the cash offer was too small and the site too far away.

The joint committee gave scant consideration to Put-In-Bay's $500 offer.

Cleveland was represented by a young yachtsman named E. W. Radder who gave a good presentation with an offer of $1,100 and had the support of Captain Nicholson of Detroit. However, the committee felt the cash offer was too low. The other representatives from Detroit supported Toledo's solicitation.

When the committee made reference to the upcoming races being the first time there would be competition between Canada and the United States, it was challenged by Captain Nicholson who stated he remembered such a race in the 1870s. Actually, Captain Nicholson was correct. In August of 1876, there was an international competition in Chicago between *Frolic* owned by Captain John Prindivillee of the United States and *Ina*, the Canadian entry. *Frolic* won the first race, but the win for the second was claimed by both yachts. The dispute was never satisfactorily settled.

Not only was there precedent for an international race on the Great Lakes but there was also precedent for allegations of ballast manipulation that Lord Dunraven had levelled against *Defender* in 1895. In the late

1870s, on the lakes the yacht *Ina* was beating all comers and had a record of twenty-seven wins out of thirty races. The Royal Canadian Yacht Club built *Brunette* to challenge *Ina*. *Ina* lost the first match race. Allegations arose as to ballast shifting and as a result scrutineers were placed on the yachts. Two men fell overboard. Years later a Mr. Marks who was the sailing master on *Ina* admitted to the ballast tampering and even explained how it was done and how quickly it was done.

Notwithstanding Captain Nicholson, most observers agreed with the *New York Sun* that the upcoming races in Toledo were to be "the first genuine international race sailed on the lakes."[1]

After Put-In-Bay came into contention, one Cleveland supporter had this to say: "It is all worse than ever. Last year we roasted, we starved. The excursionists were so numerous that they and not the yachtsmen owned the island. Three of us packed into one little room and sweltered, and the yachtsmen either lived aboard or swore onshore." He went on to praise Cleveland saying there was a brand new clubhouse and that the reception given the visitors will be "all they desire." In finishing his plea he argued, if not Cleveland, "Toledo, Sandusky or Sandy Hook (site of the last America's Cup race) but not the Bay."[2]

The Toledo group arrived in a private car. Its representatives were Commodore E. D. Potter and Robinson Locke, the eldest son of the famous "Petroleum V. Nasby."

Reverend Petroleum Vesuvius Nasby was the *nom de plume* of David Ross Locke, who was one of the leading humorists of the day. Locke a/k/a Nasby was a drinking buddy of Mark Twain and one of the nation's sharpest wits. When someone once told him that they had never seen a man as inebriated as him, Nasby replied: "Come back in an hour and a half." President Lincoln would often read a Nasby letter to his cabinet and it is said a Nasby book was the last book he read aloud before he went to Ford's Theater on April 15, 1865.

Robinson Locke had stature in his own right having served as President Chester Arthur's appointed American consul at New Castle-on-Tyne, England, in 1888 and returned to Ohio to manage the *Toledo Blade* newspaper. He was also active in the Toledo Chamber of Commerce and belonged to a Lodge of Freemasons in Toledo.

Locke and Potter told the committee that they had traveled to New York City, and had secured five Tiffany & Company cup designs ranging in price from $200 to $2,000. They tried to convince the joint committee that a cup was extremely important inasmuch as the race would be on par with America's Cup, and the Winner's Cup would also be perpetual and of great historic meaning. The joint committee, however, told them that cups and mugs were a dime a dozen and it was more interested in cash. A new offer was then made for a cash prize of $1,500 in gold, a less expensive trophy costing $200 plus all expenses including towing for both contestants.

The joint committee selected Toledo to be the site of the races. As for the Tiffany Cup, the committee said the $200 one would suffice with its cost to be split between the Royal Canadian Yacht Club and the Lincoln Park Yacht Club.

All of the other losing contenders were extremely disappointed. The *Cleveland Leader* had this to say: "Little Toledo, with a fair amount of enterprise has snatched the plum from Cleveland's grasp."[3]

After the selection and cash prize were made public, there was criticism from Caspar Whitney, a champion of amateur sports, as well as from the editors of *Outing Magazine*, a very popular sporting magazine. Whitney weighed in on the cash prize, pointing out that the international races were the first important race in the country to be sailed for a cash prize and stating that "it is hoped that the yacht clubs will in time express their disapproval of the adoption of this foreign practice."[4]

In the 1890s, cash prizes for yacht racing in Britain were more common than mugs. While no yachtsmen would race just for the money, it did help partially pay some of the expenses. The Prince of Wales's *Britannia* in 1894, entered forty-two races and won or came in second in thirty-two of them with a total cash prizes of $10,350. To this was added an additional $4,500 for cash prizes from winnings in the Mediterranean regattas.

Besides selecting the site for the international races, the meeting at the Cadillac Hotel resulted in an agreement covering many aspects of the race entered into by the Canadians and Americans. It consisted of twenty clauses with almost all the issues addressed, except for the number of professionals allowed to be part of the crews. The winner would be decided in the best of three races. The committee incorporated the prior agreement as to the length of *Vencedor* and left no restrictions for the Canadian entry. Should *Vencedor* exceed forty-five feet in length, there would be given to the competing boat a double-time allowance. The agreement stated that the competing boat would either be the *Zelma* or a new boat currently under construction providing that the selection would have to be made and the committee notified within one week of the races. A scrutineer would be placed on both yachts at a weight not to exceed 175 pounds. The Chicagoans did prevail in securing a time limit for the two out of three races to insure that there would not be a drifting match. The time chosen was five-and-one-half hours although designer Poekel had advised the Chicagoans to require a five-hour limit.

As a final recommendation, the committee agreed to add an outside yachtsman of national repute like C. Oliver Iselin, managing owner of *Defender*, or Hank Haff, its skipper, as a fifth member.

Upon returning to Chicago on May 11, Dwight Lawrence, a member of the Lincoln Park Yacht Club delegation, was pleased with the outcome of the meeting in Detroit and had this to say when interviewed: "The terms are just about even and neither side has any advantage, either as to location or conditions. It will be a good race, and I think the *Vencedor* has an excellent chance of beating the Canadian unknown. We know what our boat can do, and that it is first-class, but only one man has any idea of the Canadian craft and he is Designer Fife."[5]

As interest grew for the international race, it was reported on July 25, 1896, that the Toledo International Yacht Race Association had invited President Grover Cleveland to be present as a guest in Toledo. Another invitation went to Major William McKinley, the former governor of Ohio. McKinley, who was still referred to as Major McKinley due to his Civil War service, was already the first honorary member of the association, and currently the Republican candidate for president. It was also announced that C. Oliver Iselin of *Defender* fame was to be one of the judges.

PART TWO

CHAPTER 9

Quick in stays as a bike and stiff as a church.
                    —Observer's Comment of *Canada*

THE FAMILY OF ÆMILIUS JARVIS HAD TWO CHRISTENINGS IN JUNE OF 1896. Their one-week-old daughter was christened with the name Augusta Louisa Jarvis and their eldest daughter Mary, aged eight, on June 22 christened *Canada*. The launching occurred two hours ahead of schedule so the spectators who had sailed from Toronto on *Cleopatra* were severely disappointed to have missed the launching. Their excursion boat was too slow and perhaps better suited for the River Nile. However, a large crowd did appear cheering wildly and congratulating Captain James Andrew, who had assembled the sloop in record time.

Seeing *Canada* sail, the sailors on shore commented that the sloop was "quick in stays as a bike and stiff as a church." To interpret this description is to understand that a bicycle in 1896 was the fastest passenger vehicle. "Quick in stays" meant the boat could swiftly tack. "Stiff as a church" meant the yacht would stand up to the wind and carried a press of canvas well.

Æmilius Jarvis proved to be a tough taskmaster. He was determined to take a basically amateur crew composed of distinguished Canadian businessmen and mold them into a smoothly efficient sailing machine. There would be no towing of *Canada* by barge to Toledo but pure sailing with rigorous training days for the crew with plenty of trial races in between.

It was said that "Jarvis ruled ship and crew, syndicate and race committee, with a rod of iron, nicely polished, never flourished, seldom seen."[1] Discipline was strictly enforced on the *Canada* where Jarvis would make the crew work fourteen-hour days. His credo of "a place for everything and everything in its place" was the law on the sloop, and Jarvis enforced it. Every day after breakfast, he would make his inspections. Crew members who left pajamas, shaving gear, and shoes out on the deck saw them thrown overboard. It was reported that, as a result of Jarvis's imposed discipline, the Canadian crew "could reef the 1,000-foot mainsail in two minutes, they could shift jib topsails in 30 seconds and gybe the enormous spinnaker in a minute flat."[2]

Canada was ready to race. Its first test would come in five days in a quest for the Murray Cup.

On June 27, 1896, at 3:00 pm the gun went off in the waters near the town clubhouse of the Royal Canadian Yacht Club and *Canada* had its first trial race. Racing against *Zelma* and *Vreda*, *Canada* sailed its first race and had its first loss. The would-be entry in the international races finished three minutes after *Zelma* and only twenty-eight seconds ahead of *Vreda*. Supporters said it performed admirably and chalked the loss up to newness. Its syndicate said that its performance was satisfactory, and the yacht would perform better after it had a chance to stretch its sails a little.

Canada and *Zelma*. After *Zelma* beat *Canada* in three out of four trial races, many Canadians thought it should race *Vencedor*—Library of Congress

Saturday, July 1 saw *Canada*'s next trial race—a race for the Queens Cup on Dominion Day. That day was celebrated to mark Canada becoming a dominion of Great Britain on July 1, 1867. Since July 1, 1983, the day has been celebrated as Canada Day. This was a race for forty-two-foot class yachts. In this race, *Canada* faced a trio of competitors: *Zelma*, *Dinah*, and *Divia*. The race covered a triangular course, which was to be sailed twice for a total of twenty-five miles. This race saw *Canada* suffer its second defeat losing to *Zelma* by thirteen minutes six seconds, corrected time, and to *Vreda* by three minutes, corrected time. Now Canadian yachtsmen were no longer blaming the defeat on newness. *Canada* had two races and two losses. Speculation grew that perhaps the best challenger for *Vencedor* would be *Zelma* and not what the *New York Sun* called "the imported yacht." After all, they argued, the race was not just between Toronto and Chicago but between Canada and the United States.

But there had to be an explanation. Skipper Jarvis noticed leaks on the boat during both defeats. After the defeat in the second trial, he sailed *Canada* on July 2 to Toronto and placed it in dry dock. Numerous holes were found in *Canada*'s hull. Several plugs were loose. The bottom was thoroughly scraped and every seam tightened and black lead applied to the hull. Although some posited that the defects had been due to the hasty assembly of the yacht, Æmilius Jarvis said he felt the defects that caused the *Canada* to lose the races were not a result of poor workmanship but damage during the launching. A "second launching" took place on July 8 as *Canada* was on its way to Hamilton to again race *Zelma* for the White Wings Cup.

Besides Jarvis, as skipper, the crew of *Canada* consisted of one recognized professional in the person of Edward Roach. The other amateur crew members were some of the leading businessmen in Canada who were devoting their entire summer to the contest. They were:

J. H. Fernside of Hamilton

Gerald D. Boulton

William J. Moran

Edward Bailey (later a deputy attorney general)

W. H. (Herbert) Parsons

Sidney Small

W. M. Fertile and

W. S. Clowston of Toronto.

Amateurs in those days were referred to as "Corinthians," and according to the agreement between the R.C.Y.C. and the L.P.Y.C., there could be only two professionals—the rest had to be Corinthians.

The golden age of yachting saw the confluence of those who hired captains and crew to sail their trophy yachts and those individuals who loved yachting, who were talented helmsmen and sailed themselves. The conundrum for sportsmanlike races was should they be totally for amateurs or could professional captains and crew be hired. Also, prize money was another issue. Many agreed that good sportsmanship races were for cups and other trophies, not for cash prizes.

On July 18, 1896, off the shores of Hamilton, *Canada* and *Zelma* battled again. This time for the White Wings Cup—a race that went three miles to windward and back twice for a total of twelve miles. The two yachts were in a tight race for the entire length. *Canada* beat *Zelma* by a narrow margin of eight seconds. *Zelma* had a time allowance of sixteen seconds so in actual time *Canada* won by twenty-four seconds. Skipper Jarvis was pleased and said that *Canada* handled well both in its windward and leeward works and predicted that it would do well in Toledo against *Vencedor*.

Canada again went into dry dock and had to withdraw from the first-class race at the Royal Hamilton Yacht Club scheduled for Saturday, July 25.

Whether or not *Canada* could beat *Vencedor*, its skipper and crew became heroes on the afternoon of July 26, 1896. Approximately three miles from the Hamilton pier beaches five young Canadian boys were out sailing and capsized their skiff. They desperately clung to the skiff's keel for over an hour. As the boys were close to the breaking point, Skipper Jarvis and his crew aboard *Canada* rescued them. It was reported that all the boys were in an exhausted condition as "all had exceedingly narrow escapes."[3]

Canada had a chance to redeem itself as three more races were scheduled off Oakville for July 27, 28, and 29.

On the first day of the trials on July 27, *Canada* didn't show much improvement. Yachts *Canada* and *Zelma* finished so close to one another, they fouled, and the race committee declared it to be no race. Most observers felt that had the race continued *Zelma* would have eased out *Canada*. In this race, not only was there interest in *Zelma* but in Oakville's *Aggie* that performed very well in the trial. Oakville supporters thought it should be allowed to race against *Vencedor* until they found out that the agreement between the R.C.Y.C. and the L.P.Y.C. only provided for *Canada* or *Zelma* to face the American entry.

The preliminary races among the Canadian racing yachts on the Great Lakes ignited the pride of Canadian sports fans. It was even rumored in Montreal yachting circles that perhaps the next America's Cup challenge would come from Canada.[4]

The next day *Canada* performed better against *Zelma* and *Aggie*, winning the race by one minute thirty-six seconds. *Aggie* was pretty much out of the race when its topmast was carried away. Now, things were looking up for *Canada*.

The third trial showed *Canada* to be by far the fastest yacht with it beating *Zelma* by five-and-a-half minutes corrected time.

When *Canada* came back to Toronto that evening, Skipper Jarvis happily announced that he had received a cable informing him that Oliver E. Cromwell had agreed to be the chairman of the racing committee for the international race. Cromwell was a well-respected yachtsmen and the chairman of the racing committee at the Seawanhaka-Corinthian Yacht Club of Oyster Bay, New York. The yachting world now knew that the international races on the Great Lakes would be professionally monitored.

There was still some doubt whether *Canada* would be the boat to race *Vencedor*. Under the agreement between the yacht clubs, the Royal Canadian Yacht Club reserved the right to name the boat one week before the race. Throwing more doubt was a statement by Commodore McGaw of the Royal Canadian Yacht Club that *Canada* was not a "speedy boat," and he feared it would make a poor showing in the international race.

Canada did not sail alone for the showdown with *Vencedor* but came in a fleet of Canadian yachts from Toronto and Hamilton. The Canadian fleet were all painted black above the waterline and were dubbed the "coffin fleet" by the Americans.

Again, *Canada* went into dry dock and had to withdraw from the first-class race at the Royal Hamilton Yacht Club scheduled for Saturday, July 25.

On July 31, *Canada* sailed for Port Dalhousie on Lake Erie and prepared to enter the Port Dover Regatta on August 3 and 4.

On August 1, 1896, a final decision was made as to whether *Zelma* or *Canada* would compete against *Vencedor*. The decision was sealed by the Royal Canadian Yacht Club so the co-owner Berriman brothers would have to wait until August 17th before knowing who their crack yacht would race against.

On August 5, 1896, *Canada* raced against *Scorpion* and *Westwind* from Buffalo. Spectators packed the piers and lined the shores of Port Dover and the car ferry *Shenango* was full of spectators as hundreds wanted to see *Canada* race. The *Canada* easily won the race, the *Scorpion* wasn't timed, and *Westwind* withdrew.

At Erie, Pennsylvania, on August 6, on what was described as one of the most beautiful days for yacht racing, *Canada* beat *Scorpion* by thirty-seven minutes at the Erie Yacht Association Regatta sponsored by the Erie Yacht Club. It was reported that every race on the bill was won by a Canadian yacht.

On August 12, 1896, there was a two-day Centennial Regatta in Cleveland, Ohio. Because no one wanted to see *Canada* race *Vencedor* prior to the international races in Toledo, the yachts were put into separate races a day apart.

Up until Cleveland, the record showed that *Canada* had beaten *Zelma* four times and *Zelma* had beaten *Canada* three times. Thus, the race in Cleveland would probably determine once and for all which yacht would challenge *Vencedor*. Canada was entered in the forty-six-foot class against *Zelma* of the Royal Hamilton Yacht Club, the Detroit Yacht Club's *Surprise*, and *Czarina* from the Toledo Yacht Club. The race was a great nip and tuck battle between *Zelma* and *Canada*, with *Canada* winning but by only several seconds. *Surprise* was third and *Czarina* fourth.

The Canadian yacht *Vivia* also won its race against the American yachts *Sultana* and *Puritana*. A local newspaper would later report, "The Canadian fleet as in Erie and at Port Dover, won everything in sight."[5,6]

It was while *Canada* was in Cleveland Skipper Jarvis unleashed his temper. When one of the crew, who was a life-long friend of Jarvis, improperly hoisted a sail, Jarvis grabbed him and threw him onto the deck. The skipper was, if nothing else, a stern disciplinarian.

The next day the Cleveland Regatta would also be significant. The crack Canadian racer *Vreda* would be facing *Vencedor*. And adding to some international intrigue and unbeknownst to Captain Barbour, some members of *Canada*'s crew would be onboard *Vreda* to get a bird's-eye view of the sailing capabilities of *Vencedor*.

Although many thought *Zelma* actually had a chance of replacing *Canada* in the international races, it was whispered that Captain Jarvis had in fact been holding *Canada* in a little the whole time.[7]

On August 17, 1896, one week prior to the start of the international races and in accordance with the terms of the agreement, the Canadians officially notified the international racing committee that its entry against *Vencedor* would be *Canada*.

CHAPTER 10

As fast a boat as I have ever sailed on in fresh or salt water.
                              —Captain Irving G. Barbour of *Vencedor*

RBMCO WAS A HIVE OF ACTIVITY DURING JUNE OF 1896, IN GETTING *Vencedor* ready to launch. Besides the building of a multitude of small boats, Poekel and his workmen launched *Siren* on June 4 and *Vanenna* on June 20. Now it was reported that a large group of men were working night and day on *Vencedor*. However, there were delays and disappointments with the finishing of the yacht and the launch date was in doubt. Some Chicagoans who had planned a prelaunch banquet at the Hotel Racine had it cancelled. However, Commodore Berriman, like an expectant father, was hovering at the boatyard on the Root River awaiting the launch of his baby.

On the early evening of June 27, 1896, with a canon's roar and the incessant sounds of the blasting of factory whistles, the mahogany-sided *Vencedor* slid into the Root River at Racine. Crowds on shore shouted their approval. The fin keel weighing eight tons actually got stuck on the Root River's muddy bottom during the launch. History was being made as the spectators viewed the launch of the first international cup defender to be built on the Great Lakes. The sole decoration on the sloop was a large American flag mounted on a staff projecting from an opening for the spar.

T. Sch. Poekel had participated in many launchings at the Herreshoff yard, but he was always in the shadows of the Herreshoffs. Irrespective of the work and creative genius he brought to a yacht at that Bristol yard, he would never be in the spotlight. But now, here in Racine, he was front and center for the launching and proudly saw his creation cheered on

Vencedor under sail. For complete sail plan refer to
Appendix I.—Library of Congress

by an adoring crowd. He had been an American for only six years, but felt
a sense of national pride as *Vencedor* slid down into the Root River with
the stars and stripes waving from the topmast.

It was reported that the sloop was to be outfitted immediately and
that it would race in the regatta at Milwaukee on July 4—American Independence Day.

On July 1, 1896, with Commodore Berriman, T. Sch. Poekel, and a
group of Chicago yachtsmen onboard, *Vencedor* was towed from her moorings by the tug *Dixen* and made her first trial run. With a light wind that
day, the mahogany sloop sailed well and was easily handled. At the helm
was Irving G. Barbour, a former quartermaster on *Defender* when it won
the America's Cup race of 1895, beating Lord Dunraven's *Valkyrie III*. Barbour, who was in his late twenties, was part of the crew from Deer Isle,
Maine, which is still regarded as one of the best American sail-racing teams
ever assembled. With only the mainsail and two jibs hoisted, the yacht sped
through the water. Both designer Poekel and Commodore Berriman were
extremely pleased on how *Vencie*, as she was soon nicknamed, handled.

At about 5:00 pm on July 3, 1896, T. Sch. Poekel using the working
launch of the RBMCO towed *Vencedor* away from its mooring. There was
a slight southerly breeze. Poekel consulted with Captain Barbour who set

the big club golf sail and *Vencedor* was on its way to Milwaukee for its maiden race. Besides Poekel and Barbour, Commodore E. C. Berriman and his wife were also onboard. During the voyage, the petite Mrs. Berriman proved to everyone that she was an accomplished sailor.

It was predicted that the regatta off Milwaukee the next day would be "one of the greatest aquatic events ever sailed on fresh water."[1] It would pit *Vencedor* against her Racine stablemates *Vanenna* and *Siren*. Word spread in Milwaukee that *Vencedor* had done well under the direction of Captain Barbour in its trial runs off Racine. And according to an eyewitness account from William Hindshaw, Jr. of the Columbia Yacht Club, "was out on *Vencedor* yesterday. She glides along very smoothly. We did not have wind enough for lower canvas, which was all we had set, but she appeared to go right along. She points up very high and runs like the mischief before the wind."[2]

With only sporadic winds, *Vencedor* arrived in Milwaukee at about 4:15 am on July 4. In spite of the early arrival, *Vencedor* received a hero's welcome. The commodore of the Milwaukee Yacht Club presented it with a burgee of his club, horns sounded, and cheers went up.

After a delay due to fog, *Vencedor* got off to a flying start in its maiden race in the great Regatta of Lake Michigan. However, the fog returned and covered the course where *Vencedor* was in direct competition with *Vanenna* and *Siren*. Adding to the problems, the buoys, which marked the course, drifted and both *Vencedor* and *Siren* sailed off course. In the end, *Vencedor* was disqualified and *Vanenna* was declared the winner.

After the race, designer Poekel said he was satisfied with *Vencedor*'s performance and with a tune-up he was confident that the sloop would beat both *Vanenna* and *Siren*.

Captain Barbour was effusive in his praise saying that *Vencedor* was as fast as anything he had ever seen on salt water and was extremely confident that it would beat *Canada* in the international races.

The next morning the sun shone brilliantly and a nice breeze was in the air. Most of the yachts left early for a return to Chicago but *Vencedor* and *Vanenna*, which were headed back to Racine, remained moored next to each other all morning. Both were to be sailed back for alterations at the RBMCO. Suddenly at 12:30 pm *Vencedor* raised up its topsail and

Vanenna, which along with *Siren* was built at RBMCO—Library of Congress

headed on its twenty-five-mile trip to Racine. *Vanenna* then followed it in an apparent pursuit. A short while into the sail *Vencedor* hit the rocks of the reefs off South Point. These dangerous reefs had been the death knoll for many boats on Lake Michigan. Fortunately, Captain Barbour was able to bring the big mahogany yacht off the reefs and it kept on its way to Racine but it trailed *Vanenna*. Barbour actually began to handle *Vencedor* better than he did during the Regatta the day before. Suddenly, on that beautiful July day after clearing the reefs, he commanded, "Let's let her out." He headed straight for *Vanenna* and was able to pass it. It sailed extremely well into windward. *Vanenna* accepted the challenge but could not catch her challenger. The final result of the impromptu race had *Vencedor* reaching Racine about 7:00 pm—thirty-five minutes ahead of *Vanenna*. As many noted that *Vencedor* was remarkably fast in a windward sail someone remembered the old nautical saying that "a scow can sail off the wind, but it takes a boat to go windward."

A formal race against *Siren* in July was called off when it was discovered that *Vencedor* had a hole in its hull. After some repair work, the big racing sloop was off to Chicago.

The Lincoln Park Yacht Club Regatta took place on July 11, 1896, in a showdown between *Siren* and *Vencedor*. Even though the wind was described as catspaws, witnesses saw one of the closest races ever sailed on the Great Lakes.

Near the last turn one of *Vencedor*'s crew members, Louis Patton, was struck by the yacht's huge boom and went overboard. He was thrown a life preserver. In the water he yelled out, "Go on, go on" to Captain Barbour and *Vencedor* went on to finish the race coming on in the last minutes of the race like a charging bull. *Siren* won but by only one-and-a-half minutes with a time allowance. Most of the spectators said it was one of the finest races they had ever seen. All were extremely impressed with the performance of *Vencedor* and its captain. Concerning Barbour, the *Chicago Tribune* wrote that "he understands his business and in him Commodore Berriman has a man in whom he may place every confidence."[3] The *Racine Evening Times* commented on the blanketing of *Siren* by *Vencedor* during the final stages of the race and commented: "It was a regular Hank Haff trick, and showed under whose tutelage Captain Barbour learned to handle fin-keel."[4]

Leading the entire fleet of the Lincoln Park Yacht Club on July 17 in a sail to Kenosha was *Vencedor*. Onboard were Matthew Berriman and his girlfriend Louise Schroeder of Kenosha, as well as the commodore's wife. Commodore Berriman was following the fleet on the chartered tug *Hall*, which would tow the sailing vessels in the event of a calm. Captain Barbour ably sailed *Vencedor* past Evanston, Highland Park, and Ft. Sheridan and then guided the mahogany yacht between the piers of Kenosha. It received a tremendous salute with guns firing and whistles blowing. Not only did Miss Schroeder and Matthew Berriman enjoy *Vencedor* but apparently each other as well. Upon arrival in Kenosha, they announced their engagement. Louise was dubbed by the press as "*Vencedor*'s Queen."

But one person was not thrilled with the engagement. She was one Miss Ida Loser who shortly brought a suit against Matthew Berriman for alienation of affection. Miss Loser sought $50,000. She had been a salesperson at one of the Berriman cigar stands at the Columbian World Exposition of 1893. Besides selling cigars, she apparently had a personal relationship with Matthew who she claimed had promised marriage. He was married at the time but subsequently became divorced. Ida Loser was aptly named.

Vencedor-considered to be one of the greatest racing yachts to ever sail the Great Lakes—Library of Congress

From Kenosha, *Vencedor* sailed on to Racine for alterations.

On July 25, 1896, the Columbia Yacht Club's Regatta was to have been between *Vencedor*, *Siren*, and *Vanenna*. Reports circulated that the Joint International Yacht Committee in Toledo didn't want *Vencedor* to compete in any more races until the championship in Toledo. However, these reports turned out not to be true.

It was also reported that *Vencedor* was leaking badly in Chicago on July 25. It was thought that the yacht had leaked ever since its launching in Racine. Repairs couldn't be made in Racine because of *Vencedor*'s large keel. So the yacht sailed to Chicago for better dry-docking facilities to repair the hull. It turned out that several seams between the garboards and the waterline on the port side had opened. The entire bottom needed an overhauling. The yacht was taken to the floating dry docks of the Independent Tug Line for work, which would include scraping, papering, and painting. Only then was it put in the water before its journey to Lake Erie.

On the evening of July 30, 1896, *Vencedor* left Chicago under tow of the steamer *Madagascar*. To show their support of the American entry in the international races, the owners of the *Madagascar* waived their fee for the tow. During the journey up Lake Michigan, the boats encountered a squall and to prevent damage to his yacht Captain Barbour cut the towline. He sought shelter by sailing the yacht unaided into Port Washington. The next day at 1:00 pm the *Vencedor* left for Manitowoc. From there, on August 1, *Vencie* started for Mackinac but after running into a squall went back to Manitowoc where Captain Barbour waited until Sunday, August 2, before setting sail for Mackinac. Commodore Berriman then spent a couple of days there before getting a tow to Lake Erie. In the straits of Mackinac it was to drop its tow and pick up a tow to go down to Lake Huron. *Canada*, it should be noted, sailed to Toledo without the assistance of any steamer tow.

On August 5, 1896, *Vencedor* arrived in Port Huron, Ontario, under the tow of the steamer *James H. Prentice*. *Prentice* had picked up *Vencedor* at Thunder Bay.

The night of August 6, 1896, saw the *Vencedor* towed down to the mouth of the river by the *Lee*.

On its way to Cleveland, a squall developed and *Vencie* was forced to ride fifteen- to twenty-foot waves. Commodore E. C. Berriman's wife was onboard, and it was reported that she showed no trace of fear and that "she was a heroine in the eyes of the crew."[5] The weather in the area was so fierce that a small pleasure boat named the *Clipper* capsized. *Vencedor* along with Mrs. Berriman held its own and weathered the fifty-two-mile-per-hour winds.

Vencedor arrived in Cleveland on August 10, 1896. At noon on that day, Commodore Berriman went aboard *Nox* and asked Will and Henry Miller to be members of his crew for the upcoming races in Toledo. It was reported that they gladly accepted, as it was a testimonial to their seamanship and an honor to be asked.

Later that day, a large club topsail was set for the benefit of Charles Edwin Bolles, one of the foremost marine photographers of the nineteenth and early twentieth centuries. He journeyed from his studio in Brooklyn, New York, to take photographs of both *Vencedor* and *Canada*. The topsail was unfurled for Bolles's photograph and in taking the topsail in Captain Miller who was working on *Vencedor* had his left hand badly jammed by a wire halyard.

In early August of 1896, the *Chicago Tribune* printed a story that a group of capitalists were thinking of purchasing the RBMCO and relocating the company to Chicago. They felt Racine was ill-equipped to provide the setting for a major shipbuilding establishment. The article mentioned that the "plan includes the purchase of the present plant and its good will, together with securing the services of Theodore [*sic*] S. Poekel and the other experts now there."[6]

The first real race for *Vencedor* took place on August 13 in Cleveland. There was a chance that *Vencedor* and *Canada* would race against

CANADA   VENCEDOR
Photographs by Charles Edwin Bolles

each other prior to the international races at Toledo but, of course, no one was going to let this happen. Even though they should have been in the same class, the two yachts were entered in different classes. *Vencedor* was entered in a race for fifty-five footers and *Canada* entered in another class. Several sailors from *Canada* sailed onboard *Vreda* to observe *Vencedor* at close hand. *Vencedor* and *Vanenna* of Chicago were entered along with *Vreda* of Hamilton, Ontario, and *Neva* of Cleveland. *Vreda* was one of Canada's fastest yachts. It had lost in a race earlier in the season to *Canada* but only by one minute eight seconds. *Vencedor* beat *Vreda* in the Cleveland race by twenty-seven minutes. In a race which was reported to have enjoyed twelve-knot breeze, *Vencedor* won followed by *Vreda*, *Vanenna*, and *Neva*.[7] The official times for the twenty-one-mile race showed *Vencedor* at 2:48, *Vreda* at 3:16, and *Vanenna* at 3:18.

The next day a Canadian newspaper summarized the race as follows: "The *Vencedor* sailed a grand race, and in heavy weather, such as prevailed yesterday, may give our speedy yacht a hard time."[8] Overnight oddsmakers in Put-In-Bay gave the *Vencedor* a two to one advantage. Also, no doubt in their calculations was the fact that *Vencedor* had beaten *Priscilla*, which had handily beaten *Canada*.

On August 15, a reporter for the *New York Sun* in commenting on the *Vencedor*'s twenty-five-minute win over the steel Watson cutter *Vreda*, wrote, "Poeckel's [sic] design has a great deal of speed in her."[9] For a Canadian perspective on the upcoming international race, a writer got the comments of a Canadian yachtsman who gave the following analysis:

"If the *Canada* is only six minutes better than *Zelma* and if *Zelma* sails on fairly even terms in fresh water with the *Vreda*, what are we to think when *Vencedor* beats *Vreda* twenty-five minutes in a twelve-knot breeze?"

The Canadian added, "The *Vreda* is a mighty good boat in spite of her years, and the drubbing she received last Thursday is quite sufficient to convince me that the new Chicago challenger is little short of a wonder." His final line on the race was, "the conclusion is almost irresistable that the *Vencedor* will knock the *Canada* into a cocked hat," adding "[T]his is not a brag, because I am a Canadian and I want our boat to win."

The Cleveland Leader said this: "If the *Vencedor* can outsail the *Canada* anything like she did the *Vreda* yesterday, the Cup will never go across the lakes until another and better challenger is built."[10]

To celebrate his yacht's victory, Commodore Berriman gave a dinner at the Cleveland Yacht Club. That same evening while Berriman was feasting and gloating over *Vencedor*'s performance, Æmilius Jarvis, always searching for ways to insure his boat's success, slipped away from the Canadian fleet and sailed *Canada* up to Toledo where he took the occasion to examine the breezes on that side of the lake in the area where the races would take place. The next day the presence of *Canada* drew crowds of surprised spectators.

August 13, 1896, saw the racing of *Vencedor* against the American cutter *Vanenna* and the Royal Canadian Yacht Club's *Vreda*. *Vreda* finished second but was awarded the win on a time allowance.

The crew of *Vencedor* consisted of the following:

Commodore E. C. Berriman

Captain Irving G. Barbour of Deer Island, Maine

John Connors,

Lewis Bernard,

Ralph Hoagland,

Ed. Andrews,

Al Johnson

Roll D. Potter

Wm. Miller *

Henry Miller* (pros-Millers were engaged in boatbuilding in Charlotte of Lake Ontario).

Vencedor was to enter a race for its class in Put-In-Bay on August 18, but to everyone's surprise it withdrew its entry and was taken to dry dock in Toledo. Hundreds viewed it onshore and wished it well. Designer T. Sch. Poekel was due the following Wednesday to inspect it.

CHAPTER 11

I'll do business with anyone but I'll only go sailing with gentlemen.
Anyone who asks the cost of maintaining a yacht can't buy one.
—*John Pierpont Morgan*

THERE IS A LOT OF WATER FOR YACHTS IN THE GREAT LAKES. BETWEEN the top of Lake Michigan to the outlet on Lake Ontario there exist over 1,100 miles of open water with a maximum width in Lake Huron of 105 miles. Add this to the 60,000 to 70,000 square miles of Lake Superior and Georgian Bay and you get a lot of water.

By the 1890s, along the coasts of the five Great Lakes, there existed twenty-seven yacht clubs comprising over 5,000 members who owned between 500 and 600 yachts. In 1896, the major yacht clubs on the Great Lakes were the following:

Lake Michigan: Lincoln Park Yacht Club, Columbia Yacht Club, Chicago Yacht Club, Milwaukee Yacht Club, Racine Yacht Club, Green Bay Yacht Club, Manitowoc Yacht Club, Marinetti Yacht Club, and the Meonomonee Yacht Club.

Lake Superior: Duluth Yacht Club.

Lake Erie: Buffalo Yacht Club, Erie Yacht Club, Put-In-Bay Yacht Club, Sandusky Yacht Club, Cleveland Yacht Club, Detroit Yacht Club, Michigan Yacht Club, Citizens Yachting Association of Detroit, Ohio Yacht Cub, and Toledo Yacht Club.

Lake Ontario: Royal Canadian Yacht Club, Queen City Yacht Club of Toronto, Bay of Quinte Yacht Club, Hamilton Yacht Club, Oswego Yacht Club (NY), and Rochester Yacht Club (NY).

The oldest and largest yacht club was the Royal Canadian Yacht Club. It started small, but by 1896, it had over 800 members.

Toledo had been selected as the host port. Toledo's Maumee River flows directly into Lake Erie. Lake Erie is the fourth largest of the five Great Lakes and the eleventh largest lake in the world. It is also the southernmost and shallowest of the Great Lakes.

The races would take place at the Turtle Light Course. The course is about seven miles from Toledo and one mile east of the Turtle Light located on Turtle Island.

Turtle Island is a tiny island located on Lake Erie, named after Chief Mishikinakwa of the Miami Indian tribe who had the nickname of Little Turtle. In 1831, a lighthouse was built on the island to help ships navigating to Toledo through the Maumee River. The lighthouse was rebuilt in 1866, with the island facing a battle against erosion which decreased its size to about one acre. The lighthouse was described at the time as the finest one on the Great Lakes, and its light could be seen up to fourteen miles away. The lighthouse was decommissioned in 1904,

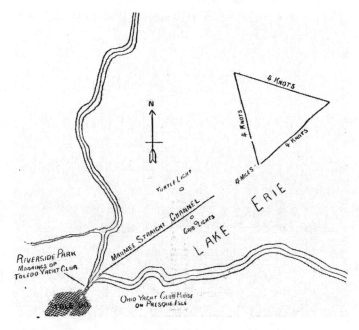

Diagram of Turtle Light course for first race

with a proud record of no shipwrecks in its vicinity in its seventy-two-year history. The island was always close to the border between Ohio and Michigan and for years both states claimed jurisdiction. It wasn't officially decided until 1973 that the island should be equally divided between the two states.

About forty miles away is Put-In-Bay, which was famous for the victory of Admiral Parry over the British fleet on September 10, 1813—it constituted the first defeat of the British fleet in the history of the world.

With *Canada* and *Vencedor* making their separate ways for their encounter with destiny in Toledo, the public's interest in Great Lakes yachting was rising on a daily basis. A reporter for the *Detroit Free Press* praised the developments for he said that up until this moment interest in yachting in the Midwest had been ebbing. In his words, the effect of the friendly rivalry of the *Canada-Vencedor* contest "will be the same to yachting as an injection of elixir of life—supposing it to exist—to the frame of a man who through neglect and years has allowed it to run to seed."[1]

On August 16, 1896, thousands of spectators lined the wharf at Put-In-Bay to watch *Vencedor* as it was pulled in by the tug *Tobey*.

The racing committee announced that it would meet on Wednesday August 19 to decide the issue of professional crews on each yacht. It was also reported that Captain "Kid" Wilds, sailing master of *Sultana*, would sail on *Vencedor*. Based on an objection from the Canadians and citing the agreement that called for no more than two professionals on each yacht, Kid Wilds and Tom Crowley were ruled ineligible to crew since William and Henry Miller on the *Vencedor* were engaged in boatbuilding at Charlotte on Lake Ontario. The Americans argued unsuccessfully that the Canadians had more than two since Captain Jarvis had once been a professional, sailing for hire on salt water. Jarvis was also successful in disqualifying Sam Cooper who was replaced by local amateur Al Scott.

On August 16, 1896, Commodore Jarvis took *Canada* for a trial run over the Turtle Light course, and afterward said he was greatly pleased with the results. He then elaborated on his views on the designs of the competing yachts:

> *Vencedor* has been built on slightly different lines, and it remains
> to be seen which designer had done the best calculating. You see,

Vencedor is built practically on the lines of *Niagara*. It is less than a foot shorter in length overall, and Poekel has copied *Niagara's* lines in many places. It may be he made a mistake in this. The Herreshoffs built *Niagara* to sail on the other side, where the winds are much lighter than we have on the great lakes. This accounts for *Vencedor's* stiffness and sheer. On the other hand, *Canada* is stiff, as is always the case on Fife's boats. The squall we had last Monday gave us abundant proof of this fact.[2]

Put-In-Bay saw the start of the Interlake regatta on August 18. Also, out in the water was Jarvis and the crew of *Canada*. It was there to stretch its canvas and held up well under standing canvas, job, and club topsails. A reporter for the *Chicago Daily Tribune*, who witnessed the tryout, wrote "ahead of the wind it ran like a scared dog."[3]

T. Sch. Poekel arrived in Toledo on August 19 and inspected *Vencedor* lying in dry dock. If any alterations are needed, he would attend to them. Commodore Berriman announced that the sloop would be released from dry dock on Friday, August 21, and that it would be sporting new sails. He added that in the event they didn't work out the old canvas might be reinstalled.

On August 20, 1896, the trophy made by Tiffany & Company arrived in Toledo from New York City. It was described as even more beautiful than

Vencedor in dry dock with designer Poekel inspecting the hull—*Harper's Weekly*

anticipated. Made of 925–1,000 fine sterling silver and consisting of a large bowl over rocks it had the American eagle and the British Lion on either side. It was ten-and-a-half inches high with a bowl that could hold thirteen-and-a-half pints. The Tiffany yacht prize was placed in a store window and drew the attention of hundreds who had come to Toledo for the races. Many commented that it was perfectly designed with the lion and eagle on opposite sides. If the Americans won it, they could display it with the lion facing the wall and *vice versa*.

Canada's Cup—Courtesy of Royal Canadian Yacht Club

Besides a look at the trophy, hundreds went by the docks to see the underbody of *Vencedor*. As excitement for the races was percolating, Commodore Berriman waited anxiously for a new boom and several small spars that had been sent from Racine but which had been mistakenly sent to Cleveland.

Although the host city was Toledo, the fact that the races were scheduled at the Turtle Light Course, Put-In Bay became the unofficial headquarters. Put-In-Bay means exactly what it says—boats and yachts can "put in" for safe boating. Over the years it was mistakenly called puddin bay. On August 22, 1896, it was a bay full of excitement and its adjacent namesake of some 200 inhabitants had a sudden population rise 100-fold to over 2,000. In Toledo all the principal buildings in the town along with the buildings on the waterfront, the lower harbor, and along the Maumee River were decked out with a combination of bunting featuring the blue yachting ensign of England and the red, white, and blue of the Stars and Stripes. The new St. Charles Hotel in Toledo served as the headquarters for many attending the event.

Sailors from the two competing yachts could be seen strolling through the town in their official uniforms and caps. It was observed that the

Canada's sailors had over a pound of gold bullion on their caps. Around the rims of their caps were R.C.Y.C. twice in gold along with six gold maple leaves. The maple leaf was the emblem for Canada but wouldn't see its way into the official flag until 1965. The American sailors had less gold on their caps with only the name "Vencedor" blazoned on them.

The largest gathering of yachts and craft in the history of the Great Lakes was predicted for the races near the Turtle Light course.

As a multitude of sailboats and steam excursion boats sailed into Toledo, one of Canada's most colorful figures appeared with his boat. He was Reverend Charles E. Whitcomb of Hamilton, Canada. The reverend was both an eloquent Episcopalian minister and an outstanding yachtsman. He came to view the big race in his yacht with the unique name of *Euroclydon* but was often called "*Parsonage.*" The *Euroclydon* was the name of the tempestuous storm that forced the Apostle Paul to take shelter with the other apostles on the island of Malta. The *Euroclydon*, which was also painted black like the rest of the Canadian fleet, had an accident on its way down Lake Erie in which it was dismasted. The boat had to pull into a south shore port on the Sabbath for repairs. In giving grateful thanks for the work in apparent violation of work on the Sabbath, Father Whitcomb gave a sermon based on Luke XIV 5: "Which of you shall have an ass or an ox fallen into a pit, and will not straightaway pull him out on the Sabbath Day?"

A reporter for the *Detroit Free Press* summarized the boats this way: "One of their ('America's') expert yacht designers drew up the plans of the *Vencedor* and with such fright were the Canadians seized on learning this, that they sent all the way to the mother country to secure a design from Fife, the man with a world-wide reputation for creating cutters."[4]

The New York Sun pointed out that the Canadians weren't taking any chances with their yacht, since "the designer of the challenging boat is Poekel whom the Herreshoffs trained for many years."[5]

On August 22, 1896, a feature article on the upcoming international race appeared through the wire services in newspapers throughout the country. The article said this about Poekel:

Vencedor was designed by Theodore [*sic*] Poekel, and built last winter to the order of the Berriman brothers of Chicago, especially for a race with the best boat Canada could produce. Poekel, the designer, just from the Herreshoff yards, had every reason to create a yacht of the first class.[6]

The official timekeeper for the races was the legendary Joseph Ruff of Chicago. Born in Glasgow, Scotland, he grew up along the Clyde and had been timing every important yacht race in Chicago since 1869. After immigrating from Scotland in 1868, Ruff had the French yacht designer Mitchell Cuson make him an eighteen-foot sailboat that he sailed on Lake Michigan. He would often comment that he paid Cuson $2 and along with three two cent internal revenue stamps for his boat.

Assisting Ruff and serving as the racing committee were H. C. McLeod of the Lincoln Park Yacht Club, E. H. Ambrose of the Royal Hamilton Yacht Club, and Oliver E. Cromwell of the Seawanhaka Club of New York.

News came that there would be a change in the course for the international race. The start was changed to be four miles from the straight channel. This would allow the yachts to be six miles east of the Turtle Light and for the first leg they would be sailing well toward Middle Sister Island. The change in the route was done for fear of the yachts approaching the shallow water on the last turn, which would have brought them too close to shoals as they raced toward the City of Monroe, Michigan.

Skipper Jarvis was equally as optimistic as Barbour and Berriman and offered this assessment: "We have just as much chance to have a light breeze as a stiff one. That is the sort of weather *Vencedor* does not want, and it amounts to an admission that we can beat her in a light breeze and smooth water. At all events, we expect a good race and feel confident we shall win no matter what the weather may be."

Joseph Ruff, official timekeeper

In preparation, Jarvis and his crew chose performance over beauty. They used their collective elbow grease in coating the fine white enamel underbody of the *Canada* with plumbago. The beauty was gone but a dark coat of lead grease would insure swiftness in the water and take off seconds from its racing time.

Spectators and prognosticators witnessed the expertise of the Canadian crew. Skipper Jarvis had trained his men to efficiently work together. It was widely believed that the crew and owner of *Vencedor* were inexperienced. In comparing the skippers, it was pointed out that Skipper Jarvis had mastered sailing on the lakes' waters as a young boy, while owner Berriman had only been identified with the sport of sailing for about a year. Mentioned also was the fact that *Vencedor*'s crew was green and inexperienced. One example that was given was seeing six or seven of the *Vencedor*'s crew attempting to take a pull at the jib in a race in Cleveland when only two men on the mast were required. Also noticed was that while *Canada*'s crew had been together since its launching, *Vencedor* had sailed most of the way to Toledo with only Skipper Barbour and a few trusty crew members. *The Chicago Chronicle* had this to say about *Canada*'s crew:

> They are as fine a lot of trained aquatic athletes as have ever been seen on the lakes, and the ease and speed with which they handle ropes and canvas is a great object lesson to the yankees.[7]

Just a couple of days before the start of the international races, Skipper Jarvis gave the following analysis to a reporter from the *New York Sun*:

> The *Canada* will sail at about three feet less corrected length than the *Vencedor*, and while there is very little difference in our lines Poekel has for the most part copied the *Niagara*, and it remains to be seen whether that was a wise course or not. The *Niagara* was built to allow Mr. Gould to enter the races on the other side of the Atlantic where the breezes are much stronger than this side. The *Vencedor*, consequently, sits higher in the

water, and as past week has shown, she is remarkably stiff in a heavy sea. She is undoubtedly a very fine boat, and the difference in type will enhance interest in the contest.[8]

Put-In-Bay and Toledo were both inundated with yachting fans from all over the Midwest and even from the East Coast who had traveled by train and boat to witness the great international yacht race.

Steamer ferries *Promise* and *Pleasure* were brought in from the City of Toledo to allow spectators to be closer to the races. Steamers *Pathfinder*, *Hinda*, and the *Pastime* from Detroit came into Toledo. Also present in the bay was Mr. Cudahy, a well-known oil and grain speculator from Chicago in his private steam yacht. It was also reported that the steam yacht *Grace* was coming with more enthusiasts and city hall officials. Steam and sailing yachts poured in from Chicago, Milwaukee, Rochester, and Oswego. Excursion trains also arrived.

On August 22, 1896, at 3:00 pm, the official measurements were made of *Vencedor* and *Canada*. Based on the lopsided agreement that Commodore Berriman had agreed to, it was feared that *Vencedor* would end up with a severe handicap.

First, *Canada* was towed from its moorings to the Craig shipyard where her measurements were taken under the watchful eye of Commodore Berriman and a scrutineer. Next *Vencedor* was taken to its slip and its measurements were taken. The respective scrutineers would stay on the yachts through the end of the races.

Rule 3 of the agreement entered into between the L.P.Y.C. and the R.C.Y.C. read as follows: "*Vencedor's* length on load waterline shall not be less than 43 feet, and her corrected length, to be ascertained as hereinafter mentioned, shall not exceed 45 feet; but should it be ascertained on measurement that this corrected length is exceeded, double time allowance shall be given on such excess, but in no event shall such excess exceed one half foot."

Rule 4 read as follows: "The boat which shall be selected by the Royal Canadian Yacht Club as its representative shall, if possible, not exceed 42 ½ feet corrected length."

Rule 3 strictly limited the *Vencedor* but Rule 4 gave wide latitude to the *Canada* with no restrictions. It was written in the *Cleveland Plain Dealer* that the "fact has become apparent that Poekel's ambition to build the challenging boat has put Commodore Berriman into a box. He has agreed to the most extraordinary conditions and if they result in the race being lost by the American boat he will have no one to blame but himself."[9]

In comparing the two rules, the *Chicago Chronicle* summed it up best: "The Canadians were shrewd enough to completely tie Poekel's hands, while they themselves were free to do as they saw best."[10]

According to the agreement, if *Vencedor* measured over forty-five feet, it had to give *Canada* double-time allowance. The measurements of the *Vencedor* were too great, and the yacht had to trim two-and-one-half feet off its main boom and shorten its club topsail yard four feet.

After midnight on August 23 scrutineers Benjamin Carpenter of Chicago and Captain George E. Evans of Toronto announced the official measurements:

It was expected that the time allowance would be about three minutes and hoped by the Americans that it might be less.

	Canada	Vencedor
Length over all (LOA)	55.21	62.73
Length waterline (LWL)	37.04	43.08
Boom	42.85	46.90
Gaff	24.12	27.80
Hoist	24.55	26.30
Sail area	2,164.91	2,283.07

Based on the above measurements, the judges ruled that *Vencedor* would allow *Canada* a time allowance of four minutes forty seconds. This was 25 percent more than expected.

When the measurements were announced, the Americans were in shock and the Canadians jubilant and the betting eased off.

Commodore Berriman and Captain Barbour appeared cheerful and confident in spite of the devastating setback.

Early on the morning of August 23, *Vencedor* was taken to the course for a trial run. Captain Barbour sailed the big mahogany sloop around the twenty-four-mile course in one hour and thirty minutes. Although news reports said that Barbour's crew was "raw" compared to that of the *Canada*, Captain Barbour came ashore in an optimistic mood. He said: "If we have a stiff breeze and a good sea, there will be no need of a third race, for *Vencedor* will win two races straight with ease."[11] Commodore Berriman joined in the analysis given by Captain Barbour.

Commodore Jarvis was equally as optimistic and offered this assessment: "We have just as much chance to have a light breeze as a stiff one. That is the sort of weather the *Vencedor* does not want, and it amounts to an admission that we can beat her in a light breeze and smooth water. At all events, we expect a good race and feel confident we shall win no matter what the weather may be."

The winner of the international yacht between *Vencedor* and *Canada* would be the winner of two out of three races. The races would take place a few miles from Turtle light where there was at least twenty-four feet of water for the yachts. The first race would consist of a triangular course of twelve knots sailed twice around with one of the legs due to the windward.

The second race would consist of the same length of the first but straightaway to leeward or to windward—the third, if needed, would be decided upon the toss of a coin.

CHAPTER 12

Turtle Light Course, Toledo, Ohio
Monday, August 24, 1896

THE FIRST DAY FOR THE INTERNATIONAL YACHT RACES ON THE GREAT Lakes was gorgeous. Bright skies and cool temperatures brought out throngs eager to see the first race. For the past two days, the wind had been blowing strongly out of the west, so most hoped there would be good breezes today. The docks and wharves swarmed with folks embarking on all types of pleasure craft, gaily decorated with flags and streamers. Around 10:00 am, a flotilla of boats left the muddy waters of the Maumee River and headed out to the Turtle Light Course—it was the largest flotilla of pleasure boats ever assembled on the Great Lakes. Thousands paid $1.50 to travel on one of the large steam excursion boats to see the races up close.

At race time over 100 boats were near the course to view the twenty-four-mile triangular race—it would be three legs of four miles each, sailed twice around. It seemed like a perfect day for a yacht race with one exception—very little wind. At 9:30 am, the press onboard *Secor* had left Dewey's Wharf.

A few thousand miles away from Toledo, Grover Cleveland, the President of the United States, who had been invited to the international races, was also in a boat. But he wasn't viewing a race; he was looking for bass in a pond located between Plymouth, Massachusetts, and his home on Buzzards Bay.

In the early morning hours of August 24, both sloops were towed out to the Turtle Light Course. As the mahogany-hulled *Vencedor* glistened in the sun with its sails down, it was reported that she looked like "a boat captured by pirates being led away."[1]

Scene of the start of the International Yacht Races captured by famed artist Carlton T. Chapman—*Harper's Weekly*

Yacht racing was not a really great sport for spectators. Those on land had limited views of the races and even those in small craft and excursion steamers only had snapshots of what was transpiring. And with time allowances, no one could even tell who won the race. But it provided an unbelievable spectacle. To witness the scene of hundreds of craft flying streamers and national flags, and then the two giant sailboats with their neatly dressed crews was a sight to behold.

Crowds sat in chairs on Dewey's Wharf, while others boarded all types of boats to get closer to the action. The famed artist Carlton T. Chapman was out on the water with his sketch pad. Chapman who had received his professional training at the National Academy and the Arts Student League had received awards for his work at Boston in 1892, Chicago in 1893, and Atlanta in 1894. Photographers were scattered in boats including those from Alvord & Sprague who were commissioned by *Harper's Weekly*. The press boat had journalists from all over the country.

Wagering was noted by the press and the bets were heavy when the odds were low. The Canadians wanted three to one odds and very few took the bet, but when some bookies approached *Pathfinder,* Fred Morgan made a bet of $100 backing *Vencedor.*

A bad omen for *Vencedor's* chances was a comment by one gadfly: "When a Canadian is willing to bet his last cent on an even-money chance the true odds must be 10 to 1 in his favor."[2]

The *Toronto Evening Star* predicted that "a slight breeze and a time allowance of almost five minutes made it appear as though Canada had the race well in hand."[3]

News reports circulated that the only concern was harsh criticism contained in a dispatch from *Vencedor's* designer T. Sch. Poekel that intimated the crew wasn't in its right senses in its handling the yacht. Poekel's criticism was that the crew was "sailing it with working topsail, with the mainsail cut and topsail carried."[4] A report surfaced in the *Inter-Ocean Daily* that Poekel "indicated that those handling the sails were not doing what the celebrated designer and boat builder thought should be done."[5]

Poekel would watch the races from the top deck of his other design, *Pathfinder,* in the presence of Mr. Morgan and his guests. Also, aboard *Pathfinder* was *Vencedor's* owner Commodore E. C. Berriman—a fact not missed by Æmilius Jarvis.

Although it was reported that Poekel's criticism was based on false information being conveyed to him, it later turned out that was not the case and that Poekel's criticism was well founded. New sails that Poekel had ordered from Racine were not used at all. The controversy in handling the sails in order to satisfy the measurements resulted in a report that the officers of the Lincoln Park Yacht Club removed themselves as sponsors and stated that *Vencedor* was racing solely under the auspices of Commodore Berriman.

Analyzing the race, the editor of Yachting Notes for the *World of New York* wrote: "There is little fear among the Chicago yachtsmen that *Canada* will capture the trophy." The article praised the secrecy in the building of *Vencedor* and added that "Mr. Poeckel [*sic*] has learned a shrewd lesson from the astute Mr. Herreshoff. No authentic information about the shape of the *Vencedor* has been allowed to become public."[6]

One of the most picturesque of all the steamers on the lake was *Sigma,* which belonged to S. C. Reynolds, president of the First National Bank of Toledo, which was serving as the judges' boat.

Promptly at 11:00 am, the gun went off from *Sigma* and the first of the best two out of three international yacht races had started.

Vencedor took the lead crossing the starting line but then *Canada* with some fancy maneuvering by Skipper Jarvis engaged in short tacking and blanketed *Vencedor*. *Canada* kept at it until it held a safe lead.

But with hardly any breeze, the two spectacular yachts inched along the course in what appeared to be a drifting match.

Canada, as predicted, kept its lead with the light winds. By 1:00 pm, both yachts were floundering in calm seas on the first leg of the three-legged race.

At 1:18 pm, *Canada* passed the first buoy or stake boat and a gun was fired. That led to a giant cacophony of horns and whistles from the multitude of boats on the lake. *Vencedor* came later at 1:40 pm and more bedlam rang out after the gun went off. A reporter from the *Chicago Tribune* wrote that "it was a noise that beat any Fourth of July celebration ever invented."[7]

At 2:40 pm, both yachts got out their spinnakers but no sails. Eyewitnesses said it looked like both yachts were anchored with no breezes. Both yachts were becalmed. The yachts had run into "Paddy's Hurricane"—a flat calm sea.

That was enough for the judges who knew that neither yacht would finish the race in the time allotted of five-and-one-half hours. The *Sigma* steamed next to *Canada* and gave three whistles—the signal that the race was over. It then headed to *Vencedor* and sounded three whistles.

When the judges called the race, *Vencedor* was nearly one mile behind *Canada*, which had only completed about six miles or one quarter of the course.

Hundreds of disappointed spectators returned back to the docks of Toledo. The consensus was that the *Canada* could outsail *Vencedor* in a mild breeze and that the Canadian crew seemed superior. A more detailed analysis was given by a crew member from *Vencedor* who made comments touching on the first day. He said that his crew wasn't prepared for the slick maneuvering by Captain Jarvis, that the time allowance still worried the crew, and that the loss of Cooper as a member was quite devastating since he was a really talented sailor. However, the crew member ended on an optimistic note saying: "Give us a stiff breeze and we will send those Britishers back to Toronto with a little less coin than they came here with."

CHAPTER 13

Turtle Light Course, Toledo, Ohio
Tuesday, August 25, 1896

As the sun rose over Toledo for the second day of racing, the crews and spectators noticed a slight breeze. The crew and fans of *Vencedor* also looked for clouds, which always preceded the squalls on the Great Lakes—but there were none. The sky was cloudless.

Overnight more boats arrived to view the races. From Boston, the steamer *Enquirer* came filled with spectators. From Cleveland, the steamers *Say When* and *Anadis* came. From Chicago, *Sentinel*. From Detroit, *Pastime* and *Nymph*. New schooners arriving were *Oriole* from Hamilton, *Priscilla* from Cleveland, and *Mistral* from Chicago.

In the morning before the race, it was rumored that T. Sch. Poekel had sent Commodore Berriman a telegram protesting the use of the old sails. He had sent down new sails. In spite of his protest, *Vencedor* entered the race with its old sails.

Because of what had happened the day before and because of the light wind blowing, there were actually fewer spectator boats in the bay for the second day of scheduled racing. There was, however, more wind—but not by much. In the words of Commodore Berriman, as his yacht was being towed to the course, "the wind was aggravatingly light" and he vowed to stay a week if necessary to get a decisive race.

Precisely at 10:50 am, a gun was fired from *Sigma* and a flag bearing the red Canadian ensign was hoisted. It was an indication that all buoys were to be kept port. At 11:00 am, a gun was fired to start the race. Today Captain Barbour was up to some tricks himself, as *Vencedor* was the first to cross the starting line three seconds after the gun was fired. At 11:05 am

Vencedor increased her lead using its balloon jib, topsail, jib, mainsail, and working gaff topsail. *Canada* used its balloon jib, topsail, jib, mainsail, and working gaff topsail. But by 11:10 am, by using what the *Ottawa Journal* called an "old trick of the Dominion boat," *Canada* drew up and passed to windward blanketing *Vencedor*.

At 11:20 am the winds died down considerably.

Canada rounded the first stake boat at 11:57:15 and *Vencedor* at 11:58:40.

At one point a reporter for the *Chicago Tribune* pointed out that *Canada* "looked like a white butterfly on the water," while at the same time *Vencedor* was tangling with its sails.

Canada continued to expand its lead over *Vencedor* passing the second stake boat at 12:45 pm with *Vencedor* passing it at 12:54 pm.

Toward the end of the twenty-four-mile race, *Vencedor* lost time when its sails got tangled when the crew was trying to get the sheet broke out.

When the winds died down, at times, the *Vencedor*'s crew's only hope was for the time to run out as on the previous day. But then the winds picked up and *Canada* finished the race before the deadline.

Vencedor was badly beaten—coming in twenty-three minutes thirty-four seconds after *Canada*. Two main reasons were given for *Vencedor*'s loss—the lack of a decent wind and the expert handling of the sails by the crew of *Canada* who had been drilled by Æmilius Jarvis for the past month. Ironically, Commodore Berriman, the man who created the race, was not onboard *Vencedor* but for the second time watched the race aboard *Pathfinder*.

	Start	Finish	Elapsed Time	Corrected Time
Canada	11.00.00	4.19.08	5.19.08	5.14.23
Vencedor	11.00.00	4.37.07	5.37.07	5.37.07

Canada received a thunderous ovation when it crossed the finish line at 4:19 pm—just about eleven minutes before the expiration of the time limit set forth in the rules.

Canadians wouldn't hear the results in the *Toronto Evening Star* until the next day. They only learned what was happening to about 12 noon, which was when the Canadian newspapers' carrier pigeons left Toledo to fly to Toronto with the update.

CHAPTER 14

Turtle Light Course, Toledo, Ohio
Wednesday, August 26, 1896

As DAWN BROKE OVER TOLEDO ON WEDNESDAY, AUGUST 26, 1896, THE weather bureau reported that there were fifteen to sixteen miles per hour winds and stronger winds expected near the Turtle Light Course—perhaps even a squall. This was extremely good news for Captain Barbour and his crew on *Vencedor*. It was also great news for the hordes of yacht aficionados who had journeyed to Toledo to see a yacht race—not a drifting match like the second race nor a cancellation like the first race.

Commodore Berriman's brother and partner, Matthew W. Berriman, arrived the night before to witness this crucial race for himself.

The judges, before leaving the wharf, said the race today would be five miles to windward and return, the course to be sailed twice thus giving the race a total of twenty miles. This race would determine if a third one was necessary or whether *Canada* would achieve victory and yachting supremacy over the Great Lakes.

The start was delayed a half hour due to an accident on *Canada* carrying away her top mast halyards. The gun was finally fired at 11:30 am for the start.

Prior to the start, Captain Barbour, as usual, did some fancy maneuvers so that *Vencedor* was first across the starting line. As usual, Skipper Jarvis luffed *Canada*'s sails in order to blanket *Vencedor*. This time, *Vencedor* did not succumb to Jarvis's tricks and took an early, commanding lead.

Vencedor was wildly cheered when it passed the first stake boat at 12:03 pm. *Canada* trailed badly passing it at 12:19:20.

The day provided a lot more wind than the first two days. *Vencedor*, as predicted, sailed swiftly in the breeze.

At noon, the rain began.

After the second turn, Skipper Barbour seemed confused as to the correct stakes boat—three boats were flying the American flag. Barbour at first headed to the correct one but then made a fatal mistake sailing to the farthest one. It was estimated that this move cost over two minutes in actual time. *Vencedor* might have made up the difference but toward the end of the last leg the winds and the seas went down.

The race ended with both yachts within seconds of each other.

Although *Vencedor* crossed the finish line first, nobody knew who had won with the time allowance afforded to *Canada*. Captain Barbour and his crew went along the judges' boat for the result. When the watches were calibrated, old Joseph Ruff announced that *Canada* won by twenty-six seconds of corrected time. The actual time was 2:11:04 for *Vencedor* and 2:44:35 for the *Canada*. *Vencedor* had beaten *Canada* by three minutes thirty-one seconds actual time.

The *New York Times* heralded the race calling it "one of the most exciting contests ever seen on the lakes."[1]

It was thought that had Skipper Barbour turned the boat properly *Vencedor* would have won the race by about one-and-one-half minutes. Instead it lost by less than a minute. In defense of Skipper Barbour, numerous small boats flying American flags were allowed to be too close to the stake boat.

Another factor causing Barbour's error was the fact that the judge's boat was not near the stake boat when *Vencedor* approached. It was felt that had it been nearby it would have been a guide for Barbour and he wouldn't have missed the correct stake boat.

	Start	Finish	Elapsed Time	Corrected Time
Canada	11.30.00	2.44.35	2.44.35	2.40.38
Vencedor	11.30.00	2.41.04	2.41.	2.41.04

It was estimated that 10,000 people witnessed the race each day with over 100 boats in the water.

CHAPTER 15

Three cheers for Skippadore Jarvis!
—Lord Mayor of Toronto, *Thomas Fleming*

AFTER THE CHAMPIONSHIP, CAPTAIN JARVIS RECEIVED A FLOOD OF congratulatory telegrams including ones sent by the New York Yacht Club and the Montreal Yacht Club. Also, awaiting in his office upon his return to Toronto was a cablegram from Fairlie, Scotland, from Will Fife Jr.

Mr. H. E. Ridley, described as an "ardent yachtsman," who had journeyed to Toledo to watch the races, arrived back in Toronto carrying two enlarged photographs of the racing yachts was interviewed by the *Toronto Evening Star*. He had this to say:

> They did themselves grand. Yesterday's was the most exciting yacht race that I ever saw in my life. The *Vencedor* is a perfect horse in a gale of a wind, and, with the choppy sea and the stiff breeze that was blowing yesterday, was picked on as the winner. But, Mr. Jarvis was quite confident that with his boat and his crew he could beat the *Vencedor* any day, and in any kind of weather, and the result fully justified his expectations. The *Vencedor*, owing to her extra length, had the advantage in yesterday's wind but the sailing abilities of the *Canada* rendered this advantage to almost nil.[1]

Concerning the missed stake boat by Captain Barbour, Ridley had this to say:

> "I was on a large excursion boat, following in the wake of the two yachts. There were fully 1,000 people on board the boat, and, without one exception, they declared they could see the stake boat clearly. In

fact, wonderment was generally expressed that Barbour was standing out so far. The old captain of the Detroit yacht *Surprise* was on board and went nearly wild. He blamed Barbour for losing the race. In language more forcible than polite." Ridley pointed out that the area around the stake boat was congested but his final analysis was that "Barbour's error was possible but inexcusable."

Captain Barbour was sore at the judges and had this to say after the race: "The judges made me lose in not having the judges' boat in the proper place. I cannot attribute the loss of the race to the Canadians; they were not at fault."

Mr. Evans, as scrutineer for *Canada* on board *Vencedor*, blamed the loss on "too much patriotism." He said that there were far too many American flags on the small boats in the area as well as on the stake boat as well as every anchored stake boat.

Matthew W. Berriman, brother and part owner of *Vencedor*, said it was the finest race he had ever seen. When asked if his brother would have another boat, he responded: "Yes and Poekel, who designed *Vencedor*, will design it."[2]

An eyewitness, however, said it was the judges' fault who were literally out to lunch. Here is the letter he wrote to the editor of the *Chicago Tribune* that was printed in its entirety:

Editor of the Tribune:

Noticing the newspaper comments that the yacht *Vencedor* in her last race with the *Canada* was not properly handled, and being an unprejudicial spectator of the race, I wish to state that the yacht *Vencedor* was well handled, her canvas was quickly and properly put on, and all through she sailed a splendid race. The race was lost by a virtue of the judges' boat not being in position to locate the home buoy on the first turn, together with the fact that there were three two-masted boats at anchor, all flying the American ensign, making it impossible to know which was the proper turning buoy. Instead of the judges' being in the proper position at the buoy they were taking luncheon, expecting to have time to reach the buoy before the return of the boats. In the two previous days' races the judges' boat was at every turning buoy, and in both of the first races the weather was very light, the buoys only four miles apart and easy to pick up, whereas in the last day's race the wind was blowing hard and the weather was thick so that in our judgment the race was lost wholly on account of the mismanagement of the judges' boat.

Signed /JUSTICE/[3]

After the race the diminutive Mrs. E. C. Berriman was inconsolable.

The next day newspapers throughout the country proclaimed the tragic loss of the *Vencedor* with such headlines: "Lost by a Fluke" (*Madison Daily News*), "Vencedor Loses on an Error" (*North Platte Semi Weekly Tribune*), "Not the Boat's Fault, the Vencedor Won but the Skipper Lost His Head" (*Detroit Free Press*), "Vencedor Unhappy Accident" (*Evening Bulletin -Ky.*), "Lost by Mistake" (*Rock Island Argus*), "A MISTAKE" (*Cleveland Leader*), "Outsailed but American Captain Lost His Bearings" (*Hawaiian Gazette*), "Lost by Mistake" (*Moline Dispatch*), "The Vencedor Not Disgraced" (*Seattle Post Intelligencer*), and "Misfortune Curses Vencedor's Cause" (*Philadelphia Inquirer*).

Many in the crowd spoke of a protest because of the confusion with the stakes boat. However, Commodore Berriman issued the following statement:

I went into the race not to protest anything, even though they should shoot a cannon ball through my canvas. We have lost, and that settles the race, but I have a challenge in my pocket for another race in 1897.[4]

Protests were fairly common in yacht racing, and actually when *America* won in the most famous race of all off the Isle of Wight in 1851, it had sailed inside the Nab lightship instead of around it and a protest was filed. However, the racing committee overruled the protest stating that insufficient instructions had been given to the contestants. If the protest had held, there never would be an America's Cup.

Part of the reason for Berriman's not willing to challenge the race was what had happened to Lord Dunraven after he had protested the America's Cup races the year before. The Irish Earl had been thrown out of the New York Yacht Club and marked as a *persona non grata* in the yachting world.

Berriman was ready with his challenge and he wrote this:

On board Yacht *Vencedor*
TOLEDO, Ohio, August 26, 1896

W. T. Boswell, Commodore Royal Canadian Yacht Club:

Dear Sir:

On behalf of Edward C. and Matthew Berriman, and through the Lincoln Park Yacht Club of Chicago, you are hereby challenged to sail a series of three matches, best two in three, on some neutral waters during the yachting season of 1897, under the New York Yacht Club rules, so far as they will apply, the arrangements governing such matches to be made by a committee of three representing the Lincoln Park Yacht Club of Chicago, and a like number representing the Royal Canadian Yacht Club of Toronto, they to choose a seventh member if necessary; the competing yachts to measure not to exceed forty-three feet as the load water line.

That evening a ball was held for the visiting yachtsmen, their friends, and families at Pythian Castle given by the International Yacht Race Association of Toledo. During the ball the trophy cup and a draft for $1,500 were presented to Commodore Jarvis by President Robinson Locke of the Association. The cash had been raised from donations from the citizens of Toledo given to the Association. The inscription on the bowl read "Presented by the International Yacht Race Association. Won by _____, 1896."

After receiving the spectacular Tiffany Silver Cup, Æmilius Jarvis was then presented with the City of Straights Challenge Cup of Detroit after which he received the challenge of Commodore Berriman.

With such a large gathering of yacht clubs represented in Toledo, a meeting was held at which time it was decided to form a Union consisting of the Yachting Associations on the Great Lakes. The sequel was a joint meeting in Buffalo of the three associations: the Lake Yacht Racing Association of Lake Ontario; the Interlake Yachting Association of Lake Erie, Detroit River, and Lake St. Clair; and the Lake Michigan Yachting Association of Lake Michigan. The result of this meeting was the creation of a new association: the Yacht Racing Union of the Great Lakes.

Before sailing *Canada* back to Toronto, Captain Jarvis gave his own comments on the race at the Cadillac Hotel in Detroit. He stated that *Canada* was about as near perfection as one of the best of the modern yacht designers could make her, praising Will Fife as well as Ratsey, the sailmakers. He added that he thought the *Vencedor* was "a crude affair" although designed by a "clever man."

At 4:15 pm on August 31, 1896, Captain Jarvis and his crew returned to Toronto Bay onboard *Canada* and received a hero's welcome.

Toronto Bay was filled with boats of all kinds in a grand welcoming celebration. Cannons roared, guns were fired, and whistles sounded as the triumphant sloop approached.

The *Toronto Evening Star* chartered the steamer *A.J. Tymon* and filled it with invited guests, draping the sides with banners proclaiming "The *Evening Star*'s Welcome to Canada," and was the first steamer to welcome Canada and its crew. Its celebratory passengers, which included dignitaries and guests, jockeyed out into Toronto Bay to spot *Canada* when it first arrived. Megaphones were used to shout out hurrahs. Among those onboard was Reverend Calvert of Oakville who the previous Sunday had preached a sermon on the international race.

The entire Toronto town council was onboard the cruiser steam yacht *Cruiser*. After the *Cleopatra* transferred a crew to *Canada*, it came alongside and Captain Jarvis and his crew hopped onboard. As soon as the transfer took place, *Cruiser*'s brass gun was fired and then pandemonium

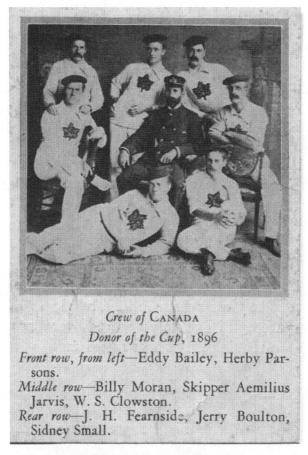

Crew of CANADA
Donor of the Cup, 1896
Front row, from left—Eddy Bailey, Herby Parsons.
Middle row—Billy Moran, Skipper Aemilius Jarvis, W. S. Clowston.
Rear row—J. H. Fearnside, Jerry Boulton, Sidney Small.

—Courtesy of Royal Canadian Yacht Club

broke out. Shots went up from *Vreda* and *Vivia*. Fireworks went off in the bay along with rifle and revolver shots.

Cruiser took the honored heroes and city officials to the newly opened Town Clubhouse of the Royal Canadian Yacht Club where Captain Jarvis and his victorious crew were feted for several hours.

At 8:00 pm, there was a torchlight procession from the yacht club to the Horticultural Gardens where a citizens' welcome and reception took place. Thousands came for the celebration and there was literally standing room only.

Toronto's Mayor Fleming, a confirmed landlubber, spoke briefly saying the race had been "fair, manly and honest" and gave a toast to "Skippadore Jarvis." The huge crowd roared with laughter. The unique moniker stayed with Jarvis forever and he would always be known as the "Skippadore."

The ladies of Toronto presented a bouquet to the handsomest member of the crew. After someone shouted out, "Give it to Fernside," others shouted it until it became unanimous. Crew member Fernside of Hamilton accepted it gracefully.

Jarvis closed his brief speech stating that he and his crew were better treated in Toledo than the Chicagoans. He then called for three cheers for *Vencedor* and her owners, which had a great response from the audience.

While the Skippadore and his crew basked in the glow of victory in Canada, analysts in the United States engaged in theories as to why *Vencedor* lost.

The *New York-Tribune* felt that Commodore Berriman had been out-foxed and had this to say: "The skipper and owner of the *Canada*, Æmilius Jarvis, is a past master in all the intricacies of yachting, both practical and documentary, and the general opinion among the assembled yachtsmen is that if Commodore Berriman got the worst of the bargain only his inexperience is to blame, and not his sportsmanlike desire to bring about a great race."[5]

On August 28, 1896, Commodore Berriman returned to Chicago and gave an interview. He said: "I have seen the finest race ever sailed on fresh water," adding "I admit that the *Canada* can beat the *Vencedor* seven out of ten races, under the conditions that governed this contest, but it is absurd to undertake to race a boat that should be classed at 49 and 50 feet racing length against a boat measuring 41 feet. I would bet $500 that Poekel's model properly canvassed will beat the *Canada* any time."[6]

As to how Captain Barbour and his crew handled the race, Berriman said: "Her crew performed excellent service throughout. Capt. Barbour distinguished himself in every race, notwithstanding that his boat was defeated. When you stop to consider that the *Canada* was in command of the veteran fresh water yachtsman, Capt. Jarvis, you can appreciate the excellent work done by the *Vencedor's* crew. We had our spinnaker out in the last race fully forty seconds before our opponent and our balloon jib was handled from fifteen to twenty seconds faster than *Canada's*."[7]

As to why *Vencedor* lost, Berriman remarked:

As to how we were beaten it is a long story to explain. When the match was first made we had a misunderstanding as to the waterline and the canvas in consequence had to be cut down. We were sailing under forty-six feet six inches racing line, and in order to accomplish it we were obliged to carry at least eighty square feet of canvas less than the *Canada*. Now, although the latter is a smaller craft than the *Vencedor* by nearly ten feet, we could not carry as much canvas. That accounts in a large measure for our defeat. But at that, the *Canada* only beat us by twenty-six seconds, which we lost in trying to locate the stake boat. The four minute time allowance also added to our handicap.

As for the *Vencedor*'s design, a reporter for the *Detroit Free Press* wrote: "Designer Poekel, who had charge of the construction of the boat, is not entirely to blame, inasmuch as he was obliged to follow certain specifications which Commodore Berriman accepted in his anxiety to make the match."

Giving his own analysis of the race was Caspar William Whitney (1864–1929). Whitney wrote for *Harper's Weekly* and was a strong advocate for amateur sports in America. In 1889, he would originate the concept of the All-American team in college football. A great outdoorsman and explorer he would be a founding member of the Explorer's Club as well as serve as chairman of the American Olympic Committee and a member of the International Olympic Committee.

Concerning the international race in Toledo, Whitney's analysis was that Berriman was outmaneuvered by the Canadians due to his lack of experience in yacht racing. He then went on to say that money purses had no place in yachting by writing this:

The offering of a $1,500 purse was another and an unwholesome feature that added to the uniqueness of this aquatic contest. The first international or interclub race ever sailed for money in American waters. And an agreement entered into by Berriman and Jarvis before the event, to divide it at the rate of 60 per cent to the winner and 40 per cent to the loser! The wonder is they did not demand some division of the excursion boat receipts to help defray their racing expenses. Yachtsmen are supposed to race for sport; If the maintenance of a racing yacht is dependent upon the hanging up of a purse, it would redound to their credit and further the best interests of sport if they retired in favor of gentlemen whose incomes permitted the luxury of yachting.[8]

After the races there continued to be a dispute as to whether different sails should have been used by the *Vencedor*. The sails that were shipped to Toledo from Racine at the request of T. Sch. Poekel were never used. Poekel said he was not misinformed during the races and that in his opinion had the shipped sails been used the outcome would have been different. He cut down the mainsail so carrying her working topsail it came with the racing length prescribed by the agreement and was not compelled to pay double-time allowance on any excess over forty-five feet. Berriman argued that using the club topsail provided the yacht with enough power to overcome the double-time allowance.

Most critics blamed the Lincoln Park Yacht Club for allowing the double-time allowance.

One of the judges even weighed in—Oliver E. Cromwell of the Seawanhaka Corinthian Yacht Club who was an eyewitness. He stated it succinctly: "The making of the match was the making of the race." He further stated that, because of the poor agreement, *Vencedor* had too much ballast and had its wings clipped. He added that the Canadian crew was superior to the Americans but said he felt in such an important international race there should be a well-trained professional crew. In his analysis of the race he stated that the sails of *Vencedor* weren't first rate, and too many fishing boats near one of the mark boats caused *Vencedor* to lose valuable time and there should have been better signage on the mark boat.

Some yachtsmen wanted to blame the designer for the loss of the races. But T. Sch. Poekel "energetically" defended his design in the *Journal Times* on August 27. He laid the blame squarely on the shoulders of the owner Commodore Berriman.

First, knowing that the sail area and waterline would be decreased, he realized *Vencedor* would not sail well in a light breeze so he wanted a time allowance of five hours for a race. The L.P.Y.C. understood this but compromised on five-and-one-half hours. If the five-hour rule had been adopted, *Canada* would not have been allowed to win the second race.

Poekel said that *Vencedor* should not have been measured or sailed with its club topsail. He said that the topsail was designed just for cruising. The measurement brought the yacht up to forty-five feet six inches and resulted in a double-time allowance. Poekel explained that "by so doing the owner changed the center of effect of the sails by bringing them too far forward, which naturally seriously interfered with both the steering and the speed of the craft."

He wanted a working topsail instead. He also wanted a new mainsail used which he had shipped down from Racine. In fact, he said, the new mainsail was a trifle larger on the beam but with the working topsail the measurements would have been below forty-five feet so there would have been no double-time allowance. He also pointed out that the old mainsail had been recently been badly stretched in a squall.

Poekel also announced that Secretary Reynolds of the RBMCO had received a letter dated before the races began that the sailing committee of the Lincoln Park Yacht Club had announced its resignation and that the races were strictly under the authority of Commodore Berriman. Therefore, if there were blame to be attributed, it should be given to owner Berriman.

According to Poekel, if his suggestions were followed, *Canada* would not have won either of the two races for the championship.

In analyzing Poekel's suggestions as to the use of sails, professional sailor and rigger Patrick Gavin-Brynes states that "Poekel was correct with his idea of optimizing the boat for maximum speed in a light wind while keeping it within the rules in order to eliminate the time allowance," and that "this is exactly what we do today." Gavin-Byrnes should know since he sails one of the last of the giant wooden sailboats that the Herreshoff yard built in 1912—*Spartan*, which is a New York Yacht Club 50. He also believes that it seems incredible that the new mainsail that Poekel shipped down from Racine wasn't used in light of the old one being severely stretched. Underlying the triumph of the races themselves came in the September 12, 1896 edition of *Forest and Stream* magazine. In the preface to its comments, it said that the "race awakened a wonderful interest on the lakes and throughout the West and it is likely to be of permanent benefit to yachting interests on fresh water."

The article disagreed with critics of the race stating the following:

> We have no sympathy whatever with the various attempts to mitigate the disappointment of *Vencedor's* defeat by blaming her owners, her designer or her builders. Messrs. Berriman have shown themselves to be spirited sportsmen and good losers, they made a fair offer in the first place, they accepted terms disadvantageous to themselves in order to get a match, and they have accepted the result in the best possible spirit, making no complaints and immediately issuing a new challenge.
>
> As to the builders, they have shown both spirit and enterprise in their original offer to build the yacht, in the securing of the best possible skill in designing and building and in the creation of a plant for the work, They have met with many difficulties incident to the inauguration of a new enterprise, and the chances of the yacht have been hurt by delays, but they have done everything in their power to make her a winner.
>
> How well the designer has done his work, it is impossible to say under the peculiar conditions of the case, the yacht has never had the sail plan which her dimensions demand, and lacking this no one can judge of the merits of the design.

The article concluded by stating that the one great mistake was the attempt at introducing such an extremely large racing machine on the Great Lakes.[9]

After the international races in Toledo, Captain Barbour and his crew sailed *Vencedor* up to Racine for minor repairs. In the vicinity of Saginaw Bay, the big mahogany yacht ran into gale-force winds and water came over the boat from aft to stern. Captain Barbour was pleased with how the sloop handled the storm even though the forward hatch and some items were washed overboard.

As for the victorious *Canada*, the *Toronto Star* announced, on September 2, 1896, that it wouldn't race any more that season and that her owners were putting it up for sale. Why? Two main reasons: (1) there was a new challenge for an international race from the Lake Erie Yachting Association and it was felt that a new yacht should be commissioned; and (2) the syndicate could not agree as to which of its members should purchase it. So it was decided to sell it at auction.

On the afternoon of September 15, 1896, a large group of yachtsmen and citizens crowded the main auction room of Townsend's Auction House in Toronto. Among those present was Æmilius Jarvis, who had skippered the *Canada* to its victory. At the outset, the auctioneer read from a prepared text:

> I offer for sale the yacht *Canada*, the purpose being to carry out the original intention of the men who formed the syndicate, which was to settle the question of ownership after the race, one of them expecting to buy it. That idea as to its disposal has been changed in consequence of the receipt of a challenge from the Lake Erie Yachting Association. The syndicate has decided to build another yacht to meet that challenge, and *Canada* will be sold for cash. If the buyer should be a Toronto man liberal terms will be offered, as the members of the syndicate want the boat to stay here.

Less than one month after its triumphant win in the International Races in Toledo, the sloop *Canada* was coming under the auctioneer's gavel.

The opening bid came from a G. A. Hamilton, an employee of the Sanford Manufacturing Company who was thought to be representing Senator Sanford, the president of the company. He bid $1,000. A stranger then bid $2,000. Will Hyslop, the owner of a large bicycle company, raised the bids to $2,500. Hamilton and Hyslop went back and forth until finally the hammer came down on $3,250 bid by Hamilton. It was estimated that *Canada* had cost over $6,500 to build less than a year before.

Neither Æmilius Jarvis nor any member of the syndicate bid on *Canada*. The group of prominent bankers and businessmen led by Jarvis, who had formed the syndicate to have the yacht designed in Scotland, built in

Canada, and win one of the greatest races in history, were unable to agree on which of its members should acquire the yacht. Senator Sanford of Hamilton became the new owner.

In December of 1897, it was speculated that *Canada* was being considered by two New York yachtsmen to be brought East to race against D. B. Burnham's *Norota*. However, this never happened. *Canada* stayed in the Midwest and never achieved a greater win than in the Canada's Cup. *Vencedor*, on the other hand, was about to achieve its greatest fame.

CHAPTER 16

That the trophy shall be known as Canada's Cup.

> —Deed of Gift
> Owners of *Canada*

UNLIKE *CANADA* AND SOME OF HERRESHOFF AMERICA'S CUP ENTRIES, *VENCE-dor* was not designed for one race. Less than a month after Toledo, the Berriman brothers, owners of *Vencedor*, issued a challenge on September 14, 1896, to Robert Hayes, managing owner of *Siren* for a best of two out of three match races. There was little opportunity for *Vencedor* and *Siren* to challenge each other prior to the races in Toledo. So there was much public interest in this match race.

Sloop *Siren* sailing off Chicago. In September of 1896 *Vencedor* would beat it to become the fastest yacht on the Great Lakes—Permission of Chicago History Museum

The competition was initially planned to be for the Lincoln Park Yacht Club championship, but since *Siren* had recently changed ownership, the Lincoln Park pennant was not possible.

The challenge was accepted with *Siren*'s owners figuring the recently defeated *Vencedor* would be an easy target. Joseph Ruff, the timekeeper from the international races, was again to be the official timer. Both yachts would have scrutineers.

On September 19, 1896, the first of the match races took place with *Vencedor* back before a crowd of 500 located both on land and on schooners in Chicago. This time the yacht's designer T. Sch. Poekel was part of the eleven-member crew.

Out for fifteen minutes that day the waters of Lake Michigan proved too rough for *Siren* and it ran for shelter. *Vencedor* also quit and the race was declared off.

The races resumed on Monday, September 20, and conditions weren't much better. There were near half gale conditions—meaning winds of between twenty-five and thirty miles per hour. Both crews got totally drenched and during the race *Siren*'s weather rigging was carried away and *Vencedor* finished the race alone.[1] The Berrimans decided to take the win as the accident occurred after the race had begun. They had learned from the races in Toledo that everything was fair in love, war, and yacht racing. Considering the stormy weather conditions, *Vencedor* finished the race alone in remarkable time.

The next race on September 21 was called off after the yachts raced for four-and-quarter hours and were becalmed.

The next attempt saw *Vencedor* soundly defeat *Siren* by about six miles. *Vencedor*'s time of 2:29:35 to *Siren*'s time of 3:07:55 left a margin of 38:25 without her time allowance of ten seconds.

Vencedor's victory over *Siren* convinced yachtsmen that *Vencedor* was the fastest yacht on the Great Lakes.

In October of 1896, the Committee of the Royal Canadian Yacht Club responsible for arranging international competitions responded to Commodore Berriman's challenge for a rematch.[2] In refusing the challenge the committee said *Vencedor* was just too big and that to compete it would have to build a big yacht which would only be used for one race.

But Berriman and the Canadians were eager for a race and Berriman made a decision to build a new challenger. Berriman said he would again turn to Racine and designer T. Sch. Poekel for a new challenger. According to the press, the smaller *Vencedor* would be forty-two feet corrected length, with a load waterline of thirty-seven feet.[3] The article pointed out that the original *Vencedor* was about forty-five feet corrected length with a load waterline of forty-three feet.

While working at the Racine yard in October of 1896, T. Sch. Poekel was seriously injured when he stepped on a nail in the yard. A doctor treated his foot but Poekel refused any anesthesia with a life-long belief that anesthetics prevent the human body from triggering its own marvelous healing system.

In the fall of 1896, the RBMCO continued designing and building boats. On October 7, it announced that it had been commissioned by the famous Civil War general Joseph T. Torrence of Chicago to build for him a forty-five-foot speed steam yacht. After the War, the military hero Torrence went into the iron and steel business in Illinois. He was responsible for City of Chicago's elevated rail system.

Poekel, who had honed his skills at designing and building steam boilers at the Herreshoff yard, would head up the building of steam boilers at Racine. The triple-expansion engines that Poekel designed at Racine were similar to the Herreshoff engines, which were recognized as excellent. Yachts using steam boilers were becoming very popular among those wealthy Chicagoans summering in Lake Geneva. One of the steamers under Poekel's charge was the *Loreto*, which was built for John M. Smyth, and named after his youngest daughter. Smyth was born in 1843 on the high seas during his parents' crossing from Ireland, and he became the founder of the John M. Smyth Furniture Company. It was as famous a retail establishment in Chicago as Marshall Field. Smyth, P. K. Wrigley, and others would turn Lake Geneva into a Chicago millionaire's paradise. And his family would use *Loreto* when they arrived by train from Chicago. *Loreto* had an extremely powerful two-cylinder compound engine. The yacht was so fast that Smyth's sons would often race it against steamers in the lake for which their father would scold them. *Loreto* stayed in the Smyth family until 1917 when it was sold by the Smyth Estate Tyrawley to E. W. Partridge. In 1918, it was sold again to investors looking for an excursion boat on the lake—the venture fizzled and in 1924, then known as *Virginia*, the boat was scrapped.

Another triple-expansion steam engine that T. Sch. Poekel designed was for *Louise*, built in 1900 as a private yacht for John Mitchell, one of the founders of the Continental Illinois National Bank. *Louise* was restored by the Gage Marine storage yard about one mile from Williams Bay and relaunched in 1978. Today it's the only large steamboat operating in the Midwest.

In November of 1897, there appeared a report in the *Detroit Free Press* that *Vencedor* because of its size was being put up for sale.[4]

The Racine Motor Boat Company continued building steam yachts and produced a quantity of them from 1896 to 1903. Most were delivered by rail to Williams Bay on Lake Geneva for wealthy Chicagoans who had summer homes on the lake and preferred traveling to them by water instead of the rough roads that circled the lake.

The Lake Yacht Racing Association met on December 20, 1896, to consider two rule changes that had been adopted by the Interlake Yacht Racing Association of Lake Erie recently in Buffalo, New York. Delegates came from Oswego, Toronto, Royal Canadian Yacht Club, Queen City Yacht Club of Toronto, the Royal Hamilton Yacht Club, and the Rochester Yacht Club. Æmilius Jarvis, as president, called the meeting to order.

Attending in an advisory capacity were E. C. Berriman of Chicago, owner of *Vencedor*, and T. Sch. Poekel, of Racine, Wisconsin, *Vencedor*'s designer.

The delegates who met until 3:00 in the morning refused the rule changes which would require yachts built in the future to have a 35 percent immersion, and a low waterline measured with the crews on board. This outcome allowed the Canadians to have their own rules.

The *New York Sun*, in wrapping up Sports of the Year for 1896, had this to say about the international race on the Great Lakes: "In the race the conditions were so manifestly unfair to the Yankee yacht that it was absolutely impossible for her to win, and no one on this side of the border takes the result seriously."[5]

As *Vencedor* ended its fall racing season, its victory over *Siren* did not go unnoticed by yachtsmen on the East Coast.

On January 17, 1897, it was announced by Æmilius Jarvis, speaking on behalf of himself, F. J. Phillips, S. F. McKinnon, George Gooderham, James Ross George H. Gooderham, and J. H. Plummer, owners of the *Canada*, that they were donating the silver Tiffany Cup they had won in Toledo to the Royal Canadian Yacht Club of Toronto to be held in trust as a perpetual international challenge cup for the winner of a yacht race between Canada and the United States. Thus was born the Canada's Cup.

PART THREE

CHAPTER 17

Harry never had so much fun at an opera before.
—Aimee Crocker Gillig
Wife of *Vencedor*'s Second Owner

THE *NEW YORK TIMES* REPORTED, ON MARCH 31, 1897, THAT A PROMINENT New York syndicate was eager to purchase *Vencedor* to bring it East to race against Howard Gould's *Niagara*.[1]

The *Chicago Chronicle*, on March 31, 1897, had this to say: "The quality of the *Vencedor* is known all over the Lakes, and her reputation for fast work in a heavy sea has traveled up and down the seacoast."[2] The *Chronicle* went on to say that Poekel had designed *Vencedor* similar to *Niagara* although with some improvements.

Vencedor as photographed by Alvord & Sprague

Niagara had a stellar record in European waters—winning forty-eight out of fifty-two races it entered. It was thought that *Niagara* would soon be traveling to America.

Both the *Times* and the *Chronicle* quoted designer Poekel that, although he thought it had an excellent chance of beating *Niagara*, he would give no guarantee. Commodore Berriman, the owner of *Vencedor*, however, would. He offered a $1,000 refund on the sale of *Vencedor* if it failed to beat *Niagara* in two out of three races.

There were other yachtsmen on the Great Lakes who were also eager to purchase *Vencedor* and keep it in freshwater. Many felt this would be the best solution, as it could serve as a test boat against a future Canada's Cup challenger.

In April of 1897, the *Racine Daily Vanguard* confirmed that the Berriman brothers were entertaining at least two offers to sell *Vencedor*.[3] Commodore Berriman said that he was sure *Vencedor* could beat *Niagara* and such a victory would soften the blow for him of seeing *Vencie* leave Chicago waters. The paper predicted that a new boat would be constructed in Racine for the next challenge in Canada's Cup.

As rumors circulated about the sale of *Vencedor*, the *Detroit Free Press* quoted this from Commodore Berriman: "The Vencedor has not yet been sold, but I expect to close the deal very shortly. She will probably go to the Larchmont Club, and should defeat easily all the boats in her class."[4]

On May 19, 1897, Commodore Berriman received a cablegram from Paris from Harry Mansfield Gillig, commodore of the Larchmont Yacht Club. He offered to purchase *Vencedor*. Gillig was a renowned yachtsman, respected amateur opera singer, and a prestidigitator. He was an early member of the Bohemia Club in San Francisco and currently married to heiress Aimee Crocker. Berriman accepted the offer. While *Vencedor* would be heading east to saltwater, Captain Irving Barbour would be staying on the lakes. For the 1897 season, he would be the captain of *Vanenna*.

Gillig was reelected commodore of the Larchmont Yacht Club on February 24, 1896. The election took place at the club's annual meeting at Delmonico's Restaurant in New York City. Larchmont, one of the most prestigious yacht clubs in the country, reported a total of 550 members with a fleet of 291 yachts for the year.[5] Sir Thomas Lipton, the greatest English yachtsman of the era, was an honorary member of three American yacht clubs: New York, Chicago, and Larchmont.

Opening day for the Larchmont Yacht Club in 1897, took place on May 29. Upon the firing of a cannon, the blue and white burgee of the club was hoisted on the club's giant mast where it would stay for the club's entire yachting season that would see *Vencedor* make its East Coast appearance. Opening day also gave members a chance to view the club's newest acquisition—one which the *New York Times* called "a fine painting"—a portrait of last year's Commodore Harry M. Gillig.[6]

This portrait of Harry Mansfield Gillig was done by the Dutch artist Hubert Vos (1855–1935).

Portrait of Commodore Harry Mansfield Gillig—Courtesy of Larchmont Yacht Club

Gillig, as a personal friend of Vos, was fortunate to get him as his portrait artist. Besides being good friends and both members of New York City's theatrical Lambs Club, Gillig often had Vos as his guest at the Larchmont Yacht Club.

Voss was born Josephus Hubertus Vos in Maastricht, the Netherlands. He had studied at the Academie Royale des Beaux-Arts in Brussels and with Fernand Cormon in Paris.

Vos's paintings are displayed at the Louvre, the Bonnettanden, the Chicago History Museum, the Fogg Art Museum, the Metropolitan Museum of Art, as well as other museums throughout the world.

Besides being the commodore of the Larchmont Yacht Club, Gillig was most famous for his marriage to Aimee Crocker in 1889.

Aimee was an eccentric heiress. She had inherited between $10 and $14 million from her father's estate. Her father had made his money developing the transcontinental railroad. Her cousin George Crocker would help fund Peary's Arctic expedition in search of the North Pole by giving him $50,000 in 1905. Peary stated that in his expeditions he had discovered a beautiful new land and named it "Crocker Land" in honor of his benefactor. He also funded Admiral Donald MacMillan's Arctic expedition to locate Crocker Land. Crocker Land was later found not to exist and some said it was a mirage that Peary saw. Others were not so charitable. Crocker money also built San Francisco's Crocker National Bank, at one time the fourth-largest bank in the United States.

Aimee, who could not be tamed by being sent to boarding school in Europe, fell in love simultaneously with both Richard Porter Ashe and Harry Mansfield Gillig. After rejecting the idea of a duel, the two young suitors decided on a game of stud poker—Ashe won out by getting four aces to Gillig's two deuces. Ashe was quite a win, himself being from the family Asheville, North Carolina, was named after and being the nephew of Admiral Farragut. But the marriage was short-lived. Aimee divorced Ashe and moved to Hawaii, lived in a grass hut, and performed hula dances so provocatively that several missionaries fled the island. King David Kalakaua became so enamored with her that he gifted Aimee an island located near Molokai, with about 300 subjects and anointed her "Princess Palaikalani—Bliss of Heaven."

Aimee returned to the states where she married Harry M. Gillig in 1889, and moved to New York City. They soon purchased a fourteen-acre estate in Larchmont near the waters where Gillig sailed. Aimee's mother lived in an adjacent villa.

The Gilligs set out to conquer the New York social world after purchasing a Manhattan townhouse. They entertained lavishly in both of their homes. *Vencedor* became Harry's fourth yacht while Aimee showed French bulldogs and became a Bohemian entertaining oriental gentlemen of all types. She could often be seen walking her dogs along Fifth Avenue. They would wear individual coats and blankets and were seldom seen in the same attire.

Aimee captured all the memories of her Polynesian and Oriental escapades in her book shamelessly titled *And I'd Do It Again*. She does allow at least one brief amusing story of a trip to Malta with Commodore Gillig. She prefaces the story stating that Harry had a great sense of humor and was an opera buff. In Malta, she relates there was a small opera house that actually had beds in its loge section. The overture had hardly begun when she, Harry, and someone unidentified went in the bed and Harry undressed. She stated that Harry had never had so much fun at an opera before.

But now after the purchase of *Vencedor*, it was widely rumored that Aimee was having multiple affairs. She and Harry grew very distant with Harry having long absences from their Larchmont villa.

Berriman accepted Gillig's terms and the great mahogany yacht would be going East. It was speculated that Gillig would try to race against some of the world's best racing yachts including *Niagara* and *Wasp*. Poekel received a huge compliment when the *Chicago Tribune* commented that "the spectacle of a big Eastern yachtsman coming out to Chicago to secure a boat to be pitted against the best yachts in the world is regarded as a tribute to Western builders."[7]

A possible race between Harry M. Gillig's *Vencedor* and Howard Gould's *Niagara* was the talk of the yachting world. *Niagara* had garnered worldwide attention by its racing against the Prince of Wales's *Britannia* and by being the most winning American yacht in English waters in history.

With the sale of *Vencedor*, Commodore Berriman was not leaving yachting—in fact, he was planning on a new yacht constructed for the Canada's Cup and for that also he would turn to Poekel at the Racine boatyard.

All the railway companies that touched New York were anxious to transfer *Vencedor* East. However, the Chicago and Northwestern and the Michigan Central won out. On June 9, 1897, at 12 noon *Vencedor* began its trip East from Chicago, having been brought down from its winter headquarters in Racine. It took two railroad cars—one sixty and the other forty feet long to carry the yacht. It was not known exactly how the train cars carrying *Vencedor* would handle the tunnels *en route*. It was surmised that the yacht might have to be taken off the cars and then reloaded after the tunnels. The *Racine Journal Times* predicted that if *Vencedor* made the trip without a mishap, "it will be one of the most successful feats of boat transportation of the century."[8]

Commodore Berriman also reiterated that he was in negotiations with the RBMCO to build a successor to *Vencedor*—this time out of aluminum for the purpose of again challenging the Canadians.[9] In spite of his promises, Berriman was never able to challenge the Canadians again on the water.

On June 18, 1897, *Vencedor* arrived in Morris Heights, New York. It had successfully made the trip by rail although its hull had cleared under some of the bridges by only two inches. *Vencie* had made the trip from

Chicago on the two railroad flat cars in seventy-two hours with Commodore Berriman riding along to insure its safe passage.

At Morris Heights, it was berthed at the Gas Engine & Power Company and Charles Seabury Company, a shipbuilding concern located on Matheson Road.

The Larchmont Yacht Club's Eighteenth Annual Regatta took place on July 5, 1897. And what a spectacle it was. Over 500 vessels appeared within a five-mile radius. *Vencedor* was one of the star attractions, making its first appearance (non-racing) on the East Coast with its owner Harry M. Gillig at the helm. Other yachts present included *Colonia* with "Wee Charlie" Barr as skipper, *Veda* skippered by Cornelius Vanderbilt Jr., the 1893 America's Cup winner *Vigilant*, *Amorita*, and *Navahoe*. The highlight of the Regatta was a match race between *Navahoe* and *Vigilant*. Owners Royal Phelps Carroll and Percy Chubb agreed to race their yachts without any time allowances. Chubb's *Vigilant* won. Chubb, who was the son in Chubb & Son, was a leader in maritime insurance and his company would grow into one of the world's leading insurance providers.

Vencedor made its East Coast racing debut on July 17, 1897, at a regatta of the Larchmont Yacht Club. The day was filled with ominous warnings as dark gray clouds, rain, and gale-force winds arrived from the southeast. Despite these conditions, eager spectators awaited the matchup between *Syce* and *Vencedor*.

Syce owned by Frederick M. Hoyt had been launched on May 4, 1897, at Wood's Yard in City Island. It was built from designs of Gardner & Cox and sported 3,200 square feet of sails made by Ratsey & Lapthorn. *Syce* had a shallow hull, a deep and short fin keel, and a bulb containing fourteen tons of lead. It had a length of sixty-nine feet with forty-five feet on the waterline.

Vencedor, racing in the waters off the Larchmont Yacht Club and sporting a new pole mast, had Hazen Morse as skipper and Gillig manning the sails. At race time the winds had died down considerably. The transplanted midwesterner lost by only four minutes eight seconds to *Syce*. According to the *New York Times*, "Although the *Syce* won, the *Vencedor* did well." The *Times* article headlined that there was little wind at

Larchmont and *Vencedor* was handicapped by new rigging.[10] Its new sails had only been put on two hours before the race.

Minutes before the start of the race in its division at Larchmont on July 21, 1897, the *Vencedor's* peak halyards carried away and her huge sail fell thunderously to the deck. Forced to sail with just its jib, *Vencedor* limped back to Larchmont Harbor and later left for City Island for repairs. *Syce* withdrew at once from the race as its owner did not want a walkover prize.

In August, *Vencedor* raced against a Fife-designed yacht with a world-class skipper. On August 25, 1897, in a special regatta of the Corinthian fleet of New Rochelle it raced against *Jessica* owned by J. M. MacDonough. The skipper of the *Jessica* was Lemuel Miller who had sailed *Vigilant* across the Atlantic and had been the right-hand man to Charlie Barr. In command of *Vencedor* was John F. Lovejoy of the Larchmont Yacht Cub Racing Committee. In rough weather *Vencedor* beat *Jessica* decisively on the twenty-six-mile triangular course winning by twenty-seven minutes forty-five seconds.

Back in the Midwest, *El Capitan*, another crack yacht designed by T. Sch. Poekel was racing. Poekel designed and built it at the Racine Motor Boat Manufacturing Company. It was built originally for F. D. Montgomery for yacht racing on Lake Delavan in Wisconsin.

Lake Delavan was a summer retreat for Chicagoans who wanted a lake cottage. Chicagoans would take the Milwaukee Road and North Western trains from Chicago to Walmoth and Williams Bay where horse-drawn buses would take them to their cottages or to one of the five resort hotels located on the lake. Although not as prestigious as Lake Geneva, where the Wrigleys summered, it had some very nice "cottages"—five of which were designed between 1900 and 1905 by the famous architect Frank Lloyd Wright. Wright also designed the first clubhouse for the Delavan Yacht Club.

On July 19,1897, *El Capitan* beat *Circe, Euliana, Mary Gladys*, and *Estelle* to win the first regatta of the Delavan Lake Yacht Club. *El Capitan* pulled ahead in the final leg in what the *Chicago Tribune* called "the prettiest and swiftest race on Lake Delavan."[11] And again on Lake Delavan on August 14, 1897, *El Capitan* was a winner beating the yachts *Mary Gladys* and *Circe*.

Lake Delavan, WI where *El Capitan*, designed by T. Sch. Poekel, often raced in the 1890s

On August 30, 1897, it was announced that *El Capitan* would test its great speed in a match race with *Mabelle* owned by the Bald Eagle Club and designed by A. C. Bower of Waukegan for a $100 cup. The two yachts would race against each other for supremacy over the Delavan lake course.

September 5, 1897 saw the opening of the Larchmont Yacht Club's fall season with a regatta featuring another race between Gillig's *Vencedor* and Hoyt's *Syce*, skippered by the famous Charlie Barr. The race saw the mammoth yachts becalmed for over two hours, but then as the wind picked up it was race to the finish with *Syce* winning by two minutes forty-one seconds.[12]

Syce's owner was Frederick Maxfield Hoyt who had inherited a fortune from his father. He was a senior partner in the importing company of Houghton, Lee & Hoyt with offices in New York City. A noted yachtsman, he also designed and owned such notable yachts as *Norota* and *Isolda*. In September of 1897, Commodore C. A. Postley of the Larchmont Yacht Club offered prizes for a series of races in a club regatta. *Vencedor* and *Syce* were both entered in the fifty-one-foot class. In order to make the races more interesting, the owners subscribed to a sweepstake and it was reported that there was heavy betting.

The first of the best of three races took place on September 21, 1897. John F. Lovejoy took the tiller of *Vencedor* with owner Gillig manning the sails. Owner Hoyt took the tiller of *Syce* with Captain Terry of the Grayling and Irving Zerega assisting. *Vencedor* lost to *Syce* by eleven minutes twenty-six seconds.

The second race between *Syce* and *Vencedor* took place at Larchmont on September 25, 1897. The race started at 12:10 pm. At the first mark *Syce* led by 5:22 and then by the second mark by thirteen minutes. With hardly any wind the yachts drifted over the course and by the end of the first round *Vencedor* was trailing by forty minutes. *Vencedor* ended up withdrawing from the race with *Syce* finishing alone.

Vencedor's losing was so bad that a reporter for the *New York Times* wrote that Gillig might very well set a bonfire to get rid of his yacht.[13]

Meanwhile, in the Midwest, the *Inter-Ocean Daily News* reported that a speed race would occur between *El Capitan* and *Mabelle* of the Baldeagle Club of Fox Lake. It was to be a race of yachting supremacy over Delavan Lake with a $100 cup trophy. *Mabelle* was designed by A. C. Bower of Waukegan. The *El Capitan*'s owner was F. D. Montgomery.

The showdown proved disastrous for *El Capitan* as reported by the *Milwaukee Journal* on September 20, 1897. It suffered an accident in the first race, capsized in the second, and was thoroughly beaten in the third. To its credit, it finished one minute faster than the Fox Lake record. *Mabelle* broke the record for all Wisconsin lakes by traversing nearly eight miles in one hour four minutes.

On March 4, 1898, with the threat of war with Spain looming, Fred W. Morgan offered *Pathfinder*, then valued at $100,00.00, to the U.S. Government. Issuing his offer, Morgan stated, "She is only fit for carrying dispatches and it is for this kind of work that I offered her to the Navy Department. She draws eight feet of water and is built entirely of the finest tempered steel." The *New York Times* was quick to endorse the offer stating that the *Pathfinder* was "one of the largest and finest yachts on the lakes as well as one of the fastest," adding that "[s]he could easily carry three or four rapid-fire guns."[14]

The year 1889 saw the Gilligs continue to step out in New York society. They often attended opening nights on Broadway as well as social charity events. On February 2, 1898, Aimee Gillig participated in the first bench show of the French Bulldog Club of America held at the Waldorf Astoria where Dimnboolaa, one of her French bulldogs, won several prizes.

The Larchmont Yacht Club had their annual clambake to celebrate the end of its yachting season on October 1, 1897. During the festivities ex-Commodore Gillig presented the club with a Japanese gong. Gillig

MR. POECKEL RESIGNS.

Severs His Connections With the Racine Boat Works.

T. S. Poeckel, who for nearly three years past has held the position as naval architect and general superintendent at the Racine Boat Mfg. Co., has resigned as such and today started for the east there to make his future home, possibly in Boston, where better opportunities await his genius. Mr. Poeckel's departude will, however, not make him lose interest in Racine, as he still retains his stock in the boat works, which he was instrumental in building up to its present dimensions. His two best known productions, and which have established his reputation as an expert boat builder, are the steel yacht "Pathfinder" and the fin-keel sloop "Vencedor."

T. Sch. Poekel's Midwest career came to an end in 1899, but he would return to the East for further triumphs.

and the other 150 members consumed 25 bushels of clams, 5 bushels of oysters, 500 hard shell crabs, 200 lobsters, 60 pounds of sausages, 200 chickens, 75 pounds of bluefish, and 500 ears of corn.

As yachtsmen discussed the next competition for Canada's Cup, the *New York Daily Tribune* on December 12, 1897, reported that there was still talk among yachtsmen that E. C. Berriman was going to give Poekel another chance to design an entry.[15]

During the month of July 1898, newspapers in the Midwest reported that T. Sch. Poekel had resigned as superintendent at the Racine Motor Boat Company and had taken a job with a Boston firm. He then returned to the East Coast where he became the chief engineer for the nation's pre-eminent shipbuilding company George Lawley & Son in Boston.

T. Sch. Poekel also designed the machinery for Thomas Lawson's magnificent sail-steamer *Dreamer*. Lawson, known as the "copper king," having cornered the copper market on Wall Street, was an eccentric millionaire who loved yachting and dairy farming. *Dreamer* was launched on September 25, 1899. It was designed by Tams & Lemoine of New York who also designed J. P. Morgan's steam yacht *Corsair*. It was built by Lewis Nixon who had designed the battleship *Oregon* at his boatyard in Elizabethport, New Jersey.

Dreamer by Thomas Willis T.Sch. Poekel was responsible for all its machinery—Author's collection

What Poekel installed for propulsion was a single screw with a triple-expansion engine with Almy boilers.

Dreamer was one of the most opulent yachts ever built. It had a crew of twenty-four and the interior was magnificent. The ladies' boudoir was decorated in the Louis XV style. Described as a floating palace, the yacht cost the "copper king" $200,000, the equivalent of about $5,500,000 today.

The artist Thomas H. Willis (1850–1925) made two magnificent paintings combining oil and silk of *Dreamer* and at Mr. Lawson's request presented one to Mr. Lawson and one to Mr. Poekel.

Lawson attempted to have his own entry in the America's Cup race with his boat *Independence*. He was refused as he was not a member of the New York Yacht Club. In his book he vehemently criticized this stating, "My refusal as owner of the American-built and American-manned yacht *Independence*, to recognize the right of the custodians of the America's Cup to compel me, or any American, to join any club in order to compete for the honor of defending an American national trophy, led to this extraordinary ruling, which dazed the yachting world and at once brought into asking the question: "Has one of the great sports of America, yachting been syndicated."[16]

In August of 1898, Irish-born tea baron Thomas Lipton decided to commence a life-long attempt to win back the America's Cup and issued a challenge from the Royal Ulster Yacht Club to the New York Yacht Club, which was accepted. Springing into action were the two Morgans—John Pierpont and Edwin D. They immediately contacted N. G. Herreshoff to design and construct a contender. Captain Nat at that point did not have T. Sch. Poekel in his employ and needed another talented naval architect to come to his assistance. He found such a person in Alpheus Appleton Packard.

It had been about two years since Poekel had left the Herreshoffs and with a future Cup defender on the horizon a recent graduate of MIT would be just the ticket.

Alpheus Appleton Packard graduated from MIT in 1898, majoring in naval architecture and mechanical engineering. As a boy of fourteen,

Packard had built an English cutter all by himself. He was just the sort of man that the Herreshoffs needed.

In Edward Burgess's original field of entomology, he became acquainted with Professor Alpheus Spring Packard of Brown University. Professor Packard had studied at Bowdoin and Harvard. He was re-nowned in his field.

A. A. Packard wanted to go to Germany to obtain his doctorate, but, according to his son, he received an offer from the HMCO "that he couldn't refuse."[17]

At the HMCO, Packard was primarily involved with the design and construction of *Columbia*, which was being built to compete with Lipton's *Shamrock* for America's Cup. Packard focused on developing and perfecting a novel topmast that could be raised and lowered within Columbia's mainmast. According to Bror Tamm, the renown foreman of the Lawley yard, Packard was "brilliant," "outstanding," and "a wonderful engineer."

Columbia went on to defeat *Shamrock* and *Shamrock II*, winning America's Cup in both 1899 and 1901. Packard would "never forget Capt. Nat's praise for his supervision of the entire construction job on *Columbia* and his part in her two successful defenses."[18] But apparently Herreshoff's son ignored the praise, and there was no mention of Packard's role in Francis's biography of his father.

According to Packard's son, his father would leave the Herreshoff Manufacturing shortly after the victories of *Columbia*, since he had "too often been caught in the crossfire of conflicting orders of Capt. Nat and J.B. Herreshoff." Packard would leave the Herreshoffs and become a partner with Starling Burgess forming the firm of Burgess and Packard. No doubt, the two had teamed up partly due to their academic fathers.

Back in the Midwest, the Poekel-designed *El Capitan* won a regatta on Lake Delavan beating three other yachts in a drenching rainstorm and light winds by fifteen minutes. *El Capitan* was now owned by Charles A. Stevens of Chicago who had one of the largest retail silk businesses in the country.

In 1899, John F. Duthie, protégé of T. Sch. Poekel and a fellow Herreshoff alumnus, was working at a shipbuilding concern in Portland, Oregon. Because of his work on plating *Defender* in 1895, he was involved with the use of metals. In January 1899, he had an idea which he felt was revolutionary in nature for sailboats. He wrote a letter directly to C. Oliver Iselin, who had been the principal owner of *Defender*. He proposed to sell his invention to Iselin. His only stipulation was that Iselin could choose any manufacturer to make it except for the HMCO. In his letter he reminded Iselin that "Mr. N.G. Herreshoff stated to you they could not make a steel boom and gaft."[19] Duthie reminded Iselin that he actually did what Herreshoff said couldn't be done. There is no indication that Iselin followed up on Duthie's offer. Remarkably *Columbia*, Herreshoff's 1899 and 1901 entry and winning yacht for America's Cup, had a steel boom.

In June of 1900, it was reported that *Vencedor* may be coming back to the lakes. An article in the *Rochester Democrat and Chronicle* reported, on June 17, 1900, that arrangements were well under way to bring *Vencedor* back for a match race on July 4 with *Siren*, owned by George R. Peare. The article stated that the Berriman brothers were instrumental in getting the sloop back to Chicago and, if it happened, it "will give an impetus to the sport that few things could."[20]

While Gillig hadn't yet given up on *Vencedor*, he did give up on his marriage to Aimee Crocker. A referee in a divorce case granted a divorce to Aimee on December 14, 1900. It was reported that at the time Gillig was in Paris and had not been in either the couple's Larchmont villa or New York City townhouse at all during the previous summer.[21]

Mrs. Gillig apparently was not lonely, surrounding herself with Japanese and Chinese servants, Irish coachmen, footmen, and a French maid.

According to Captain A. J. Kenealy, a writer for the Trend and Drift of *Yachting Outing Magazine*, Volume 31 for December, Gillig was undeterred with the lackluster performances of *Vencedor*, writing in December that "Gillig does not despair of extracting from the *Vencedor* the latent speed which he confidently believes lurks somewhere in the sleek hull of this good-looking lake craft, whose salt-water experiences have not been at all inspiriting."

Gillig spent thousands of dollars on alterations on it but it sailed only that season and the yacht ended up for three years in dry dock in the Hawkins Boatyard in City Island, New York. At one time while at Hawkins, *Vencedor* was moored next to *Defender* and *Columbia,* both Herreshoff America's Cup winners.

The United States succeeded in winning Canada's Cup in 1899, when the Chicago Yacht Club's *Genesee* beat *Beaver* of the *R.C.Y.C.* and skippered by Aemilius Jarvis.

Back East, T. Sch. Poekel became the chief engineer at Lawley's boatyard in South Boston, and later in Neponset. There he designed engines and boilers and was in charge of steel construction. Bror Tamm, another Dane, was one of the Lawley's chief foremen and, according to late Louis Howland, when discussing yacht designers would always speak of Poekel in reverential tones.

The Lawley yard had built two winners of America's Cup, both designed by Edward Burgess, *Puritan,* which was launched on May 5, 1885, and *Mayflower,* which was launched in 1886.

On December 23, 1900, the *Boston Globe* reported that "Mr. Poekel is a very clever engineering draftsman and has full charge of the construction of the torpedo boats *Blakley* and *DeLong.*"[22]

USS *Blakley*—Author's collection

The USS *Blakley* (Torpedo Boat No. 27/TBp-27) was launched at Lawley's on November 22, 1900. After completing dock trials at the Boston Navy Yard, the ship was moved to Newport, Rhode Island, where it was fitted with ordnance and electrical equipment. At Newport, the boat would be tested and inspected.

On September 30, 1901, off of Newport, Poekel was representing Lawley in test runs of USS *Blakley*, accompanied by representatives from the naval board of inspection and survey. The boat was brought up to 25.8 knots per hour, just shy of its desired goal of twenty-six. But just then the blower engine broke down and T. Sch. Poekel was forced to withdraw it from further trials. This caused a week's delay, but everyone was pleased with the performance overall.

In the morning of June 19, 1902, USS *Blakley* was taken out into Newport Bay, Rhode Island, for a test for the standardization of its wheels. The ship was doing well on the measured one-mile course cruising at about twenty-three knots per hour with steam pressure of 200 pounds.

In the engine room were three nautical engineers of the Lawley firm sent to observe the machinery: Alex Mason, Henry Pryor, and T. Sch. Poekel—all skilled machinists and engineers.

Suddenly, there was a hissing sound and then a jet of steam appeared from under the cylinder. In a flash, the engine room filled with hot vapors, which increased in heat, and filled the room. Machinist Mason ran at once to the throttle and turned it off but suffered severe scalding to his bare arms as he came in contact with the hottest volume of steam. Pryor's bare arms were also badly burned. Poekel, who was wearing a heavy sweater, was saved from any injury and took charge—saving the boat from further damage. The story of the scalding incident made the front page of the *Boston Globe*.

USS *Blakley* was part of the Third Torpedo Flotilla, U.S. Atlantic Fleet prior to World War I, and then during the war years the ship was part of the Patrol Force based in New London, Connecticut, and patrolled the waters of the First and Second Naval Districts. The ship was scrapped in 1920.

USS *DeLong*—Author's collection

T. Sch. Poekel designed the engine for *Scud*, one of
the fastest boats afloat—Library of Congress

The USS *DeLong* was launched on November 23, 1900. Doing the
christening was Lt. Commander DeLong's daughter, Mrs. Mills of New
York City.

For its first two years in service, USS *DeLong* was assigned to the Reserve Torpedo Flotilla at Norfolk, Virginia, and later had torpedo training and practice along the Atlantic seaboard in the Gulf of Mexico. During World War I, the USS *DeLong* was refitted and served as a minesweeper. Later it was an escort for patrol duty in Halifax, Nova Scotia, where the ship escorted seaplanes for the Naval Aero Squadron. The ship remained in service until 1920.

William Randolph Hearst wasn't alone in wanting the fastest steamer in the world. There were many yacht owners who demanded high speeds. In 1901, one owner with similar desires was stockbroker Edmund Randolph of New York City. Randolph was an avid yachtsman and member of the New York Yacht Club. He had a steamer named *Scud* designed by the firm of Tams, Lemoine & Crane, the same firm that had designed *Dreamer* for Thomas Lawson. It was going to be built by Lawleys, and he wanted the fastest engine. Poekel was brought in to design the engine. This engine was faster than the engines Poekel had worked with while at the Herreshoff yard. The *Scud* was eighty-five-feet long, eighty-one feet in waterline, with eleven feet beam, six feet and ten inches deep and draught of four feet and six inches.

The contract for *Scud* was for $20,000 and had a forfeiture clause in the event that the yacht was not completed by June 1, 1901, providing for a price reduction except if the delay was not the fault of the builder. There was a delay and Randolph withheld $4,000. In October of 1901, Lawleys brought a suit for the money due.

Randolph sailed another steamer, *Apache*, in the transatlantic race for the Kaiser's Cup in 1905. Unfortunately, *Apache* came in last, trailing the winning *Atlantic* by six days.

In 1903, Randolph sold *Scud* to the forty-five-year-old lawyer Samuel Untermyer. He was a partner in the New York City law firm of Guggenheimer, Untermyer & Marshall and became famous for being the first lawyer to make a million dollar fee.

When international mining expert Lawrence P. Gray of Boston, in late 1900, wanted a unique yacht for his personal use on the Surinam River in the wilds of Dutch Guyana, he turned to T. Sch. Poekel as his designer and George Lawley & Son as his builder. Poekel designed a fifty-foot steamer with a twelve-foot beam, and an eight-foot draft. It had a unique design with a hull that was peculiarly constructed with a keelson running up near the stern. It had double bilges and a propeller underneath the boat. It had a very nice pilot house with sleeping accommodations and was named *Bostonia*.

The *New York-Tribune* on December 30, 1900, wrote the following about a new design by Poekel:

> T.S. Poekel, who has charge of the engine and machinery department of Lawley's, has designed a novel shape for a steam yacht, which contains part of the Duggan idea put into the double bilged *Dominion*. At the after part of the keel the keelson is raised, so that there is a hollow underneath it, and double bilges are thus obtained. In this space the propeller will be placed underneath the hull.[23]

Poekel, while at Lawleys, drew up plans for several reciprocating steam engines.

Bostonia was built in the remarkable short span of five weeks. The normal time for such a steamer would have been two-and-one-half months. In January of 1901, the *Boston Globe* reported that the flush plating was being applied and soon was going to be shipped to New York. There it would be loaded onboard the Royal Dutch India Lines's *Prins Frederick Hendrick* and shipped to Dutch Guiana on February 2.

Meanwhile in England it was reported that Sir Thomas Lipton was very confident of winning that "family plate," which he called America's Cup, in the fall with *Shamrock II* designed by George Lennox Watson. Watson had performed hundreds of tank experiments to determine the highest speed. When Capt. Nat was asked why he didn't do tank testing, he replied, "phooey—they're just worthwhile for steamers—not racing yachts."

On February 6, 1901, it was reported that *Vencedor* had been sold by Commodore Gillig to Fred A. Price of the Chicago and Columbia Yacht Clubs and would return to the Great Lakes for racing in the next season.[24] Price was a partner in the firm of Conklin, Price & Webb of Chicago and fairly new to yacht racing—having only gotten involved in it the year before.

The *New York Times* reported, on February 28, 1901, that the recently sold *Vencedor* was undergoing preparations to be shipped back to the Midwest. The *Times* reported that the fin keel had been taken off along with other paraphernalia and was being prepared for shipment to Chicago. The article said the boat and fixtures would be put on a derrick scow at City Island and shipped via rail from Jersey City to Chicago.[25]

In March of 1901, formal plans were made to bring the *Vencedor* back to the Great Lakes.

But how to ship *Vencedor* by rail? Due to the technical difficulties, William Cothrall, the official measurer of the Chicago Yacht Club, was sent to City Island to assist in bringing Price's new acquisition back to the Great Lakes. A March *Chicago Tribune* article described the proposed train trip:

> The limit of width of freight allowed to be carried by the railroads is six feet ten inches and '*Vencedor's*' greatest width is over 10 ft. By tilting the boat on edge the yacht was still found to exceed the permissible limit. By careful measuring, however, it was found that the boat could be carried through except in the event of meeting some of the large Pullman dining cars at some of the

Vencedor being loaded on railroad cars for its return to the Midwest—Courtesy of Chicago Yacht Club

narrower parts in the road. In this emergency special permission was sought and obtained of the railroads, the schedule being so arranged that the yachting freight would not encounter any of the broad cars at the narrow points.

Vencedor's career in salt water was mixed.

But *Vencie* was far from finished with racing as we shall see.

After returning to Chicago, *Vencedor* immediately outshone most of the racing yachts on the lakes. On June 8, 1901, the great mahogany yacht won the Michigan City Cup by beating *Josephine* in a race from Chicago to Michigan City by fifteen minutes. Finishing third was *Valiant* with *Siren* finishing fourth. *Siren's* owners A. W. Masters and George Webb were among the first to congratulate *Vencedor* on its win.

August 17, 1901, was double-regatta day in the City of Chicago. Both the Chicago Yacht Club and the Columbia Yacht Club had regattas on that day. The C.Y.C. Regatta pitted the three veteran stablemates *Vencedor*, *Vanenna*, and *Siren* against each other. As the race started, the wind was blowing at twenty miles per hour. The signal service gave the warning not to go out but the warning was ignored by the skippers of all three yachts.

The Poekel designed *Pathfinder* as the judges' boat for the Canada's Cup races in 1901—Library of Congress

The race was triangular for a twenty miles and the finish was the closest ever seen on the course. *Vencedor* was first at 4:07:45, *Vanenna* second at 4:08:47, and *Siren* third at 4:08:50. *Forest and Steam* reported that *Vencedor* was ably skippered by Hank Goble, a Western man, and it called the race "the hardest battle these two ancient rivals have ever fought out together" in what was called the closest race ever on a twenty-mile course.[26]

Although *Vencedor* would not get another crack at Canada's Cup in 1901, the other Poekel-designed boat *Pathfinder* served as the judges' boat during the race. That year saw the Canadians with Captain Jarvis again win the Cup with the R.C.Y.C.'s *Invader* beating *Cadillac* of the Detroit Yacht Club. This would be the second win for Skippadore Jarvis and his last.

On June 14, 1902, under the auspices of its new owner Fred A. Price, *Vencedor* won the tenth annual Michigan City race of the Columbia Yacht Club. It beat both *Siren* and George R. Peare's *LaRita*, and set the record for the thirty-two nautical mile race and won for Price the permanent possession of the trophy. Captain Abe Farrell ably handled *Vencedor*, which had been the underdog to *Siren*. This was the second win in a row for *Vencedor* in the annual Chicago to Michigan City race. The races that year were marred by a fatality in the person of George M. Finnery, a crew member of *Tartar*, who was struck by a gybing boom and knocked overboard. His death by a broken neck pointed out the inherent dangers of yacht racing.

In what was supposed to be another great showdown between *Vencedor* and *Siren* on July 5, 1902, in a race at Chicago for the Pfister Cup, *Vencedor* unfortunately lost her main mast at the start and fell out of the race.

Also, in 1902, Commodore Price offered $500 to any boat that could beat *Vencedor* in a match race run according to the rules of the Lake Michigan Yachting Association. William Ferguson Cameron, the president of a Chicago insurance company, accepted the challenge on behalf of his sloop *Vanenna*. *Vanenna* won the race and became, at least for a brief period, the champion racing yacht of Lake Michigan.

In a regatta sponsored by the Columbia Yacht Club on May 30, 1903, which was then celebrated as Decoration Day, *Vencedor* won in twenty-five miles per hour winds and heavy seas. Decoration Day was established by Major General John A. Logan, head of the Grand Army of the Republic, who wanted a day devoted to putting flowers on the graves of dead Union soldiers. In the twentieth century, the day was changed to Memorial Day as a day to honor those who died in all the wars.

Sailing in the Columbia Yacht Club Regatta on July 4, 1903, long-time rivals *Vencedor* and *Vanenna* were again matched against each other. The match race almost finished until an accident occurred. *Vencedor*'s throat halyard block gave way and its huge mainsail crashed down on the deck. At that point *Vencedor* was over one minute in the lead and probably would have won the race and received the Pabst Cup.

Capturing the William Hale Thompson Trophy on July 11, 1903, *Vencedor* soundly beat *Vanenna* in the postponed Independence Day Regatta of the Chicago Yacht Club. On July 25, *Vencedor* won the Captain A. W. McMasters Cup for forty-five footers beating again *Vanenna*.

On August 3, 1903, *Vencedor* made the best actual time in the Lake Michigan Yachting Association race from Chicago to Milwaukee in spite of the fact that it suffered a severe accident when metal rods that held the mast from pushing through the keel broke, causing a leak that required the crew to bail water the entire time of the race which took place in gale-force winds. *Vencedor* eclipsed all prior records for the eighty-five-mile race finishing it in seven hours forty-eight minutes—an average of eleven miles per hour.

August 8, 1903, saw *Vencedor* achieve an easy win in the Lake Michigan Yachting Association Regatta—it had no competitors but sailed the course.

On August 13, 1903, *Vencedor* lead its class in the South Haven Regatta.

Back at Lake Delavan, on August 31, 1903, *El Capitan*, now owned by H. N. Norton, who was one of the largest tin can manufacturers in the country, won the Delavan Yacht Clubs' championship beating *Ruth II* owned by Dr. E. R. Kellogg by four-and-one-half minutes corrected time. *El Capitan* enjoyed an eight-and-one-half-minute time allowance.

On September 5, 1903, *Vencedor* won the Columbia Yacht Club's cruising race to Indiana Harbor defeating a fleet of twelve other boats. In so doing, it set a new record for the race, eclipsing the old record by almost thirty minutes.

It was always a great yachting event on the lakes when any of the former stablemates from the RBMCO competed with one another. One such event was the first match race between W. F. Cameron's *Vanenna* and Commodore Price's *Vencedor* for the championship of Lake Michigan. The races were the best of three. The first race was on September 11, 1902. Measurements gave a slight time allowance to *Vencedor*, but Commodore Price graciously waived it and called for a flat race. It was tightly fought and *Vanenna* led most of the way, but *Vencedor* nipped it at the finish line winning by fifteen seconds. It was called one of the closest and most exciting races ever on Lake Michigan. In the second race on September 13, *Vencedor* broke its peak halyard. The last and deciding race was on September 20, and *Vanenna* was able to win by a few minutes.

September 12, 1903, saw *Vencedor* winning in thirty-six miles per hour winds and taking home the Murray Cup at the annual fall Regatta of the Columbia Yacht Club.

The championship of Lake Michigan Yachting was held on September 17 and 18, 1903, between *Vencedor* and *Vanenna*. Abe Burrell was the professional skipper of *Vencedor*, while Pete Elefson was the pro at the helm of *Vanenna*.

The first day the two sloops raced in forty miles per hour gale-force winds and saw *Vencedor* win by almost twenty minutes.

The second day of racing was on a triangular course with each leg of seven miles for a total of twenty-one miles. *Vencedor* won the race by five minutes forty-five seconds even after a bad start in which Skipper Burrell crossed the starting line five seconds before the gun was fired which required *Vencedor* to redo the start costing it about two-and-a-half minutes.

The official times were *Vencedor* (4:50:10) and *Vanenna (*4:55:55), and owner Price had another handsome silver cup to bring home.

On December 5, 1903, Fred A. Price, *Vencedor's* owner, was elected commodore of the Columbia Yacht Club. At that time, the Columbia Yacht Club was one of the three yacht clubs in Chicago and was headquartered on a floating structure in Lake Michigan. It was known for its convivial members and fine cuisine.

On June 11, 1904, *Vencedor* was entered in the thirteenth annual cruise to the resort Michigan City, Indiana, given by the Columbia Yacht Club. It would be the yacht's fourth consecutive victory.

Back at Lawley's, Poekel became the general superintendent. In 1904, he supervised the building of *Visitor*, which was the fastest boat of her length in the world. On June 28, 1904, he accompanied the designers Swesey & Raymond along with the owner Commodore W. Harry Brown of Pittsburgh on a trial run from Provincetown, Massachusetts, to the New England docks. Captain Coleman with a crew of twelve brought the steamer in at speeds that sometimes reached twenty-one knots per hour. The owner, Commodore Harry Brown, would later become famous with his successor yacht *Visitor II* which on November 23, 1910, he sailed through the Panama Canal to the Gatun Locks, making history of sailing the first boat in the canal.

Independence Day 1904 saw *Vencedor* win two important races but unfortunately suffer an accident on its third consecutive Fourth of July—a day which was called a "hoodoo day" in the vernacular of the times.

Vencedor won the Pabst Cup in its match race against *Vanenna*. After that race, *Vencedor* was dismasted. Fortunately, there were no crew injuries (although two of the crew had to jump overboard not to be hit by the sails). The previous year's Independence Day accident saw *Vencedor*'s peak halyards part and two years before its mast was carried away.

Vencedor continued its winning streak on July 24, 1904, coming in first in the cruising race from Chicago to the Michigan resort of Macatawa Park for the second time. *Vencedor*, in the lead, enjoyed a regal escort by the yachts *Collean* and *Snipe* of the Macatawa Bay Yacht Club. Many launches and small craft blew whistles and horns, as it passed through Saugatuck Piers. For winning this race, *Vencedor* received the beautiful silver Waukazoo Cup, which was presented by Commodore C. M. Camburn of the Macatawa Bay Yacht Club. In the evening, the press reported that the town was turned over to the Columbia yachtsman and a dance was held in the newly opened lake front park.[27]

Chapter 18

Oh Mackinac, la belle, we love you so,
Tho' years may come and go,
We'll constant be,
Mackinac, la belle, our Mackinac,
So we sail north upon our inland sea.

MICHILIMACKINAC ("BIG TURTLE") WAS THE ORIGINAL NAME TO AN island and the area near the straits of Mackinac between Lake Huron and Lake Michigan. Eventually called Makinaw and Mackinac the island ended up being called Mackinac (pronounced Mackinaw).

While Yellowstone National Park was the first national park, Mackinac National Park was the second. It was created when a bill was signed into law by President Ulysses S. Grant in 1875. The 1,000 acre national park lasted until 1895, when it was decommissioned and became a Michigan state park.

With a course of 332 miles, the Chicago-Mackinac yacht race is the longest freshwater sailing race in the world. And it is tough. In 1937, for example, only eight of the forty-two boats entered completed the race. The Chicago Yacht Club describes it best: "Stripped down to its essence, the Mac like all sailboat races is still primarily a test of strength, endurance and willpower."

The first race to Mackinac took place in August 1898. The winner was *Vanenna* which finished in fifty-two hours seventeen minutes and fifty seconds. An hour later *Siren* arrived in second place. Both sloops had been built at the RBMCO when T. Sch. Poekel had been superintendent.

Ten yachts were entered in the 1904 race from Chicago to Mackinac Island, seeking the winner's pennant from the Chicago Yacht Club for the 332-mile marathon. Included in the fleet were the three stablemates from Racine—*Vencedor*, *Vanenna*, and *Siren*. *Vencedor* and *Neva* were sailing under the auspices of the Columbia Yacht Club. All the rest of the entries were sailing out of the Chicago Yacht Club. *Vanenna*, the race's first winner in 1898 had been a three-time winner over *Siren* in major lake races.

Vanenna, flying the colors of the Chicago Yacht Club had Vice Commodore Atkin on board, and *Vencedor*, flying the colors of the Columbia Yacht Club had its owner Commodore Fred A. Price onboard.

Just after 5:00 pm on Wednesday, August 3, 1904, the race began as boats passed through Chicago's Van Buren Street gap and began to leave behind the smog filled skyline of the City of Chicago.

Vencedor got off to a slow start with the winds blowing about twelve knots. But by 4:00 am, *Vencedor* was clearly in command but with *Vanenna* close at hand.

At no time during the race were these two sloops outside of sight of each other. Often the sloops were so close to each other that the crews would converse with each other.

As the sloops approached Mackinac, the crew of *Vencedor* almost made a fatal error. They spotted what they thought was Fort Mackinac and hauled the sloop's spinnaker in and changed course. But after realizing their error, they corrected and fixed their course. Half an hour later, the stake boat was sighted.

Vencedor was able to live up to its name by beating *Vanenna*. *Vencedor* finished the race at 7:06:00 am and *Vanenna* at 7:10:40 am—a difference of less than five minutes between the two sloops for the 332-mile race that took over thirty-seven hours. The race which saw *Vencedor* and *Vanenna* almost inseparable for the entire race was said to be one of the closest races ever sailed on fresh or salt water.

Commodore Price, gave this analysis of the race: "I am fully satisfied with the race. I defeated *Vanenna* last year in Chicago and also in the present race. Over the whole present course we were sailing directly with the wind, which favored the *Vanenna* more than *Vencedor*. The *Vanenna* is 2 feet longer and has a foot greater beam, which with wind, gives the

Vanenna a greater advantage. In close weather work and going to windward the *Vencedor* is better than sailing before the wind."[1]

Not only did *Vencedor* win the Chicago Yacht Club pennant for finishing first but it also broke the course record for the best time of thirty-seven hours forty-six minutes greatly surpassing the previous record of fifty-three hours set in the 1898 race. Besides the pennant, *Vencedo*r took home the Grand Hotel Cup and $100 in gold.

A few weeks after Mackinac, there was a race scheduled for the Sir Thomas Lipton Trophy, which was a silver cup donated in 1901 by the great Irish-born yachtsman. In 1904, George R. Peare had won the race the two previous years with his crack yacht *LaRita*.

The yacht *LaRita* had won the cup in 1902 and 1903. Naturally, the owner wanted to win it again. Peare, unlike other yacht owners such as Sir Thomas Lipton, actually sailed the yachts he owned. He was a broad-shouldered man with an athlete's build, an excellent yachtsman, but known to have a fiery temper. On the night of August 14, 1904, he showed up at a banquet held by the Columbia Yacht Club and confronted Commodore Fred A. Price, owner of the club's flagship *Vencedor*. He asked why he wasn't invited. Price tried to explain the banquet was a complimentary dinner for visiting yachtsmen from out of town. Soon voices grew louder, and Peare punched Commodore Price in the face. He was subdued by fellow members of the club who thereafter went into session, and barred Peare's yacht *LaRita* from participating in the upcoming Lipton Trophy Regatta. The expulsion was based on the yacht owner "not acting as a gentleman."

According to his wife Genevieve, the same held true at home. She brought an action for separate maintenance a few weeks later. One of her grievances was that her husband preferred his boating trophies to his marriage.

In October 1904, Commodore Price announced that he was "getting out of the racing game." He planned to dismantle *Vencedor* and use some of its pieces to build a new yacht—probably in the East. This startling announcement caused the press to write: "The passing of *Vencedor* will be much like the parting from an old and faithful friend to the yachtsmen. The yacht for several years has earned and sustained the reputation of being the crack racing craft of Lake Michigan, and has won a number of trophies for its owner and for the club under whose burgee she sailed."[2] But for whatever reasons, Commodore Price remained in the racing game and *Vencedor* was not dismantled. It did not have a premature death and went on to win many more trophies, burnishing its reputation even more.

In July of 1905, Billy Cameron of the Chicago Yacht Club challenged Fred A. Price to a series of match races between *Vanenna* and *Vencedor*. To sweeten the pot Cameron announced he was putting up $500 cash for the winner. The challenge was widely reported to be a joke emanating from a squabble on July 4 between the two men since *Vencedor* had been beating *Vanenna* so often.

Thirteen vessels entered the Macatawa Bay Yacht Club race from Chicago to Mackinac Macatawa Piers on July 30, 1905. The race saw *Illinois* drop out due to an accident and the *Vencedor* battle *Juanita* to the end. The result was that *Vencedor* not just won beating *Juanita* by over two minutes but finished the race ahead of the yachts of all classes.

T. Sch. Poekel had kept his promise to his parents by bringing them to America to live. They settled in Dorchester, Massachusetts, where unfortunately, on September 7, 1905, his mother Anna C. Poekel died from pneumonia at age sixty-seven.

The year 1905 saw the American entry *Temeraire* beat the Canadian *Iroquois* in the fifth racing of Canada's Cup and for the first time a defending country's boat won. Through 1905, the history of the race was as follows:

	Challenger	Defender
1896	*Canada* (C)	*Vencedor* (A)
1899	*Genessee* (A)	*Beaver* (C)
1901	*Invader* (C)	*Cadillac* (A)
1903	*Ironde* (A)	*Strathcona* (C)
1905	*Temeraire* (A)	*Iroquois* (C)

Watching the Canada's Cup races off Charlotte, New York, that year were Æmilius Jarvis as a spectator for the first time and Will Fife Jr. who journeyed over from Scotland to view the races.

In the annual fall Regatta of the Columbia Yacht Cub on September 16, 1905, *Vencedor* beat *Neva* and established a new record for the Tom Murray Cup. At the helm was the owner Fred A. Price who the night before had resigned his position of commodore of the Columbia Yacht Club. He had been stung by criticism that he had not taken the club's bid for the Lipton Cup seriously with his yacht *Quien Sabe*. The press also reported that *Vencedor* was on the market, and because of his increasingly busy business schedule Price was planning to devote his time cruising his *Juanita*.

Commodore Price finally sold *Vencedor*, and the yachting season of 1906, saw George R. Tramel, an executive with the Aetna Insurance Company, become the big mahogany yacht's fourth owner.

June 16, 1906, saw the start of the Fifteenth Annual Columbia Yacht Club race to Michigan City. The *Chicago Daily Tribune* predicted the race would be "the greatest event of the kind ever held in the history of western yachting." A lot of hype surrounded four-time successive winner *Vencedor* and its skipper George R. Peare. The race was a complete dud with *Vencedor* getting stuck in the mud and all the sailing yachts becalmed. *Vencedor* had set the record in 1902 by sailing the thirty-two-mile course in 3:38:55. In 1906, *Pilot*, which won the race, did it in three hours ten minutes.

On July 4, 1906, *Vencedor* won the Eleventh Annual Regatta of the Lake Michigan Yachting Association setting a new course record of 1:18:40—beating the previous record of 1:27 flat, also set by *Vencedor* two years before. The crew of the victorious yacht consisted of George Tramel, owner; Abe Burrell, skipper; Dr. J. B. Palmer; George McCullough; Dr. T. N. Dickinson; T. S. Kelly; L. Y. Cowan; Dick McGurn; and Burt Levis.

July 21, 1906, saw the third annual Mackinac race, and it was remarkable by having eight of the twelve entering yachts finishing within an hour of each other. *Vencie*'s old rival *Vanenna* was far in the lead by North Manitou Island but ran into bad luck in the final leg going aground off Skilligalee Light. Winning Skipper Steere of *Vanadis*, thinking *Vanenna* had won, crossing the finish line to cheers he yelled out, "We get second money." *Vencedor* took home honors in the sloop class. That year saw the magnificent $1,500 Mackinac Cup of the Chicago Yacht Club presented to the winner.

Mackinac Cup—Courtesy of Chicago Yacht Club

The cup is twenty-three-inches high, twenty-four-inches long, and stands in the Chicago Yacht Club. It was purchased in 1906, by Chicago Yacht Club members headed by Eugene Sullivan, Ernest Puttkammer, and Dr. W. L. Baum to provide a fitting perpetual trophy for the annual Chicago to Mackinac race.

Forty-six boats were entered in the Chicago Regatta of October 6, 1906, which honored the visit of the famed Irish yachtsman Sir Thomas Lipton. It was one of the greatest assemblages of yachts in the history of the Great Lakes. It was a joint effort of the Chicago, Columbia, Jackson Park yacht clubs, and the Chicago Athletic Association. Steamers flew the private burgee of the "shamrock" to honor the Irish baronet.

As Lipton watched through his binoculars from the deck of USS *Dorothea*, *Vencedor* took a long lead over his former Racine stablemate *Vanenna*. But suddenly it tragically broke its gaff about three feet from jaws and was put out of the running. She had been expected to receive time prize honors. That was not the only pain she suffered—her course record was beaten by *Vanenna* as well as *Juanita*.

After the regatta at a reception at the Columbia Yacht Club, Sir Thomas Lipton had this to say:

I was greatly pleased with these races, which I understand were especially arranged for my entertainment.

I have seen many regattas but never one that was more interesting or better handled. There are some fine boats in the fleets of the Chicago clubs and they are manned by skillful sailors I feel as if I have been paid an undue honor by so many of the boat owners keeping their yachts in commission until such a late date in the season, and I assure my friends that I appreciate their efforts.[3]

In the June 15, 1907, annual race to Michigan City, *Vencedor* was first to arrive but because of its heavy time allowance, gave victory to *Chloris*.

July 5, 1907, saw *Vencedor* win the time prize in the Independence Day Regatta on the Great Lakes. Sailing for owner George Tramel with McCullough as skipper the big mahogany yacht beat forty-five of the best boats in Chicago.

The next day, *Vencedor* raced from Chicago to Milwaukee for the G. G. Pabst Cup offered by the Columbia Yacht Club. Again skippered by George McCullough there was a crew of eleven along with the owner's son James H. Tramel. Sailing under the colors of the Columbia Yacht Club, *Vencedor* finished first in the joint regatta of the Columbia Yacht Club, Jackson Park Yacht Club, and the Chicago Yacht Club. *Vencedor* sailed to victory arriving in Milwaukee over four hours ahead of the sloop *Pilot*, which came in second with corrected time, with *Illinois* finishing second in actual time.

Having such a successful season in 1907, *Vencedor* was the favorite in the upcoming Mackinac race.

This year the race was known as the second race for the Chicago Yacht Club's "Mackinac Cup"—a perpetual challenge trophy that was valued at $1,000. Fourteen yachts started the race with the one gun start at 4 pm on Saturday, July 20, 1907. Thirteen would finish. *Vencedor* and *Illinois* went for an early lead making for the open lake. *Illinois* was expected to be the biggest rival for *Vencedor*, but after a close beginning it dropped back considerably. The next day *Vencedor* pulled ahead, but then in late morning it had to deal with a tremendous squall. Even with the squall encounter, *Vencedor* set the record for the fastest Mackinac race (forty-three-and-a-half hours) except for its own record of thirty-seven hours set previously. *Vencedor* finished the race two hours and nine minutes ahead of the second place *Hawthorne* owned by Fox, McConnell, and Clinche. *Vanenna*, which was a late entry, sailed one of the worst races of its career and trailed *Vencedor* by six hours.

According to the *Chicago Tribune*: "It is the general opinion among the Chicago men here that *Vencedor* never sailed a better race and Skipper McCullough is given no small measure of credit."[4]

Donald Prater, a chronicler of the Mackinac races, said, "Victory of *Vencedor* stamps it undeniably as one of the greatest yachts on fresh water."[5] Owner George Tramel sailing for the Chicago Athletic Association walked away with three trophies: the Mackinac Cup, a silver tea service for having the fastest elapsed time, and a cut glass liquor set for *Vencedor*'s first place in the sloop class. All those skippers that didn't win anything received watch fobs. Included in the losing group was the skipper of *Vanenna*, which received one of biggest losses of its career.

J. M. Handley of *Yachting Magazine* called the *Vencedor* the "Queen of Lake Michigan" and added that the record she set when she first won "will probably never be equaled in the history of this trophy."[6] And the *Chicago Tribune* stated, "The victory of the *Vencedor* stamps it undeniably as one of the greatest yachts on fresh water."[7]

August 24, 1907, saw *Vencedor* win top honors by finishing with the best flat record over the course in the open regatta of the Chicago Athletic Association—just thirty-eight seconds more than its record the year before. The great mahogany yacht with Skipper McCullough at the helm again defeated *Vanenna*. The victory of *Vencedor* was even more incredible,

Vencedor's 1907 win became a permanent part of the Mackinac Cup—Courtesy of Chicago Yacht Club, Jesus Santos, photographer

since it sailed the race with the jaws of its gaff broken and the upper part of the mainsail spilling past the wind.

Illinois edged *Vencedor* by a hair when she won the first leg of the triangular race from Chicago on September 2, 1907, by three minutes of corrected time. However, *Vencedor* went on to beat *Illinois* on the last two legs and won the entire contest with a total of seventeen points over *Illinois*'s fifteen points. The race covered 115 miles between Chicago, St. Joe, and Michigan City and return.

Back on the East Coast, 1907 saw T. Sch. Poekel, living in Dorchester, Massachusetts, continue to enhance his reputation and became active socially being accepted into Dorchester's prestigious Colonial Club. On January 22, 1908, the club hosted a reception honoring fellow club member and Mayor of Boston George Albee Hibbard. Punch at the dinner-dance reception was served by the daughters of members, including Poekel's daughter Anna B. Poekel.

March 14, 1908, saw George Tramel elected commodore of the Chicago Athletic Association.

The 1908 Mackinac Race saw a narrow escape at disaster for the venerable *Vencedor*. On the eve of the race when the boat was in dry dock, one

Valmore and *Vencedor*—Permission of Chicago History Museum

of the shorns with which the boat was braced forced through the planking below the waterline on the starboard side. Subsequently, tons of water
filled the yacht from the dry dock just prior to floating. All the water was
pumped out but not before the entire boat was soaked.

While Poekel was working at the Lawley yard, he would see a boat
built that would race his beloved *Vencedor*. *Valmore* was designed by Fred
D. Lawley and built by George Lawley & Son for John P. Lawrence of
Providence, Rhode Island. In 1908, it was purchased by William Hale
Thompson. Unlike the train trips for *Vencedor*, *Valmore* was sailed, mostly
by Thompson at the helm, over 3,000 miles from New London, Connecticut, in the Atlantic Ocean to the Gulf of St. Lawrence, along the St.
Lawrence River and through the Great Lakes, and on to Chicago, where
it would be entered in the Mackinac Race of 1908.

Valmore won the "Mac," beating the prior year's champion *Vencedor*.
It would be the first of three successive victories for the William Hale
Thompson's eighty-one-foot schooner. The race saw nine boats race over
a period of four days in what was described as "probably as unsatisfactory
a race as the club had ever run."[8]

During the Lipton Cup Regatta week it was decided to have a match race
between Chicago Athletic Association commodore George Tramel's *Vencedor* and Illinois Athletic Association president William Hale Thompson's
Valmore. The race under the auspices of the Chicago Yacht Club took place
on the afternoon of August 21, 1908. At the tiller of *Vencedor* was its former
skipper Abe Burell as George McCullough, its usual captain, was called away
on business. At the helm on *Valmore* was its owner and future mayor of Chicago William Hale "Big Bill" Thompson. The race was one of the closest on
freshwater. The yachts finished within seconds of each other, after a six-hour
contest. However, the time of four hours set for the race had expired and the
judges declared the race to be "No Contest." *Vencie* would have won by thirty-
one seconds with its time allowance had the race not been called.

August 22, 1908, saw *Vencedor* achieve the fastest actual time in the
annual regatta of the Chicago Athletic Association.

On July 5, 1909, *Vencedor* won the annual Lake Michigan Yachting
Association Regatta sailing under the auspices of the Chicago Athletic
Association and under the direction of Skipper George McCullough. The

Chicago Daily News reported that starting last of all "the crack mahogany fin keeler plunged through the area like a thoroughbred and rapidly overhauling one after another of the pacemakers that had started before."[9] *Vencedor*, referred to as the "Big Train" in some news reports, set the regular triangular course record by traversing the course in 1:13:35 beating the previous record set by the *Juanita* of 1:14:25.

A famed *Chicago Tribune* sportswriter who went by his initials HRK, captured the uniqueness of *Vencedor* when he wrote: "There is no single sticker out there on our water front that has anything on *Vencedor*. That good old ship is almost human."[10] Of course, he had in mind the fact that many in the sporting world referred to it as *"Vencie."*

Eleven boats left Chicago on July 24, 1909, in the race to Mackinac. Thousands lined the shore of Lake Michigan to see the start with hundreds in small crafts in the water. The *Amorita*, *Valmore*, and *Vencedor* were the first to cross the starting line. These three were the favorites, and betting was extremely high at their respective clubs, the Chicago Yacht Club, the Chicago Athletic Association, and the Illinois Athletic Club. *Amorita* finished first followed by *Valmore* five minutes six seconds later, but the win was given to *Valmore* on time allowance. *Vencedor* finished third. This was *Valmore*'s second consecutive win of the Mac.

After over twenty-five years of shipbuilding in South Boston, George Lawley & Son, considered to be the best known yacht-building company in the United States, closed title on land fronting the Neponset River in Neponset, Massachusetts, for establishing a new shipyard. The company was able to use the existing brick waterfront building, wharves, and marine railways. Neponset was selected over sites in Belfast, Maine, and St. Augustine, Florida. The company at that time employed between 300 and 400 skilled mechanics, carpenters, ship joiners, iron ship workers, blacksmiths, riggers, caulkers, painters, plumbers, and tin smiths.

By 1910, *Vencedor* had the most wins of any yacht sailing on the Great Lakes.

June 18, 1910, saw the Eighteenth annual cruising race of the Columbia Yacht Club to Michigan City. Although the top prize went to *Invader*, *Vencedor* won in the fifty-five-foot sloop class.

In the summer of 1910, a growing number of yachtsmen were advocating the Mackinac race be changed. Some wanted it to be Chicago to Detroit. Some said it was too dangerous for the yachts to go to Mackinac since there were no safe harbors along the way. Still others just wanted a change for the sake of change. But tradition prevailed and Mackinac Island remained the destination.

Twenty-mile-an-hour winds were present when the gun was fired on July 24 for the start of the 1910 race to Mackinac. With such a wind blowing, it was speculated that *Vencedor*'s 1904 record of thirty-seven hours fifty-four minutes for the 1904 race might be broken. And it was, with William Hale Thompson's *Valmore* cutting about five-and-one-half hours off the record time. *Valmore* finished the race with a time of 31:24:06.

August 11, 1910, saw *Vencedor* take top honors for its class in the Knights Templar Regatta held under the auspices of the Chicago, Columbia, and Jackson Park Yacht Clubs. It won the time trophy offered in the sixty-five-foot schooner and fifty-five-foot sloop class.

September 5, 1910, saw the recently rebuilt *Vencedor* win three more trophies for George Tramel, in winning the annual long distance cruising race from Chicago to St. Joe, Michigan City, and back. A trophy was awarded for winning each leg of the race.

After working for the HMCO, the RBMCO, and George Lawley & Son, T. Sch. Poekel wanted his own boatyard.

On April 30, 1911, the *Boston Daily Globe* reported that Poekel, after spending nearly a dozen years with Lawley as a superintendent and engineer and designer of engines and boilers and supervisor of steel construction, would open his own shipyard at the site of the Sheldon boatyard in Neponset, Massachusetts.[11] Poekel left Lawley's as of May 1 and opened the boatyard of T. Sch. Poekel & Co. on the banks of the Neponset River adjacent to Lawley's boatyard. Bror Tamm, one of Lawley's senior engineers, would comment that among yacht designers Poekel was one of the best.

Business was off to a good start at the Poekel yard in Neponset. A few weeks after opening, T. Sch. Poekel had been commissioned to build a thirty-foot auxiliary ketch for a prominent New York yachtsman from a design by A. P. Homer.[12]

The year 1911, on the West Coast saw T. Sch. Poekel's protégé John F. Duthie also start his own shipyard known as J. F. Duthie & Co. The yard covered over twelve acres of the Seattle waterfront. During its inaugural year, the boatyard built the steel whaling steamers *Kodiak* and *Unimak* as well as the fishing steamer *Starr*.

Three months after opening his own boatyard in Neponset, Thorvald Sch. Poekel would read about *Vencie*'s attempt to win its third Mackinac Cup. He was, however, very content with life. With his own boatyard, he didn't have to share his reputation with anyone. His experience defined his business philosophy: "I would rather make fifty cents for myself than a dollar for someone else."

CHAPTER 19

One of the prettiest starts ever seen in the Mackinac event.
—*The Inter-Ocean News*

IN MAY OF 1911, IT WAS REPORTED THAT *VENCEDOR* MAY NOT RACE FOR the season quoting its owner George Tramel who said he may not go in for the sailing game that year.[1] However, that was about to change as in June a syndicate approached Tramel and took over the racing of *Vencedor* for the summer. The syndicate consisted of Rear Commodore William A. Lydon, John G. DeLong, C. A. Briggs, and Hugh E. Keough. Lydon was the founder of the Great Lakes Dredge and Dock Company of Chicago. News accounts reported that *Vencedor*'s racing in 1911, would preserve its record of a clean slate in being in commission every year, since it was built in 1896.

When the syndicate took over *Vencie*, it was just out of dry dock in the South Chicago Dockyard. Skipper George McCullough was put in charge of overhauling the yacht. The syndicate entered the sloop in the Milwaukee race where it did well and then in a race for the Thomas Lipton Trophy. *Vencedor* was driven hard in that race and afterward had to be sent back to dry dock for repairs. It seemed its fifteen-year-old age was beginning to take a toll as *Vencedor* prepared for another attempt at Mackinac.

In a race for the Herbst Cup, *Vencie* finished second, minutes behind E. M. Mills's *Mavourneen* in the seventy-five-mile race from Milwaukee to Chicago.

July 22, 1911, saw eleven yachts and 142 crew leave from the Chicago Yacht Club in the eighth annual Mackinac 332-mile race. The *Inter-Ocean News* reported that it was "one of the prettiest starts ever seen in the

Vencedor at the start of the 1911 Mackinac race—
Permission of Chicago History Museum

Mackinac event." There was a moderate southeast breeze blowing between twelve and fifteen miles per hour when the race started at 3:00 pm.

Vencedor was looking for its third Mackinac win and was sailing under the command of its Skipper George B. McCullough with Stanley Thorne and John P. Brady onboard along with eight professional sailors. Brady was a reporter for the *Inter-Ocean News* who would later give an eyewitness account of his time of the yacht during the race. Most of the professionals onboard had come from the East to enjoy a "picnic" on Lake Michigan.

In the race were *Mavourneen*, *Illinois* that had won the Canada's Cup, the Herreshoff-designed *Shark*, *Polaris* from the East Coast, *Juanita*, *Capsicum*, and *Amorita*. Also, in the race was one of the favorites—William Hale Thompson's *Valmore*, which had a string of three straight wins in the Mackinac. Initial reports indicated that there were no clear favorites in the race. According to the *Chicago Tribune*, "Never in the history of the race was the winner so uncertain."[2] However, one thing was certain, the fifteen-year-old *Vencedor* was in the worst shape of its career.

The big yachts were set to leave at 3:30 pm and *Vencedor*, through the talented maneuvering of Skipper McCullough, was the first to cross the starting line.

However, shortly after the start, *Vencedor*'s lead was taken away when its balloon jib got stuck and the great mahogany yacht's entire rigging almost landed in the waters of Lake Michigan. Soon *Amorita, Valmore, Juanita, Mavourneen*, and six other entries passed the old champion by.

But Captain McCullough wasn't conceding anything and before the first evening, *Vencedor* had passed *Iroquois, Prairie,* and *Illinois*. Now *Vencedor* set its sight on the leaders *Valmore* and *Mavourneen*. But something else was happening. Overnight the temperature dropped to thirty-two degrees and gale-force winds started blowing.

At 4:00 am, the crew spotted land but more ominously, a red watery sky and scores of white caps.

An interim report from the Chicago Yacht Club, on the night of July 23, announced that the yacht *Amorita* was in the lead forty-five minutes over the yacht *Valmore*. *Polaris* was third and *Vencedor* fourth ahead of *Juanita* and *Mavourneen*.

The reported accounts said that the weather was pretty rough and "made Lake Michigan look like a bad night off Cape Hatteras."[3]

The violent storm affected all of Michigan. Across the lake, which is a little smaller than the state of West Virginia, it created a marine disaster.

Conditions in the northern part of Lake Michigan turned into gale conditions. The boats were not just racing but racing to survive.

Gale-force winds and torrential rain continued as the yachts fought their way up the lake. The eleven yachts that had left Chicago under a moderate southerly breeze were now in a storm that was becoming the worst summer storm in the history of the Great Lakes. Tremendous winds battled the boats as they attempted to reach Mackinac.

The crew of *Mavourneen* had hired a professional cook to accompany them. At the last moment, the hired chef couldn't go and got a replacement. The new chef was seasick at the start of the race and was useless during the voyage. When the storm arose, he asked the captain where he should go. The captain told him "go below since you would be the first to die when the boat sank."

A sailor from *Vencedor* would later say, "I have sailed many years on fresh and salt water and never experienced such seas."

George Brady, a reporter from the *Chicago Tribune*, who was on the yacht *Polaris* stated that during the storm "we clung to the rail and had all the delirious sensations of trying to ride a submarine bronco."[4]

The U.S. Weather Bureau telegraphed the Chicago Yacht Club with the news that the winds had reached hurricane force of eighty-two knots per hour.

The storm was one of the worst in the history of the Great Lakes. Besides marine disasters all over Lake Michigan, the storm hit land and William Wither's windmill was blown down and Joe Guild's silo was completely destroyed in Marin Township.[5]

The storm created damage to other boats on the lakes as well. The lumber barge *Lucky Lucy* was picked up in Traverse City without a crew and the barge *Hattie Wells* had its starboard side ripped apart and lost one-third of its deck load of 8,000 cedar posts.

Vencedor rode the mountainous waves well but the mainsail and the working jib were providing too much canvas. For the first time in *Vencedor*'s history, Skipper McCullough ordered them stripped and had the storm trysail or spencer sail hoisted. The yacht was sailing with only 10 percent of its normal canvas size, but still traveling at over twelve knots per hour.

Except for the leaders, the other yachts were sailing the race in pairs. The *Juanita* with Captain Andrews at the helm was the closest yacht to *Vencedor*.

Captain McCollough decided to seek refuge from the mighty storm by heading to the nearest port with a marina, Charlevoix, thirty miles away. The problem was that in order to get there *Vencedor* had to cross Grand Traverse Bay. The Skipper knew mountainous waves were awaiting his fifteen-year-old mahogany yacht. The crew of ten were thinking of the lifeboat aboard that could hold six at most. The weather was so thick you couldn't even see the bowsprit. The tender was unlashed.

Crossing Grand Traverse Bay in rough seas Captain Andrews of *Juanita* noticed that *Vencedor* was heading directly into the shoals but being about a half mile away he had no means to give it a warning signal.

The yacht approached a buoy, which marked shallow water, and the crew spotted Fisherman's Island a few times but lost sight of it. Suddenly seeing shallow water McCullough yelled, "For God's sake, hold her off,

Harry." Suddenly there was a loud crash. The yacht had hit a boulder and the decks were inundated with water with the crew hanging on for dear life. The Skipper rushed for the tiller and yelled: "Up forward there, you fellows, and put the jib on her." The crew with their freezing and wet hands were able to hoist the jib. The Skipper was hoping that with the strong winds the yacht would sail free but it didn't happen. Instead, the yacht nestled in between two boulders and its 16,000 pounds of lead ballast created a permanent anchor. The thought on everyone's mind was that the boulders would surface right through the planked deck.

Next, Skipper McCullough gave the order: "Get ready the dinghy and get out the life preservers!" Stanley Thorne, one of the amateurs on board, quickly passed out live preservers to the crew. At that point they could only hope and pray for a rescue by the nearby *Juanita*. However, in the flash of an eye, *Juanita* sent up its own distress signals. Real praying was needed now.

Just then a speck appeared on the horizon. It grew larger and the crew realized their prayers were answered as the steamer *Arapahoe* approached at full speed. And it approached just in the nick of time as dusk was fast approaching. *Arapahoe*, skippered by "Hawk" Davis, had been trailing *Vencedor* on its way to Georgian Bay and after seeing it hit the shoals immediately steamed over.

Because of the tremendous waves, *Arapahoe* couldn't come close to *Vencedor*. It went astern of *Vencedor* and threw out a bowline. The waters were choppy and the ten members of crew of *Vencedor* leapt for their lives across the tumultuous waters onto the deck of the adjacent *Arapahoe*.

Arapahoe made several unsuccessful attempts to extricate *Vencedor* from the shoals before bringing the rescued crew into Charlevoix.

One of the amateur members of *Vencedor*'s crew, after the rescue at Charlevoix, left his crewmates and took the steamer *Manitou* to go to the finish of the race in Mackinac. He drew widespread laughter when racing officials asked him how many of the crew got on *Arapahoe* and he replied: "Nine of them got on after me."[6] As for Captain McCullough, he followed seaman rules and was the last to leave—he shrugged off his bravery off saying that he was hesitant to board a "stinkpot."

The only possible way to salvage *Vencedor* was with a tugboat. When McCullough got ashore, there were four tugs in port, and he persuaded one operator to try to extract *Vencie* from the rocks. The tug left port at 4:00 am but faced monstrous waves from the storm. It soon turned around and headed back to port as the seas were too rough to handle.

Vencedor was left stuck between two boulders on Frenchman's Reef being ground into little chips. The legendary yacht was totally destroyed. Its wooden remains slowly rode the waves onto a beach at Charlevoix.

John Brady, a talented yachting reporter who also served as part of the crew of *Vencedor* described the end as follows:

> The old boat died in battle as such a gallant old ship should. Her time was nearly up and her death in the Mackinac race was much to be preferred to having her rot in a junk heap. So declared owner Tramel. There never has been a boat on the great lakes driven throughout her career as was the *Vencedor*. Ever since her launching in 1896 she has been in race after race. She won the Mackinac race twice and would have stood well this year had her finish line been drawn at the Island instead of on Fisherman's Reef.

Thankful that the entire crew was saved, George Tramel, *Vencedor*'s owner, stated, "I would rather see *Vencie* go the way she did than any other way."[7]

Vencedor's former owner Edward C. Berriman would later say, "the good ship *Vencedor*, after a glorious life, died in action, as such a yacht should die."[8] And as John Brady said it, "The old yacht died with her boots on." T. Sch. Poekel, *Vencedor*'s designer, would also say for the rest of his life that that's the way he wanted to die "with his boots on."

The next day at about 4:00 pm Captain McCullough gathered his crew together to scour the Charlevoix beach to gather up the remains of

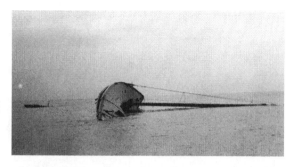

Wreck of *Vencedor*, off Charlevoix, Michigan
July 25, 1911—Permission of Chicago History
Museum

The end of *Vencedor*

Vencedor in the form of pieces of canvas, mahogany, deck planking, riggings, and ropes that had washed ashore. Just in case they encountered any souvenir hunters, the captain carried a loaded rifle.

Although all 142 sailors in the 1911 race to Mackinac survived, the *Chicago Evening Post* urged the end of the Mackinac race, given what happened to the mythical *Vencedor*. Only seven out of eleven yachts that started finished the race. The four that didn't finish were *Capsicum*, which sought safety in Frankfort Harbor; *Iroquois*, which went into Manitou Island; *Juanita* stood by after seeing *Vencedor*'s distress signals; and *Vencedor*.

The thirty-foot *Mavourneen* was the winner but dragged its anchor at Mackinac taking a brutal beating against the rocky shore and sustained tremendous damage.

William Hale Thompson, the owner of the *Valmore*, sent a telegram to the Chicago Athletic Club describing the situation to his fellow members:

> Sailing the Mackinac race in half a hurricane with no fatalities is a tremendous compliment to Chicago sailors. Loss of the yacht *Vencedor* and injury to *Illinois* and *Mavourneen* and minor accidents to most yachts sink into insignificance when compared with the courage, seamanship and nerve displayed by our yachtsmen in driving their yachts to Mackinac in tremendous winds, blinding rain and fog with all hands well and accounted for.

Vencedor has the unique distinction of being the only boat lost in the Mackinac race.

And someone even wrote a poem:

The Wreck of the Vencedor
By Maurice Beam

The gun is raised in the starter's hand; the white fleet nears the line!
And now a flash—a roar! They're gone! These lithe, pale ghosts of the
   brine.
Ten glis'ning prows on the Northeast Run to Old Fort Mackinaw,
Like ivory arrows, siren-shaped, fresh leapt from a hickory maw.

That milk-white hind that sniffs the wind—'tis Vencedor, out ahead!
See! Bellying full, her white sails pull; hungry, by East Wind fed.
Thus is the royal race begun—now trophy mounts in dreams.
The ships are kissed by the evening mist, warmed by the sun's last
    beams.

And now night falls like a dream upon the waters' waste.
And through the dark the long hulls slip like timid maidens, chaste,
But strong-caressed by slithering hand of lapping, hungry Sea,
Who may betimes woo gentle-like or lust most passionately.
The running lights, dim red-green sprites, dance on the liquid swell.
The quivering boom in the eerie gloom, spews up its canvas shell,
Hark! Out the East as the sun lifts up, wails now a ribald wind,
Grim harbinger of Storm-King's ire that white sails yet defy him!

Look! Vencedor quails as the seas pile high, but never a falter nor hitch!
She logs fourteen 'cross Traverse Bay! she flies like a pirate's bitch!
The waves lap high and the lightning spits and the thunder rolls aloft.
The billows boil within her wake as she leaps from crest to trough!
Her forestays moan and her backstays groan with the song of that
    lunatic wind.
Her rigging shrieks, her deck planks creak, in an alto requiem.
Thus she hums a song as she rides to death that makes the Storm-
    King rage.
Thus Vencedor, like her sires of yore, goes down with her canvas
    raised!

Now the giant racer fought and pitched and slammed into the Run!
Her loyal crew sat dry-eyed, tense, full knowing her race was done!
For three men now at her tiller-bar scarce held her on the sea.
On the starboard bow loom'd Fisher's Reef, and a murderous surf alwa!
And now wild surge becomes a dirge, chanting a last refrain,
As the gaunt white throat of the faithful boat is turned to sea again.
To sea she strained! Here safety lay, away from treach'rous shore.
For surging wave but formed her grave, 'twas land killed Vencedor!

And ghastly figures, beck'ning, rose from up stark Fisher's Reef.
Voluputurous froms with virgin's eyes, that hid ghouls vampire teeth.
Thus did dread death-march then begin for graceful Vencedor,
By orchestra of wind and wave—the Sea-Gods' troubadours.
In vain brave hands like iron bands strain on that tiller-bar.
Not twenty men could hold her when she came that last sick'ning jar,
As mighty racer, fleet to death, crashed full upon the reef
And rose no more. The Vencedor sleeps now her last long sleep.

Close-wedged between two giant rocks that white throat quivering lies,
While seas break fierce o'er sodden decks and wind with water vies
To rent askew that quiv'ring mast, to batter down the strakes,
To humble more this sriken Queen, erstwhile Pride of the Lakes,
Whose fame is known where sailors roam, from island Sil 'galee
To Saugatuck and Bay de Noc and back to Manistee.
From Beaver Isle to Waugoshance, from Gary to Death's Door –
From Mackinac to Chi and back, they loved fair Vencedor!

By the first week of August, 1911, four of the Mackinac entries that had survived the violent storm were back in Chicago: Commodore William Hale Thompson's *Valmore*, which had come in fifth; Henry Higginbotham's *Shark*; *Prairie*, which had come in third; and E. O. Mills' winning *Mavourneen*.

Meanwhile, back in Charlevoix, George Tramel arrived from Mackinac where he had been a judge of the race, who didn't see his yacht finish. He collected what remained of *Vencedor* that had washed ashore. He vowed to take the lead that was salvaged from the keel, some of the remaining mahogany timbers, and even the canvas sail for the rigging to build a new boat. The new yacht would be called *Vencedor II*.

Probably Tramel's plan was more wishful thinking, providing salve to an emotional wound. Many yachtsmen on the lakes as well as observers suffered from the loss of the great mahogany yacht. There would never be a *Vencedor II*, but what did remain were the memories of the original *Vencedor* that for fifteen years provided some of the greatest racing memories during the golden age of yacht racing.

In yachting circles, it was speculated that due to the lack of safe harbors on Lake Michigan there would never be another race to Mackinac. In fact, for the next three years, the destination was changed to Grand Traverse.

John G. DeLong, a reporter for the *Chicago Daily Tribune*, perhaps wrote the best eulogy: he said that to so many yachtsmen the loss of the yacht was like the loss of a close friend and "Vencedor was one of the most famous yachts on either fresh or salt water, and its remarkable string of victories had made its name a byword among yachtsmen all over the United States."[9]

Epilogue

On August 1, 1925, T. Sch. Poekel, after injuring his back at an accident at his boatyard in Neponset, transferred his business to the employee who had saved his life. He then retired to Green Cove Springs, Florida, where, after the premature death of his daughter Anna, he raised his three grandsons—Irving, Charles, and Carl. His engineering traditions inspired Irving to become a chemical engineer and Charles an electrical engineer. His toughness inspired Carl to be a prizefighter. Both Irving and Charles carried on the T. Sch. Poekel genius of designing and inventing. Charles for his Master's Thesis designed the lighting system for Florida Field at the University of Florida and during World War II invented a device for de-icing airplane propellers that became the industry standard. Irving helped design the gas masks used in World War II. Carl inherited his grandfather's tough independence and worked for himself. All three would honor their grandfather by changing their names from Brown to Poekel or Pockel.

On a foggy Halloween morning in 1940, while crossing a street in West Caldwell, New Jersey, T. Sch. Poekel was struck and killed by a taxi cab achieving his wish and, just like the *Vencedor*, dying "with his boots on." He is buried in Cedar Grove Cemetery in Dorchester, Massachusetts, alongside the Neponset River—within sight of where his boatyard stood.

Will Fife Jr., the designer of the "kit boat" *Canada* that beat *Vencedor* in 1896, continued his family tradition of designing yachts and during the 1890s averaged over fifty a year. He went on to design the *Shamrock I* and *III*, the first and third of Sir Thomas Lipton's America's Cup entries. He designed the *Hispania*, a yacht for King Alfonso XIII of Spain. He never married and had no children. On June 26, 1903, he and Sir Thomas Lipton sat next to President Theodore Roosevelt at a luncheon in their honor at the White House. He died in 1944, and his once famous boatyard was taken over by his nephew Robert Balderston who sold the business after World War II. Today, there is little left to remind anyone of the once world-famous Fairlie boatyard except for a weathervane depicting the yacht *Latifa* his two sisters had placed on top of the steeple of St. Columba's Church. The yacht was said to be one of Fife's best designs and his personal favorite. There is also a ceramic sign on the Village Inn, formerly the Mudhook Inn, that reads as follows:

> The famous boatyard of William Fife and Son was situated along the shoreline opposite of this Inn from the early years of the 19th century until 1939. Three generations of William Fifes designed many fine yachts which were built and launched by the Crafts-men of Fairlie to sail and race with great distinction worldwide.

After a remarkable life as a yacht builder, and businessman John Brown Herreshoff died in 1915.

In 1920, Nathanael Greene Herreshoff, the "Wizard of Bristol," would see *Resolute,* his sixth defender of America's Cup win. From 1893 to 1920, he had designed and built every America's Cup defender: *Vigilant* (1893), *Defender* (1895), *Columbia* (1899 and 1901), *Reliance* (1903), and *Resolute* (1920).

On August 22, 1924, the HMCO, which at one time was valued at over $1 million and where Thorvald Poekel learned his trade, was auctioned off in a liquidation sale. Capt. Nat died on June 2, 1938, in his beloved home of Love Rocks in Bristol.

Edward Burgess's son Starling Burgess continued his father's tradition of designing America's Cup contenders and designed the winning yachts *Enterprise* in 1930, *Rainbow* in 1934, and *Ranger* in 1937. Together the Herreshoff and Burgess families won twelve consecutive America's Cups. Fagnani's "Erato" for which the wife of Edward Burgess posed for hangs today in the Metropolitan Museum of Art in New York City.

Poekel's protégé John F. Duthie emigrated to the West Coast where he worked for the Wolf & Zwicker Ironworks in Portland, Oregon. He then went to Seattle, Washington, in 1912, and formed the J. F. Duthie & Company, shipbuilders. Under Duthie's direction, the company became a major shipbuilding concern in the State of Washington where Duthie designed and built thirty-four boats and ships. At one time, the company employed over 4,000 workers. The company built the ferry *Leschi*, steam whalers *Kodiak* and *Unimak*, holders for the most whales caught one season, the steamer *Star* that held the world's record for the most halibut caught, and the stern-wheeler *K.L. Ames* that operated on the Copper River in Alaska. During World War I, the company constructed several steel ships for the war effort.

He became a millionaire as the owner of J. F. Duthie & Co. and acquired major ore mines in British Columbia. He was a prominent member of the Rainier Club in Seattle. Unfortunately, his only son Wallace died at the age of twenty-three, and there was no one left to carry on the family business. Duthie passed away in Medina, Washington, on April 25, 1945, at the age of seventy.

Thomas Lawson, the "copper king," made and lost millions and had built the *Dreamer*, considered to be the most luxurious yacht in the world with all its intricate machinery designed by T. Sch. Poekel. The man who tried to enter his own yacht in the trials for America's Cup but was turned down by the New York Yacht Club wrote his own story about it and had it circulated at his own cost. He created a magnificent estate named Dreamwold only to see it come under the auctioneer's gavel. The man who carried emeralds and diamonds in his suit pocket and who always kept a spare $7,000 in his wallet died in a Boston hospital on February 8, 1925, at age sixty-eight. His grandson Thomas Lawson McCall would go West and enter politics serving as Oregon's governor from 1963 to 1975.

Frederick Mayfield Hoyt whose *Syce* beat the *Vencedor* and tarnished its reputation on the East Coast continued in yachting and lived in Stamford, Connecticut, and Marblehead, Massachusetts. After spending several years in Europe, Hoyt and his wife Jane booked first class passage to New York on the *Titanic* leaving on April 10, 1912, from Southampton, England. According to reports, the ship's Senior Surgeon Dr. William Francis Norman O'Loughlin went to the Hoyts' cabin (No. C-93) and told them to prepare to leave in the lifeboats. The doctor assisted Mrs. Hoyt into a lifeboat. After his wife's lifeboat was launched, Mr. Hoyt jumped into the icy waters and was pulled into it by the occupants. The Hoyts were rescued by the *Carpathia* and arrived back in New York on April 18. Dr. O'Loughlin went down with the ship.

Kaiser Wilhelm II, whose threat to build a contender for America's Cup prompted T. Sch. Poekel and some Chicago yachtsmen to say that they could do the same in Racine, was out sailing on *Meteor* on June 28, 1914, when someone threw onboard a cigarette pack with a message inside saying that Archduke Ferdinand had been assassinated which resulted in the beginning of World War I and the end of the Edwardian era and the golden years of yachting. He would be the last emperor of Germany.

Fred W. Morgan who was the original owner of the *Pathfinder* took his invention of a bicycle tire into the automotive area and would see his company become the largest tire manufacturer in the world, Uniroyal. He died on May 27, 1921, at age sixty-seven. Besides leaving four children, he left his wife, Mary Wright Morgan, the daughter of his former partner.

Darwin Almy, another unsung Herreshoff hero, inventor of the Almy water tube boiler—an invention that revolutionized steam yachts—died on March 9, 1916, at age sixty-eight. He left behind three children as well as his third wife.

Samuel Curtis Johnson, who took the parquet floor division of the Racine Hardware Manufacturing Company and went into a different direction from the RBMCO, saw his floor business flourish and then as an accommodation to his customers developed a cleaning wax in his bathtub and turned his company into Johnson Wax. The company would grow and produce such iconic products as Raid, Pledge, Ziploc, and Shout. In 2017, the company, still family-owned, had over 13,000 employees worldwide with gross sales of over $10 billion.

William Hale Thompson, known to Chicagoans as "Big Bill," whose schooner *Valmore*, a yacht that won the Mackinac race three times in a row and often raced *Vencedor*, would enter politics and was elected Chicago's forty-first and forty-third mayors serving from 1915 to 1923 and 1927 to 1931. His reputation would be tarnished when it surfaced that he had accepted a $150,000 campaign contribution from Al Capone and then after his death in 1944, when $1.8 million in cash and bonds were found in his safe deposit box.

George Warrington, who was the consulting engineer for the machinery on the *Pathfinder*, was appointed by President Theodore Roosevelt as under-secretary of Commerce in 1902, and later served as director of Lighthouses and Lightships until his death in 1925.

Aimee Gillig, having married and divorced Commodore Gillig, the second owner of *Vencedor*, continued her Bohemian lifestyle and married at least three more times—twice being to Russian princes. When asked if Prince Galitzine was her fifth or sixth husband, she replied: "The prince is my twelvth [*sic*] husband if I include in my matrimonial list seven oriental husbands, not registered under the laws of the Occident." She died on February 7, 1941, at age seventy-eight.

In 1898, Howard Gould, still infatuated with actresses, married actress Catherine Clemmons, the former mistress of Buffalo Bill Cody. Cody, incidentally, was another member of the Craft that is a Freemason. Cody backed her in several productions although she lacked any theatrical ability. Gould spent his honeymoon on his steamer yacht *Niagara* and, because of Jay's Gould's will, he forfeited half his inheritance for marrying someone who the majority of his brothers and sisters didn't approve of. This amounted to $5 million. When she wasn't on stage, Mrs. Gould was most of the time inebriated, starting to drink cocktails before breakfast.

Gould would later divorce Catherine on the grounds she was still seeing Cody. He, however, had to pay her a record-setting $36,000 in alimony.

Edward C. Berriman, the cigar manufacturer who as the first owner of *Vencedor*, had challenged the Canadians to an international race on the Great Lakes, lived in Chicago for forty-six years before he split his time spending winters near his factories in Tampa, Florida, and summers in Delavan Lake, Wisconsin. He died from pneumonia while on a business trip to Cincinnati on August 2, 1925. His obituary in the *Chicago Tribune* stated that he was owner of the *Vencedor* and a personal friend of Sir Thomas Lipton.[1]

Robinson Locke, the president of the International Racing Committee that ran the races between *Vencedor* and *Canada* in 1896 and as a member of the Toledo Chamber of Commerce had campaigned for the races to be in Toledo, died in 1920. Later that same year the Robinson Locke Lodge No. 659 was instituted and consecrated in West Toledo honoring Locke who had been a thirty-third degree Mason.

Samuel Untermyer, the second owner of the swift steamer *Scud* with the Poekel-designed engine, would have a stellar legal career at the firm of Guggenheimer, Untermyer & Marshall for forty-five years. He was a strong Democrat and an ardent Zionist. Representing a former love interest of President Woodrow Wilson, he presented the president with damaging correspondence and his client's request for $40,000 to help her stepson. When the president said he didn't have the money, Untermyer said he would personally give it to his client with the stipulation that he would be consulted if a vacancy arose on the Supreme Court. When one did, Untermyer recommended Louis D. Brandeis, who Wilson appointed as the first Jewish jurist on the court. Most of the land from Untermyer's palatial estate Greystone in Yonkers, New York, was bequeathed to the State of New York and is now known as Untermyer Park.

The Lincoln Park Yacht Club that challenged the Royal Canadian Yacht Club in 1896, for an international race on the Great Lakes, continued as a yacht club until 1920, when it merged with the Chicago Yacht Club. Although it lost its name, its blue and white flag lives on as the burgee of the Chicago Yacht Club.

There have been twenty-three Canada Cup competitions with the United States winning fourteen and the Canadians twelve. It is now a biannual contest but the winner still receives a plaque on that great Tiffany silver trophy with the lion and the eagle intertwined. The next race of Canada's Cup is scheduled for September of 2020.

Æmilius Jarvis kept on winning yachting races and horse-jumping events. However, he would only win the Canada's Cup one more time—in 1901. He would lose in 1899, 1903, and 1907. During his fantastic sailing career, the "Skippadore" would serve seven times as the commodore of the Royal Canadian Yacht Club. He would also gain fame as Canada's leading foxhound rider.

However, he suffered a major setback in 1924, when he was indicted and convicted of conspiracy to defraud the government in a bond trading case. He ended up having to pay a fine of $200,000 (originally $600,000.00) and served six months in a Canadian jail. One visitor he had in jail was Sir Thomas Lipton.

Jarvis would spend the rest of his life trying to clear his good name and remained active as a sportsman. At age seventy-nine, he broke his collarbone when the horse he was jumping fell on him. Upon turning eighty, he quipped that he was not yet old enough to take up golf.

On the eve of his eightieth birthday, in a question and answer colloquy with Gordon Sinclair of the *Toronto Evening Telegram*, Jarvis gave his retrospective views on his spectacular life. Asked about good health, Jarvis stated that it came from your parents and also its important to keep active since its "far better to wear out than rust out." Asked what triumph in sports gave him the most satisfaction, he said, "The winning of Canada's Cup near Toledo in 1896." Jarvis died on December 19, 1940, in Toronto.

Freemasons and other fraternal organizations like the Odd Fellows would never again see the rise in their numbers as they did during the golden age of yachting. In 2017, there were less than 1 million Freemasons in the United States.

The Poekel-designed *Pathfinder* changed hands many times. During Prohibition, it was used to catch rum-runners on the Great Lakes and in the Atlantic. In 1940, the Canadian government used it as a naval training ship. After World War II, it went back into private hands.

Its last owner attempted to sell it and gave a deadline of November 16, 1946, for all prospective buyers. When there were no offers and with restoration impossible, instead of scrapping the huge steel steamer, he had it towed into Georgian Bay, where he opened the sea cocks and allowed it to find a final resting place at the bottom of Penetanguishene Harbor. There it remains to this day and is often visible from the air. It serves as an everlasting monument to one unsung Herreshoff hero.

GLOSSARY OF NAUTICAL TERMS

AFT: Toward, at, or near the stern.

AHOY: Seaman's call to attract attention.

BALLAST: Weight at the bottom or the lower portion of the boat to give it stability and/or to provide satisfactory fore-and-aft trim. Ballast can be placed inside the hull of the boat or externally in a keel.

BEAM: Greatest width of a vessel.

BEAT: To sail toward the direction from which the wind blows by making a series of tacks.

BOAT: A small craft carried aboard a ship.

BOW: The forward-most or front part of the vessel.

BOWSPIRIT: A spar projecting from the bow used as an anchor for the forestay and other rigging.

BROAD REACH: Sailing with the apparent wind broad on the beam (quarter).

BULKHEAD: Below deck partition separating one part of a boat's interior from another.

BUOY: An anchored float marking a position.

BURGEE: A small rectangular flag flown from the top of the mast, serving as an indicator of apparent wind. Usually a term for the flag or pennant of a yacht or boat club.

CATAMARAN: A twin-hulled boat consisting of two narrow hulls connected by two beams and a trampoline or rigid deck. The word is believed to come from Tamil (South Indian) *kattamaram*.

CAT BOAT: A boat with one mast and one sail.

CAULK: To make watertight by driving in any or various appropriate materials.

CENTERBOARD: A sailboat keel that can be raised or lowered; either the only keel or a supplement to a fixed keel.

CLIPPER: The famed and fast square-rigged ships, of very fine lines, of the mid-to-late nineteenth century. Term used before this time was the BALTIMORE CLIPPER.

COCKPIT: The working area, usually toward the stern of a boat, from which the boat is steered.

CORINTHIAN: An amateur sailor.

CRAFT: All ships and boats, large and small.

CREW: Ship's people other than captain and officers.

CUTTER: Small boat, similar to a sloop but with the mast further aft providing a larger area for headsails, normally sets two headsails, a forestay sail, and a jib.

DINGHY: A small boat, powered by sail, oars, or an outboard motor; usually designed to be used by one or two people; often carried on a larger boat.

DOCK: The planked floor of a vessel resting upon the beams.

DRY DOCK: A narrow basin or vessel used for the construction, maintenance, and repairs of ships, boats, and other watercraft that can be flooded to allow a boat to be flooded in and then drained to allow that load to come to rest on a dry platform.

FIN KEEL: A keel that looks like an inverted fish fin.

FLEET: A large body or group of ships.

FLOTILLA: A small group of ships.

FORE: Located in front of the vessel.

FOREMAST: Forward mast in all vessels with more than one mast, except yawls and ketches.

FURL: To roll a sail up snugly on a boom and secure it; also called "furling."

GALLEY: A boat's kitchen.

GARBOARD: The strake next to a ship's keel.

GROMMET: A ring made of line, cloth, or metal sewed into a sail.

GYBINH: Turning the stern of a boat through the wind; opposite of tacking.

HALYARD or HALLIARD: A rope or wire that is used to hoist a sail (or to hoist a flag or other signal).

HEEL or HEELING: A sideward inclination normally of a temporary duration.

HELM: Where you steer the boat. Usually this is a big wheel, but on smaller boats it can be a tiller, which is basically a long wooden stick.

HELMSMAN: The person who steers the boat.

HOIST: To raise a sail or flag.

HULL: The main body of a boat.

JIB: A triangular headsail (a sail set in front of the forward mast). Unlike the mainsail, it does not have a boom.

KEEL: The keel is a large, heavy fin on the bottom of the boat that sticks down into the water. It prevents sideway drift and provides stability.

KETCH: A two-mastered yacht with the aft mast (mizzen mast) smaller than the main mast and stepped ahead of the rudder post.

KNOT: The unit of speed at sea, defined as one nautical mile per hour.

LANYARD: The line by which a sailing ship's shroud is secured.

LEECH: The trailing (back) edge of all sails.

LEEWARD: Direction away from the wind; opposite of windward.

LENGTH OVERALL (L.O.A.): The maximum length of the hull from the forward-most point on the stem to the extreme after end.

LIST: The tipping of a vessel.

LUFF: The leading (fore) edge of all sails.

MAINSAIL: The big triangular sail just aft of the sailboat's mast. As the name suggests, this is the boat's largest and most important sail running along its bottom age, the mainsail has a thick pole called the boom.

MAINSHEET: The rope attached to the boom and used to trim (or adjust) the mainsail.

MAST: A vertical pole to which sails are attached.

MIZZEN: The aftermost mast and its sails and gear.

PORT: The left-hand side of a boat, when looking forward.

QUARTERMASTER: A petty officer, who attends the helm, binnacle, and similar bridge duties.

READY ABOUT: Order to "stand by" in preparation to taking the vessel; also called "about."

REEF: A group of rocks or coral generally at a depth shallow enough to present a hazard to navigation.

REGATTA: An occasion of boat racing.

RIGGING: All the lines that secure and control the sails, masts, and spars on a sailboat.

RUDDER: A moveable underwater blade that is used to steer the boat, controlled by a tiller or wheel.

SCHOONER: A sailing vessel with two or more masts with the tallest mast stepped aft.

SEACOCK: A valve in the hull of a vessel, below the waterline, for admitting seawater or pumping out bilge water.

SHROUDS: The wire ropes on either side of the mast, which support it sideways.

SKIPPER: A nickname for the captain.

SLOOP: A small- to mid-sized sailboat larger than a dinghy, with one mast bearing a mainsail and head sail and located farther forward than the mast of a cutter.

SPARS: Masts, booms, gaffs, yards, and poles used in sailboat rigging.

SPINNAKER: A large three-cornered sail used in downwind sailing.

SPOON BOW: An overhanging bow of a ship whose underside is somewhat spoon-shaped.

SQUALL: A sudden and often violent wind, sometime with rain and snow, and of short duration.

STAND BY: A command, to be prepared to act at once.

STARBOARD: The right-hand side of a boat, when looking forward.

STAYS: Rigging used to support the masts in a fore-and-aft direction.

STAYSAIL: A sail usually triangular, set on a centerline stay.

STEAMER: A ship propelled by steam.

STEM: The bow or prow of a boat.

STERN: Rear end of the boat.

STINKPOT: Term for a powerboat.

TACK: (1) To change direction; (2) the course you are on relative to the wind.

TACKING: Turning the bow of a boat through the wind so that the boat turns from one tack to the other.

TENDER: A vessel used to provide transportation services for people and supplies to and from shore for a larger vessel.

TILLER: A lever attached to the rudder post that is used to steer the vessel.

TIME ALLOWANCE: The amount of time a boat must allow another. In theory, if the allowance is correct, all the competing boats will be exactly equal.

TON: A measure of weight ashore and a measure of capacity on a vessel.

TONNAGE: A measure of a vessel's interior volume. The weight of displacement of a ship.

TOPSAIL: Second sail above the deck.

TRIM: (1) Way in which a vessel floats. (2) Setting and adjusting the sails and rigging.

TRYSAIL: A small triangular fore-and-aft sail, strong replacement for a cruiser's mainsail that is used in severe weather; also known as Spencer's sail on storm trysail.

UPWIND: All courses that are closer to the wind (heading more directly into it) than a beam reach are called upwind courses; opposite of off-wind or downwind.

WATERLINE: (1) Any of the several lines which may be marked on the outside of a vessel and which correspond with the water's surface when the vessel is floating evenly. (2) Intersection of the hull and the water's surface.

WHEEL: Device used for steering a boat when sailing.

WINCH: Device to provide mechanical advantage for pulling in sheets and halyards.

WINDWARD: Toward the wind. "Sailing to windward" means sailing toward the wind.

YACHT: A sailboat or powerboat used for pleasure, not a working boat.

YACHTING: The use of recreational boats and ships called yachts for sporting purposes. Originally from the Dutch word *jacht* ("hunt").

YAWL: A two-mastered yacht with the mizzen mast stepped aft of the rudderpost. A ketch is similar but its mizzen mast is forward of the rudderpost.

APPENDIX I

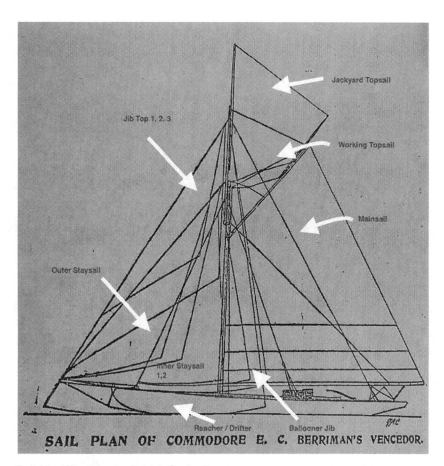

Sail identifications by Patrick Gavin-Byrnes.

APPENDIX 2

EVOLUTION OF A YACHT

Construction of a Modern Craft as Shown by Pathfinder

It is a feat Requiring Infinite Care and Nicety of Calculation –
How Displacement, Speed, Equilibrium, and Arrangement Are Determined-
Real Work of Building – The Motive Power- Description of F.W. Morgan's New Yacht

The publication of an item in the daily press announcing that Mr. Blank has ordered a first-class steam yacht, to cost ____, to make ____ speed, and to be finished at a certain date is about all the pubic knows of one of the most difficult problems in designing and engineering that confronts the modern shipbuilder.

The first thing to be done is to determine the size or length of the vessel, the amount of room needed by the owner, and the speed desired. The designer is then left to figure the beam or width of the yacht, the draft, the amount of room necessary to accommodate the boilers and machinery, and the requisite number of officers and crew to sail the boat and handle the machinery. It is not always an easy task to harmonize these conflicting elements.

When F.W. Morgan gave the order for building the Pathfinder he gave the designer every opportunity to build the finest yacht ever seen on the great lakes. Mr. T.S. Poekel, in designing the Pathfinder, found that it would be necessary to build a vessel about 140 feet long by 18 feet 3 inches beam, with a draft of 8 feet. These dimensions were made necessary to give the owner the requisite amount of cabin room for his family and guests, and to allow sufficient room for machinery and accommodations for officers and crew.

This much having been decided upon, Mr. Poekel set to work in earnest for the plans of the yacht. The first thing made was an estimate of he size and weight of the proper amount of boiler and machinery needed to drive the vessel at the required speed of eighteen miles an hour. This was done, and the results were entered in a special book, used only for the work on Pathfinder. Next, the midship section of the vessel was designed. In figuring out this part of the boat the following points were kept in view:

The smallest amount of wetted surface, or the portion under water, that will give the amount of displacement required to carry the weight of a vessel, machinery, crew, passengers, and stores is the best for speed. The largest amount of wetted surface of the Pathfinder is show by the lines BBB. When it is remembered that every inch of wetted surface of a yacht means a certain amount of friction, which must be overcome by the use of steam, the desirability of decreasing the wetted surface is readily seen.

Determining the Power.

The next calculation made was the size and pitch of the propeller required to drive the boat at desired speed. This is usually determined by the proportion of the propeller to the amount of wetted surface or the coefficient of the midship section. There is no fixed rule for this, each designer using his own ideas and the results of his long experience.

In calculating this point the speed of the engine was first determined. Then came the size and pitch of the propeller. By the pitch it meant the theoretical distance which each turn of the propeller will drive the boat ahead. The diameter of the propeller is usually about two-thirds of the pitch. The Pathfinder propeller having a pitch of ninety-four inches, the diameter is sixty-six inches. With the engine running at a speed of 300 revolutions a minute the speed of the yacht should be 300 times ninety-four inches a minute, less 15 per cent allowance for slip.

After these points were determined the rest of the hull was designed with a view to parting the water at the bow and allowing it to fall gradually into place at the stern, thus gradually filling up the hole made by the passage of the boat through the water in such a way as not to drag the water after the vessel. This gives the propeller a chance to revolve in solid instead of dead r slack water and makes a great difference in the speed of the vessel.

The next move was the building of the model, made on a scale of one-half inch to the foot. It represented one-half of the yacht, thus:

How Displacement is Computed.

The model was made to fit the working drawings or design of the yacht, and was repeatedly tested and measured to insure its accuracy. When the model was completed it was varnished and polished and then immersed in a tank of water with a carefully constructed overflow pipe. When the model was immersed to the designed water line the amount of liquid that had been displaced by it and had overflowed into a receptacle was carefully weighed. This weight was figured out in proportion to the scale of the model, and it gave the displacement of the vessel in cubic feet, Dividing this result by thirty-five for salt water and thirty-six for fresh the weight of the vessel in tons was found.

Locating Center of Gravity.

The next thing done was to exactly locate the center of gravity of the boat, or to find exactly the distance from the stem to the center of the weight of the vessel. This was accomplished by dividing the length of the boat into fifteen or twenty sections by the use of vertical lines from keel to water line. The curves of the boat at each line or section were taken off by special instruments and the are of each section calculated. These areas having been multiplied by their distances from the stem, then all added together and divided by the sum of the area of all the sections, gave as a result the distance of the center of gravity from the stem. Similar methods were used to find the center of gravity of the machinery, cabins, and other parts.

The centers of gravity of the boat, machinery, cabins, and other portions of the whole must be in the same point in order to fulfill the determined conditions of water line and displacement. When they had all been adjusted to the same point the distance of the point below water line was found by similar processes.

TO FIND CENTER OF GRAVITY

M – Metacentre.
F – Center of Gravity of Ship.AZA1Q
E – Center of buoyancy below water line.
E 2 – Center of buoyancy of submerged portion.
F K – Length of righting lever.

Balance Nicely Determined.

The heeling angle of the boat was next ascertained. To do this the model was heeled 15 degrees and the center of gravity determined. Then the model was heeled 25 degrees, and the process repeated until a number of angles have been covered. The different centers of gravity found by these manipulations had vertical lines drawn up from each until all intersected the center line of the model. This point where they all cross the center line is called the "metacenter." If it is too high, it means the boat will recover itself after a roll too quickly, making it liable to heavy strains in a seaway. If the metacenter is too low, then the boat will be top-heavy, will recover itself too slowly in rolling, and will be liable to capsize. This last defect has been strickenly shown in several foreign torpedo boats.

After the model and drawings were found to agree in every particular the lines of the sections were taken from the model by special instruments and transferred to the book. They were then enlarged to the full size of the ship, and laid out on two boards, those forward on one board and those aft on the other. Then came preparations for framing.

The distances between ribs, r the centers of the frames, are governed by Lloyd's insurance rules. The stem, stern-piece, and keel can each be made in one piece. The first two are usually made of forged steel. The stern-post is perforated by the hole through which passes the propeller shaft.

How the Frame Is Made.

The pieces of angle steel to be made into frames were heated in a long furnace and were bent on a heavy grating or floor. A full-sized wooden pattern or templet was laid on the floor and its outline marked in chalk. Then iron pins were placed at the angles of the outline and the hot bars for the frame were bent on them until the shape of the pattern was conformed with.

When the frames were completed the keel was laid and the ribs were joined to it. All rivet-holes were punched beforehand from the mold. From the wooden patterns the exact location of each rivet-hole was shown. Then the plates were rolled cold to fit the exact size, the edges trimmed, and the rivet-holes pinched to fit the model or pattern. The plate was then bolted into position., and when a number were in place all were riveted securely.

Next in order the deck beams were bent to the curve of the deck and riveted to the frames and gussets.

The deck was next laid, the planks being fastened to the deck beams by screws which passed through holes in the beams and were imbedded in the under part of the planks. The deck was then calked with oakum and the cracks filled with marine glue.

Machinery and Boilers.

Next in order came the cabin floors, which were laid on angle irons placed for that purpose. After them coal bunkers and steel bulkheads were put into place to make a stiff and water tight job.

While this work was under way the machinery and boilers were approaching completion in another part of the shop.

While the plating was in progress, the workmen built a bed of steel angle plates in the bottom of the ship to hold the boiler and engine, placing them so as to prevent vibration. Then the boiler and machinery were placed into position., Auxiliary machinery consists of an air pump, circulating pump to force cold water through the condenser, boiler feed pumps, pumps to supply the lavatories and bath rooms, and the electric light plant.

The deck-houses were by this time finished by a different set of men, and were next placed into position where they were securely bolted. The deck-houses and interior furnishings were made of mahogany and were polished like pieces of furniture.

The bulkheads, or partitions, the after cabins, and state rooms, the cabinets, desks, lockers, lavatories, and a multitude of smaller fittings were then placed in their proper positions.

At the same time, the outside of the yacht was being painted, the bottom finished in copper paint to prevent the vessel from rusting and to stop the growth of moss. The propeller and rudder being placed in position, the yacht was ready for launching.

The ceremony for launching, of course, included the usual array of interested spectators. The young woman broke the decorated bottle of champagne over the stem of the vessel as it glided into the water. A lunch followed, during which every one drank to each other's health. The masts were then stepped, the rigging set up, sails bent, and after a general overhauling, the yacht was ready of its trial trip.

Pathfinder is a Success.

The Pathfinder has shown that it will do everything that its designer, Theodore S. Poekel (sic), claimed for it. Before the yacht was launched it was painted white down to the designed water-line, and below that copper paint was used. When it was in the water, and stores and coal on board, it floated at exactly the water-line the designer had drawn, thus proving his calculations correct.

Principle of Triple Expansion.

The principle on which the triple expansion engine and condenser, such as furnish the power for the Pathfinder, work s as follows: The steam enters the high pressure cylinder at a pressure of 250 pounds to the square inch. After it has moved the first piston the valves admit it to the second cylinder, where it expands still more and moves the second piston. The low pressure is divided in two cylinders in order to balance the engine more perfectly. From the low pressure cylinder the steam passes through large copper pipes to the condenser. When there it comes in contact with a great number of small brass tubes, through which a powerful pump is forcing cold water. This cools the steam so that it turns into water. The water it forms is then pimped into a hot well or tank, from which it goes into the boiler, to be used over and over again.

When the steam leaves the low pressure cylinder and enters the condenser it takes 1,500 cubic inches of steam to condense into one cubic inch of water. An air pump is constantly at work taking this small amount of water out of the condenser, thus helping to create a vacuum. The rarefaction materially helps the efficiency of the low pressure cylinder.

The engine of the Pathfinder is of the type known as the triple expansion, with four cylinders. It makes 300 revolutions a minute when running, but the entire engine shaft, and cranks are so evenly and well distributed as to weight that no motion is felt on deck even at full speed. There is a special condenser, an air pump, automatic oiling devices, and every modern feature in the way of accessories.

The boiler is also of the most approved and latest type. It is of the tubular type and occupies a floor space of ten feet square. Owing to its modern construction it is practically non-explosive, since if tube bursts the damage done in such an event will be trifling.

The subsequent performances of the yacht have more than satisfied Mr. Morgan. On a recent trip from Holland, Mich., the Pathfinder, carrying several members of the Holland Society and their guests, made the return trip averaging eighteen miles an hour for the entire distance. At that time the yacht had been in commission less than a week and the machinery was new and stiff.

Yacht of Fine Appearance.

In appearance the yacht resembles a small cruiser or a large torpedo boat. It is the first strictly modern steam yacht built on Lake Michigan. The entire forward portion of the vessel below is given up to the galley, or ship's kitchen, and to the accommodations of the crew. The Captain, engineers and officers are provided with staterooms and a messroom. The rest of the crew have every comfort that experiences can suggest.

On deck, forward of the engine and boiler rooms, is the main deck saloon. The top of this house is used as a bridge, from which the boat is navigated. Patent steering wheel and gear, engine-room, telegraph, and signals, chart stands, search light and other necessary apparatus complete the equipment of the department.

Abaft the engine-room are two large staterooms for guests. Behind these rooms is located the main saloon or sitting-room. It is sixteen feet long by the full width of the yacht. Numerous cabinets, writing desks, and lockers line the walls and fill the corners of the room. On either side is a long divan upholstered in Russian leather. The floor is covered with a velvet carpet.

Aft of this room is a stairway, which reaches the deck above through the deck house. On the starboard side is a bath-room, while the port side is occupied by a single state-room. A passageway leads aft between these rooms to the owner's quarters, which consists of a large room extending the full room width of the boat, and two state-rooms for the children. All these rooms are fitted with every luxury and convenience. In hot weather they are cooled with electric fans, run at night by a storage battery, which is powerful enough to run fifty incandescent lights eight hours.

The usual equipment of lifeboats and a naphtha launch is provided, together with an ample supply of life preservers. It is probable that Mr. Morgan will take a cruise in salt water in the Pathfinder next season.

Notes

Chapter 1
1 *The Chicago Chronicle*, July 8, 1895, p. 8.
2 *The Compass* of the Rochester Yacht Club, May 1924, p. 4.
3 *The Evening Star*, January 28, 1896, p. 4.
4 *Chicago Daily Tribune*, January 26, 1896, p. 7.
5 *Detroit Free Press*, February 29, 1896, p. 6.
6 *Chicago Daily Tribune*, February 27, 1896, p. 8.
7 *Forest and Stream*, February 28, 1896.
8 *Chicago Times Herald*, February 28, 1896.

Chapter 2
1 *Racine Daily Times*, August 22, 1896.
2 Gunther, *Boat Manufacturing in Racine*, p, 15.
3 *Chicago Daily Tribune*, March 29, 1896, p. 49.
4 *The New York Times*, January 21, 1894, p. 20.
5 *Chicago Tribune*, February 10, 1896.
6 *The Globe Magazine*, February 28, 1896, p. 6.
7 *The Chicago Chronicle*, December 3, 1895, p. 8.
8 Herreshoff, L. Francis. *Capt. Nat Herreshoff: The Wizard of Bristol*, p. 139.
9 *Buffalo Morning Express*, February 28, 1896, p. 10.
10 *Detroit Free Press*, February 18, 1986, p. 6.
11 *Racine Daily Journal*, March 10, 1896.
12 *Chicago Daily News*, March 22, 1896, p. 4.
13 *Calgary Herald*, March 17, 1896, p. 3.
14 *The New York Times*, March 22, 1896, p. 6.
15 *Portland Press Herald Maine Sunday Telegram*, June 24, 2007, p. 1.
16 *New York Sun*, July 27, 1896, p. 9.
17 *Detroit Free Press*, April 13, 1896, p. 8.
18 *Racine Daily Times*, August 22, 1896.
19 *The Saint Paul Globe*, June 21, 1896, p. 8.
20 *Chicago Tribune*, June 11, 1896, p. 8.
21 Wheeler, Stephen E. "The Racine Boat Manufacturing Company," September, 2001, Vol. 46, No. 3.
22 *Racine Daily Journal*, May 25, 1897.
23 Larkin, Larry. *Full Speed Ahead*, pp. 57–58.

Chapter 4
1 *Harper's Weekly*, 1899, p. 846.
2 D'Antonio, Michael. *A Full Cup*, p. 160.
3 *The New York Times*, June 26, 1876, p. 4.
4 Carter III, Samuel, *The Boatbuilders of Bristol*, p. 73.
5 Nathanael Herreshoff diary, January 6, 1889, Manuscripts Collection, G. W. Blunt Library, Mystic Seaport Museum.
6 *The New York Times*, September 12, 1891, p. 1.
7 Whyte, Kenneth, *The Uncrowned King*, p. 229.
8 Samuels, Peggy and Harold, *The Collected Writings of Frederic Remington*, p. 359.
9 Herreshoff, Francis book, pp. 150–151.
10 Dickie, John, *The Craft: How the Freemasons Made the Modern World*, p. 344.
11 Carter, Samuel II. *The Boatbuilders of Bristol*, p. 71.
12 Herreshoff, Francis L., *Capt. Nat Herreshoff: The Wizard of Bristol*, p. 321.
13 Howland III, Llewellyn, *No Ordinary Being*, p. 26.
14 Stephens, William Picard, *Traditions and Memories of American Yachting*, p. 221.
46 Brooks, Jerome E., *The $30,000,000.00 Cup*, p. 112.
16 Burnett, Constance Buel, *Let the Best Boat Win: The Story of America's Greatest Yacht Designer*, pp. 192–194.
17 Herreshoff, Nathanael G., *Recollections and Other Writings*, p. 58.
18 *The New York Times*, September 16, 1893, p. 2.
19 Stephens, William P., *Traditions and Memories of American Yachting*, p. 145.
20 *The New York Times*, August 19.1903, p. 2.
21 Herreshoff, Nathanael G., *Recollections and Other Writings*, p. 109.
22 Lawson, Thomas W. and Winfield M. Thompson, *The Lawson History of America's Cup*, p. 29.
23 Brady, Laurence, *The Man Who Challenged America*, p. 116.
24 *The New York Times*, October 10, 1893, p. 1.
25 Herreshoff, Francis L., *The Golden Age of Yachting*, p. 106.
26 *Outing Magazine*, September, 1903, p. 624.
58 Brooks, Jerome E., *The $30,000,000.00 Cup*, p. 124.
28 Carter III, Samuel, *The Boatbuilders of Bristol*.
29 *Glasgow Herald*, September 9, 1895, p. 7.
30 Holm, Ed, *Yachting's Golden Age: 1880–1905*, p. 152.
31 Bagley, Clarence B., *History of Seattle*, pp. 140–141.
32 *Boston Herald*, June 30, 1895, p. 1.
33 *Boston Daily Globe*, November 24, 1895, p. 27.

Chapter 5
1 Jarvis, Edward and Æmilius, Robert, *Æmilius: The Last Viking*, Royal Canadian Yacht Club, 2014, p. 1.
2 Royal Canadian Yacht Club, Hall of Fame, Æmilius Jarvis.

Chapter 6
1 Tuchman, Barbara W., *The Proud Tower*, pp. 122–123.
2 *Boston Daily Globe*, November 24, 1895, p. 27.
3 *Bristol Phoenix*, December 17, 1895.
4 *Bristol Phoenix*, May 26, 1896, p. 2.

Chapter 7
1 *Outing Magazine*, May, 1899, p. 143.
2 *Chicago Daily Tribune*, July 12, 1896, p. 31.
3 *Toronto Evening Star*, May 16, 1896, p. 4.

Chapter 8
1 *The New York Sun*, August 22, 1896, p. 8.
2 *Detroit Free Press*, March 28, 1896, p. 6.
3 *Cleveland Leader*, May 11, 1896, p. 3.
4 *Outing Magazine*, September, 1896, p. 124.
5 *Chicago Daily Tribune*, May 12, 1896, p. 5.

Chapter 9
1 Townsend, Robert B., "When Canvas Was King," *Scuttlebutt Sailing News*, August 23, 2011.
2 Ibid.
3 *Toronto Evening Star*, July 27, 1896, p. 1.
4 *Toronto Evening Star*, July 28, 1896, p. 2.
5 Annals of Royal Canadian Yacht Club, p. 117.
6 Jarvis, Edward and Æmilius, Robert, *Æmilius: The Last Viking*, Royal Canadian Yacht Club, p. 201.
7 *The New York Sun*, August 22, 1896, p. 8.

Chapter 10
1 *Chicago Daily Tribune*, July 3, 1896, p. 8.
2 Ibid.
3 *Chicago Tribune*, July 12, 1896, p. 11.
4 *Racine Evening Times*, July 13, 1896.
5 *Rochester Democrat and Chronicle*, August 11, 1896, p. 11.
6 *Racine Journal*, August 6, 1896, p. 2.
7 *The New York Times*, August 14, 1896, p. 6.
8 *Toronto Evening Star*, August 14, 1896, p. 3.
9 *The New York Sun*, August 15, 1896, p. 4.
10 *Cleveland Leader*, August 14, 1896.

Chapter 11

1 *Detroit Free Press*, August 3, 1896, p. 8.
2 *Chicago Daily Tribune*, August 17, 1896, p. 8.
3 *Chicago Daily Tribune*, August 19, 1896, p. 8.
4 *Detroit Free Press*, August 24, 1896, p. 8.
5 *The New York Sun*, August 22, 1896, p. 8.
6 *The Saint Paul Globe*, August 22, 1896, p. 5.
7 *The Chicago Chronicle*, August 24, 1896, p. 4.
8 *The New York Sun*, August 23, 1896, p. 8.
9 *Plain Dealer* (Cleveland), August 24, 1896, p. 3.
10 *The Chicago Chronicle*, August 24, 1896, p. 4.
11 *Detroit Free Press*, August 24, 1896, p. 8.

Chapter 12

1 *The Nashville American*, August 25, 1896, p. 3.
2 *The New York Sun*, August 24, 1896, p. 8.
3 *Toronto Evening Star*, August 24, 1896, p. 1.
4 *Chicago Tribune*, August 25, 1896, p. 3.
5 *Daily Inter Ocean News*, August 25, 1896, p. 5.
6 *The World*, August 24, 1896, p. 8.
7 *Chicago* Tribune, August 25, 1896, p. 3.

Chapter 14

1 *The New York Times*, August 27, 1896, p. 9.

Chapter 15

1 *The Evening Star*, August 27, 1896, p. 1.
2 *Chicago Tribune*, August 28, 1896, p. 8.
3 *Chicago Tribune*, August 31, 1896, p. 8.
4 *Evening Star*, August 27, 1896, p. 2.
5 *New York-Tribune*, August 27, 1896, p. 9.
6 *Racine Daily Tribune*, August 29, 1896.
7 *Detroit Free Press*, August 29, 1896, p. 2.
8 *Racine Evening Tribune*, September 9, 1896.
9 *Forest and Stream*, September 12, 1896, Vol. XLVII, No. 11, p. 213.

Chapter 16

1 Plin Dealer (Cleveland), April 1, 1901, p. 3.
2 *The New York Times*, October 7, 1896, p. 3.
3 *The Globe*, October 10, 1896, p. 26.
4 *Detroit Free Press*, November 18, 1897, p. 6.
5 *The New York Sun*, December 27, 1986, p. 7.

Chapter 17
1 *The New York Times*, March 31, 1897, p. 5.
2 *Forest and Steam*, April 10, 1897, p. 294.
3 RRDV, 4–2–1897.
4 *Detroit Free Press*, May 6, 1897, p. 6.
5 *The New York Times*, February 21, 1896, p. 6.
6 *The New York Times*, May 30, 1897, p. 6.
7 *Chicago Tribune*, May 20, 1897, p. 12.
8 *The Journal Times (Racine)*, June 5, 1897, p. 1.
9 *Racine Daily Journal*, June 5, 1897, p. 1.
10 *The New York Times*, July 18, 1897, p. 4.
11 *Chicago Tribune*, July 290, 1897, p. 5.
12 *The New York Times*, September 5, 1897, p. 3.
13 *The New York Times*, September 26, 1897. p. 6.
14 *The New York Times*, March 5 1898, p. 2.
15 *New York Daily Tribune*, December 12, 1897, p. 3.
16 *Boston Daily Globe*, August 11, 1902, p. 1.
17 Howland, Llewellyn III, *No Ordinary Being*, p. 46.
18 Ibid.
19 Letter to C. Oliver Iselin from John Duthie, January 17, 1899, Mystic Seaport Museum, In. Coll. 85, Box 1, Fol. 7.
20 *Rochester Democrat and Chronicle*, June 17, 1900, p. 19.
21 *Chicago Tribune*, October 29, 1900, p. 5.
22 *Boston Globe*, December 23, 1900, p. 26.
23 *New-York Tribune*, December 30, 1900, p. 8.
24 *The New York Times*, February 6, 1901, p. 7.
25 *The New York Times*, February 28, 1901, p. 7.
26 *Forest and Stream*, August 24, 1901, p. 155.
27 *Chicago Daily Tribune*, June 12, 4, p. 11.

Chapter 18
1 *The Inter Ocean*, June 7, 1904, p. 3.
2 *Forest and Stream*, October 8, 1904, Vol. LXIII, No. 115, p. 311.
3 *Chicago Daily Tribune*, October 7, 1906, p. 1.(?)
4 *Chicago Daily Tribune*, July 23, 1907, p. 1.
5 Prater, Donald Fry, *There Will Always Be a Mackinac Race*.
6 *Yachting*, September, 1907, Vol. II, No. 3.
7 *Chicago Tribune*, July 23, 1907, p. 11.
8 Prater, Donald Fry, *There Will Always Be a Mackinac Race*, p. 49.
9 *Chicago Daily News*, July 6, 1909.
10 *Chicago Daily Tribune*, July 8, 909, p. 13.
12 *Boston Daily Globe*, April 30, 1911, p. 62.
13 *Boston Daily Globe*, May 14, 1911, p. 57.

Chapter 19

1 *Chicago Daily Tribune*, May 22, 1911, p. 15.
2 *Chicago Daily Tribune*, July 22, 19, p. 12.
3 *The Lake County Times*, July 24, 1911, p. 3.
4 *The First Hundred Years*, Annals of the Chicago Yacht Club, p. 113.
5 *Charlevoix Courier*, July 26, 1911.
6 *Tales of the Mackinac Race*, p. 13.
7 *The First Hundred Years*, Annals of the Chicago Yacht Club, p. 113.
8 *The Compass* of the Rochester Yacht Club, May, 1924, p. 4.
9 *Chicago Daily Tribune*, July 25, 1911, p. 13.

Epilogue

1 *Chicago Tribune*, August 5, 1925, p. 12.

BIBLIOGRAPHY

Archival Sources
Herreshoff Manufacturing Company
Records (copy) 1868–1944
1 Vol., Ms. 83, pp. 4 to 12.
From the Collections of the Rhode Island Historical Society

Books, Periodicals and Dissertations
"Annals of the Royal Canadian Yacht Club—1852–1937," with a record of the Club's trophies and the contests for them—compiled by C. H. J. Snider, Club Archivist, Rous & Mann Limited, Toronto, Canada 1937.

Bagley, Clarence B. *History of Seattle: From the Early Settlements to the Twentieth Century*, S.J. Clarke Publishing Co., Seattle, WA, 1916.

Barrault, Jean-Michel. *Yachting the Golden Age*. Hachette Illustrated. London, 2004.

Brady, Laurence. *The Man Who Challenged America: The Life and Obsession of Sir Thomas Lipton*. Birlinn Ltd, Edinburgh, 2007.

Bray, Maynard and Claas van der Lind. *Herreshoff Masterpieces*. W.W. Norton & Company, New York, London, 2017.

Brooks, Jerome E. *The $30,000,000.00 Cup: The Stormy Defense of the America's Cup*. Simon and Schuster, 1958.

Burnett, Constance Buel. *Let the Best Boat Win: The Story of America's Greatest Yacht Designer*. Cambridge, Houghton, 1957.

Carter III, Samuel. *The Boatbuilders of Bristol: The Story of the Amazing Herreshoff Family of Bristol, Rhode Island/Inventors, Individualists, Yacht Designers, and America's Cup Defenders*. Doubleday & Co., Garden City, New York, 1970.

Chappelle, Howard I. *The History of American Sailing Ships*. Bonanza Books, New York, 1935.

Chevalier, Francois and Jacues Tagland. *1851 America's Cup Yacht Designs 1986*. Francois Chevalier & Jacques Tagland, Paris, France, 1987.

Clark, Christopher M. *Kaiser Wilhelm II: A Life in Power*. Penguin, London, 2009.

Compton, Nic. *The Anatomy of Sail: The Yacht Dissected and Explained*. Adlard Coles Nautical, Bloomsbury Publishing Plc., London, 2014.

Conner, Dennis and Michael Levitt. *The America's Cup: The History of Sailing's Greatest Competition in the Twentieth Century*. St. Martin's Press, New York, 1998.

Connett, Eugene V. *Yachting in North America: Along the Atlantic & Pacific & Gulf Coasts and on the Great Lakes and on the Western and Canadian Lakes & Rivers*. D. Van Nostrand Company, Inc., Racine, Wisconsin, 1948.

Crane, Clinton H. *Clinton Crane's Yachting Memories*. D. Van Nostrand Company, Inc., New York/Toronto, 1952.

Crocker, Aimee. *And I'd Do It Again*. Head of Zeus, Ltd., London, 2017.

Curwood, James Oliver. *The Great Lakes: The Vessels That Plough through Them: Their Owners, Their Sailors and Their Cargoes Together with a Brief History of Our Inland Sea.* G.P. Putnam's Sons, New York and London, 1909.

D'Antonio, Michael. *A Full Cup: Sir Thomas Lipton's Extraordinary Life and His Quest for America's Cup.* Riverhead Books, New York, 2010.

Dickie, John. *The Craft: How the Freemasons Made the Modern World.* Public Affairs, New York, 2020.

Gabrielson, Mark J. *Deer Isle's Undefeated America's Cup Crews: Humble Heroes from a Downeast Island.* The History Press, Charleston, 2013.

Gunther, Fred. *Boat Manufacturing in Racine, Wisconsin.* Racine County Historical Society and Museum, Inc., 1989.

Hasselbalch, Kurt, Frances Overcash, and Angela Reddin. *Guide to the Haffenreffer-Herreshoff Collection: The Design Records of the Herreshoff Manufacturing Company, Bristol, Rhode Island, The Francis Russell Hart Nautical Collections,* MIT, Cambridge, Massachusetts, 1997.

Herreshoff, L. Francis. *Capt. Nat Herreshoff: The Wizard of Bristol, The Life and Achievements of the Yachts He Designed.* Sheridan House, 1981.

Herreshoff, L. Francis. *The Golden Age of Yachting.* Sheridan House, Dobbs Ferry, New York, 1963.

Herreshoff, Nathanael G. *Recollections and Other Writings.* Herreshoff Marine Museum, 1998.

Hoch, Edward Sebastian. "Yachting on the Great Lakes," *The National Magazine,* Vol. IV, No. 5, August, 1896, p. 411.

Holm, Ed. *Yachting's Golden Age: 1880–1905.* Alfred A. Knopf, New York, 1999.

Howland, Llewellyn III. *No Ordinary Being: W. Starling Burgess: Inventor, Naval Architect, Poet, Aviation Pioneer, and Master of American Design.* David R. Godine, Publisher, 2015.

Jarvis, Edward and Robert Æmilius. *Æmilius: The Last Viking.* Self-published, March 2, 2015.

Jobson, Gary. *An America's Cup Treasury: The Lost Levick Photographs, 1893–1937.* The Mariners' Museum, Newport News, Virginia, 1999.

Jones, Gregory O. *Herreshoff Sailboats.* MBI Publishing Company, China, 2004.

Krejci, William G. *Haunted Put-In-Bay.* Haunted America, Charleston, S.C., 2017.

Larkin, Larry. *Full Speed Ahead: The Story of the Steamboat Era on Lake Geneva.* Larry Larkin Publishing, June 1, 1972.

Larsson, Lars and Rolf E. Eliasson. *Principles of Yacht Design.* Adlard Coles Nautical, London, 1994.

Lawson, Thomas W. and Winfield S. Thompson. *The Lawson History of America's Cup, a Record of Fifty Years,* Southampton, Ashford Press Publishing 1986 (a reprint of the original version published privately in 1902), Hampshire, England.

Lipton, Sir Thomas. *Lipton's Autobiography.* Duffield & Green, New York City, 1932.

McCallum, May Fife. *Fast and Bonnie—a History of William Fife and Son Yachtbuilders.* John Donald Publishers, Edinburgh, 1998.

McCutchan, Philip. *Great Yachts.* Crown Publishers, New York, 1979.

Newell, Gordon. *The H.W. McCurdy Marine History of the Pacific Northwest (1895–1965)*. Superior Publishing Company, Seattle, Washington, 1966.

Oppel, Frank (Ed.). *Tales of the Great Lakes: Stories from Illinois, Michigan, Minnesota and Wisconsin*. Castle/Book Sales, Inc., New York, January 1, 1986.

Pastore, Christopher. *Temple to the Wind: The Story of America's Greatest Naval Architect and His Masterpiece, Reliance*. The Lyons Press, Guilford, Connecticut, 2005.

Prater, Donald Fry. *There Will Always Be a Mackinac Race: A History of the Races for the Mackinac Cup*. D.F. Keller & Co., Chicago, Illinois, 1925.

Rogers, John C. *Origins of Sea Terms*. Mystic Seaport Museum, Mystic, Connecticut, 1985.

Rohl, John C. *Kaiser Wilhelm II, 1859–1941, A Concise Life*. Cambridge University Press, 2014.

Samuels, Peggy and Harold. *The Collected Writings of Frederic Remington*. Doubleday & Company, Inc., Garden City, New York, 1979.

Shelak, Benjamin J. *Shipwrecks of Lake Michigan*. Trails Books, Black Earth, Wisconsin, 2003.

Simpson, Richard V. *Herreshoff Yachts: Seven Generations of Industrialists, Inventors and Ingenuity in Bristol*. History Press, Charleston, South Carolina, 2007.

Sleight, Steve. *The Complete Sailing Manual*. DK, London, New York, Munich, Melbourne Delhi, 2012.

Stephens, William P. *Traditions and Memories of American Yachting*. Motor Boating, Hearst Magazines, Inc., New York, 1942.

Stephens, William Pixard. *American Yachting*. Macmillan Company, New York, 1904.

Stone, Herbert L. *The "America's" Cup Races*. Outing Publishing Company, New York, 1914.

Streeter, John W. ed. *Nathanael Greene Herreshoff and William Picard Stephens: Their Last Letters, 1930–1938*. Herreshoff Marine Museum, Bristol, Rhode Island, 1988.

Swierenga, Robert P. *Dutch Chicago: A History of the Hollanders in the Windy City*. Eerdmans Publishing, Grand Rapids, Michigan, 2002.

Townsend, Robert B. *Who Was Canada's Greatest Yachtsman?*, Odyssey Publishing, Ontario, 2002.

Tuchman, Barbara W. *The Proud Tower: A Portrait of the World before the War; 1890–1914*, Macmillan, New York, 1966.

Van Mell, Richard and Wendy. ed. *The First 100 Years, a History of the Chicago Yacht Club—1875–1975*. Carl Gorr Printing, Chicago, Illinois, 1975.

Whyte, Kenneth. *The Uncrowned King: The Sensational Life of William Randolph Hearst*. Counterpoint, Berkeley, California, 2009.

Index

About the Author

Charles Axel Poekel Jr. is a graduate of the George Washington University and Washington College of Law of American University. He is a former member of the New Jersey State Historical Commission and is currently the chairman of the Elisha Kent Kane Historical Society of New York City. He is a member of the National Maritime Historical Society, the Association of Yachting Historians, the Sippican Historical Society, and the Sailing Museum of Newport, Rhode Island.

His other books are *West Essex* and *Babe & the Kid: The Legendary Story of Babe Ruth and Johnny Sylvester*. Visit him online at www.charlesaxelpoekel.com.

Together with his wife, Lynn, and their flame-pointed Himalayan Mr. Whiskers, he alternates his time between Marion, Massachusetts, and Palm Beach, Florida.

He is the great-grandson of Thorvald Julius Schougaard Poekel.

ABOUT THE COVER

THE COVER IS A COPY OF AN OIL PAINTING BY PATRICK O'BRIEN. PATRICK O'BRIEN IS AN award-winning artist whose striking paintings depict the classic age of sail. The National Maritime Historical Society awarded him its Distinguished Service Award in recognition of his body of work, and the U.S. Naval Academy Museum mounted an exhibition of his paintings. He has won the top prizes at the prestigious Mystic International Marine Art Exhibition, and his paintings have been used many times on the covers of books and magazines.

www.PatrickOBrienStudio.com